The Making of 'Cash Maoism' in Nepal: A *Thabangi* Perspective

by

Pawan Patel

ADARSH BOOKS

The Making of 'Cash Maoism' in Nepal: A *Thabangi* Perspective

ISBN-10: 81-8363-142-8
ISBN-13: 978-81-8363-142-6

First Published: 2019

***Published by*:**
ADARSH BOOKS
New Delhi

***Distributed by*:**
ADARSH ENTERPRISES
4393/4, Tulsidas Street, Ansari Road,
New Delhi-110 002
Ph: 011-23246131, 23246132
email: adarshbooks@vsnl.com
Visit us at: www.adarshbooks.com

***Graphics by*:**
Jay Mata Graphics

***Printed by*:**

"यह काम समर्पित है अम्मा को
उपजाया जिसने मुझमे बप्पा को
मनई रूप दिया जलनी को
जन्माया इक थबांगी मन को"
(16-17 अक्टूबर, 2016)

Preface

What is the point of one minute mourning?
In every minute mourning,
I feel amused half a minute
In the other half, my heart weeps.

(Swapnil Smrati, Nepali poet)

Thus, a young Nepali poet succinctly grasps the essence of decade-old People's War. The so-called Maoist Revolution concluded without accomplishing even a single demand from their "Forty Points Demand". The armed struggle finally ended by signing a Peace Treaty in June, 2006. The Maoist movement was long over and there is also no chance that it would get repeated in near future after abolishment of Shah Monarchy through a ballot box (i.e., first Constituent Assembly in 2008). However, the first constituent assembly could not deliver a new constitution for many years until it ended up in coma and finally dead. A second constituent assembly was convened in November, 2013. Due to internal bickering, Nepali Maoist lost this election. Then Prachanda utilize his pragmatic wisdom to sit in opposition.

An earthquake in form and content arrived in 2015. The rural heartland of country faced harsh cold winters amid living in tents and murmuring of debris of their houses after 2015 earthquake. Instead of giving a minimum help to its people, the ruling class made a declaration of a regressive Constitution. The six month old blockade by Indian government in guise of patron of Nepali Madhesi population made really this earthquake effective. This established this fact clearly that Nepal remains a protectorate state of inheritor of British Indian Empire. Moreover, it proved also that without consent of 'big brother', even anti-people measure of Nepali ruling class would not be entertained.

Previously, only one king ruled over Nepal. Now, Nepal got many kings found in every political party's right from the Maoists, Nepali Congress, CPN (UML), and the Madheshi front. Thus a republic has been established in Nepal but it is without nail and tooth. But it is only in form and its content is missing. In this sense, it is a wretched republic which does not show willingness to address social, economic and political demands of proper representation of hitherto oppressed groups including Janjati, Madhesi, Dalit, and women in polity. These demands are in no sense revolutionary or radical but essential demands to establish bourgeois democracy in Nepal.

And finally after riddling of Chinese tilting of CPN (UML)'s 'left' Prime Minister KP Sharma Oli's nationalist rhetoric; Prachanda's 'Cash Maoist' formed a coalition government through a 'common minimum program' with their former 'class enemy' of Nepali Congress. This Maoist government formation had finally led to other small faction of 'Cash Maoism' syndrome to be get unified by a "Unity Conference" by accommodating breakaway small factions led by Badal, Matrika Yadav & Mani Thapa. Now the Unified CPN (Maoist) is called CPN-Maoist United or unity centre. Two factions led by Prachanda's Guru Mohan Baidya 'Kiran' and Netra Bikram Chand 'Biplav' remains out of this fold following parliamentary road but in no sense they are out of purview of 'Cash Maoist' politics. They are roaming here and there to set a new road of future struggle to liberate Nepal from 'expansionist' Indian state, but unable to get a right track since so-called enemy of Nepali people, the king is no more. On the other side, another 'Cash Maoist' character once celebrated Maoist ideologue Dr. Baburam Bhattarai had denounced philosophy of liberation publicly. He is happy to be identified as former Marxist and 'Mustang Prime Minister'[1]. According to him, now Nepal needs *Naya Shakti* on the lines of learning from 'big brother' India's Aam Aadmi Party. He wants people to believe that Mr. Karl Marx has become redundant for Nepal and the NGO politics is necessary to reclaim power for welfare of poor people.

The leader of Maoist Revolution, Prachanda, now is called Pushpa Kamal Dahal but no more 'fierce one'. Because the fierce one syndrome had reproduced warlord as a necessary outcome of 'Cash Maoism' which made 13,000 people get killed, thousands get disappeared and hundreds of thousand families displaced to make sure only one thing that the Maoist officially enter into bourgeois parliamentary path and to make Nepal a 'Switzerland of South Asia'.

Moreover, he turned out to be a true flag bearer of Nepali ruling class by adhering to be a *Brahmanical* prophecy to make sure Nepal a 'secular' republic where constitution would protect an eternal *Sanatan* Hindu religion. This way, even the so called 'achievement' of Nepali people (i.e. end of Hindu monarchy) by establishing minimum level of bourgeois democracy became redundant. This is whole truth of 're-structuring of state' that is building of a federal republic without altering anything.

---

1 The Mustang model of development was propagated in tenure of Dr. Baburam Bhattarai as being Prime Minister of Nepal in 2012. The Mustang Jeep is considered safe and easy vehicle for riding in hilly region of country. It is made in Nepal but not by manufacturing but by assembling engine from China and tyre-tube from India. By riding a Mustang Jeep, he argued that Nepal should utilize its strategic position from economic boom of two neighbor giant markets of China and India.

Acknowledgements

This kind of a work was never possible without my journey as a political activist. My journey of Nepal had began from left student politics at the University of Allahabad via Balia since 1999 and subsequently studying at Jawaharlal Nehru University, New Delhi which made me travel finally to Thabang. Therefore, my past, present and future (if I have!), everything was focused on one point, on completing this work.

The settings of JNU bestowed on me two *Gurus*, Prof. Anand Kumar and Prof. Avijit Pathak who jointly supervised my Ph. D work which this book is based on. I am indebted to both of them. While in this unusual journey from India to Nepal, I met my "unconventional Guru" Stephen Lawrence Mikesell. Though, I could not do justice to his suggestions over the manuscript but they remain with me for future projects.

I am indebted to Dr. Gilbert Sebastian, (Dept. of International Relations & Politics, Central University of Kerala) for appreciating my work and giving me the courage to publish this "imperfect" draft.

On this occasion, I would like to express my gratitude to Ekraj Thapa of Chandranigahpur & Kumar Shah of Ghodagaun, Rolpa, Nepal.

Thanks to Nepali Maithili progressive poet Roshan Janakpuri for translating my poem "Prachand Maya" in Nepali. Beside this, my gratitude to Rajendra Maharjan (senior journalist, Kathmandu) and Arun Baral (editor, onlinekhabar.com) for translating my

Hindi articles into Nepali. Their appreciation of my work assured me that I am on the right track to become a worthy student of Nepal.

Meeting Mary Des Chene in 2009 was a joy but could not heed her advice. In spite of that, her writings on Nepal inspires me. I fondly remember her.

Dr. T. Kumar (Xavier University, Orissa), Dr. Amir Ali (CPS/SSS, JNU), Dr. Gideon Shadang (Rajdhani College, DU), Dr. Ziaur Rahman, New Delhi, Dr. Dhiraj Kumar Nite (Ambedkar University, Delhi), Sanjay Kumar (Central University of Bihar, Motihari) and Uncle Ji (of Suman Villa, Budh Vihar) used to take away my tensions whenever I was entering a trouble zone.

Ashok Kumar Majumdar alias Dada (proprietor of Jawahar Books, JNU) introduced me to my publisher, Nirmal Kumar Karn of Adarsh Books. While thanking them, I also appreciate Ramanuj Chaube who edited this work.

Dr. Abdul Rafey (Budding Urdu Literary Critic) and Abhijit Sonal persuaded me in many ways to publish this work. Many thanks to them.

Finally, I shall remain indebted to Baba Sheomangal Siddhantkar, Prof. Anand Kumar and Com. Narendra Kumar who gave me a new lease of life.

However, I shall alone be responsible for any limitation of this work.

401/3, Suman Villa, Budha Vihar,
Munirka, New Delhi
15 April 2017

Abbreviation

CDO:	Chief District Officer
CPN:	Communist Party of Nepal
CPN (M):	Communist Party of Nepal (Maoist)
CPN (UML):	Communist Party of Nepal (Unified Marxist-Leninist)
I/NGO:	International/Non Governmental Organization
MLM:	Marxism-Leninism-Maoism
NC:	Nepali Congress
NDR:	New Democratic Revolution
PLA:	People's Liberation Army
RAW:	Research & Analysis Wing
RIM:	Revolutionary International Movement
RNA:	Royal Nepal Army
SJM:	Samyunkta Janmorcha
UNMIN:	United Nation Mission in Nepal
URPC:	United Revolutionary People's Council
VDC:	Village Development Committee

CONTENTS

CHAPTER 1

Analytical Framework to Study People's War in Nepal

> *Do not say that social movement excludes political movement. There is never a political movement which is not at the same time social.*[1]

Peasant mobilizations in Third World, in general are known for its radical fervour and transformative socio-political project. This is more specifically true for a region like South Asia which is a birth-place to many peasant movements particularly from times of anti-colonial struggle and Chinese revolution. However, this is a bitter fact, that once peasantry as a class fought epic struggle to run over existing state machinery, its communist party leadership left the struggle in between and went into what is known in Communist discourse worldwide as revisionism. India's Telengana and Naxalbari movement are prime examples of this type of peasant mobilization. Recently, it was Nepali People's War added a new count in this series of betrayal of people's aspiration which had truly shaken not only Nepali society but the whole region for a serious attempt to accomplish transformative Socialist project.

The present work is an attempt to do a political-sociological analysis of the decade-long People's War[2] in Nepal. It is been considered that Maoist movement contributed to the ouster of Shah Monarchy but it made a partial role because of monarchy's own incompetence and geo-strategic power balance. In this

---

1 Karl Marx (1955), *The Poverty of Philosophy*, Moscow: Progress Publishers, p. 197.

2 The terms 'People's War', 'armed struggle' and 'Maoist movement' are used interchangeably throughout this work.

context, the CPN (M) and the Seven Political Parties joining hand together to bring down monarchy by an uprising of April Movement in 2006. However, it cannot be said that the Maoist project was successful in a revolutionary takeover of the State following a decades-old armed struggle.

By this work, I conceptualize People's War as a political movement which was significant for not only Nepal but the whole of South Asia. The People's War however erupted in Nepal in an unpropitious international situation when the so-called project of 'End of History' was being celebrated after the demise of Soviet Union, the world's 'first actually existing Socialist State'. The end of history also suggested an end of revolutionary political mobilizations based on Marxist theory and building of the Socialist Project. The demise of "actually existing socialism" had a profound impact as many renowned scholars changed their political-ideological loyalty by calling off "impossibility of socialism in one country".[3] The world was projected again as unipolar world by imperialist triumph that capitalism has no alternative.

It was also a period, according to the Maoists; they were facing acute state repression in their attempts to organize villagers and solve their problems in the area of influence that they came to see, there was no other choice but only People's War. Coincidently, it was a period just after the restoration of multiparty democracy after a popular people's movement in early 1990s. The present work shall attempt to present a critique of the social movement approach and to show its limitations by placing it in context of decade-long political mobilization done by the CPN (M) in Nepal. This research raises question over whether the People's War fits in framework of social movement developed by various scholars and attempts to present an analytical framework. However, before proceed further, it is important to discuss about mobilization and social movement.

---

3 Randhir Singh (2011), *The World After Collapse of Soviet Union*, Delhi: Aakar Books, p. 27.

1. MOBILIZATION DEFINED

The study of political mobilization has been conceptualized in different ways as; protest movement, rebellion, social movement, insurgency and revolution. All these concepts have been central to the discourse of social science literature and have been termed as collective behavior in general. The discipline of Sociology, however, has been overwhelmingly dependant on few conceptual frameworks in understanding this phenomenon in contemporary world scenario. Among them, the concept of social movement is a central one which focuses on studying single issues such as political and social rights, changes in policy, and so on.

In any kind of protest, social movement, rebellion, revolution etc. mobilization is a necessary dimension. The process usually manifests in gatherings like mass meetings, protest marches, processions and demonstrations, etc. However, often the ruling classes or the state too use this process in its favour. The term mobilization was first used, in context of military perspective, in order to describe the preparation of the Russian army during the 1850s and later on in context of the French Revolution. Mobilization is called as a process in which a group of people actively participate from being mere passive onlookers. Etzioni (1968) defines mobilization in the military sense as, "... the process by which a unit gains significantly in the control of assets it previously did not control as mobilization...."[4] In his conception, "assets" consists of three elements: coercive (i.e. weapons, armed forces, manipulative technologies), utilitarian (i.e. money, goods, information services), normative (i.e. loyalties, obligations). Following this, he argues that a group mobilizes in a condition when it gains substantial control over coercive, utilitarian and normative resources but demobilizes if it loses such a control.

4 Amitai Etzioni (1968), *The Active Society*, New York: Free Press, pp. 388-389.

The concept of mobilization also connotes wider social efforts for modernization and development. This process of mobilization activity consists of three processes: the process of interest formation, the process of community building, and process of employing means of action. Following this, Deutsch (1961) theorize mobilization as macro-level process by which traditional commitments of people i.e., social, economic and psychological are eroded and the people are socialized in new patterns of behaviour.[5] Tilly (1978) has reformulated this concept and used it to explain collective action of large-scale social movements, and revolutions. He defines mobilization as a process: "...by which a group acquires collective control over the resources needed for action. Those resources may be labour power, goods, weapons, votes and any number of other things, just so long as they are usable in acting on shared interests."[6]

Draper (1978) notes the importance of the contribution made by Marx and Engels made in conceptualising of mobilization while explaining class conflict in the capitalist societies. According to him, mobilization is a social mechanism in the process of attaining revolutionary change of society. Economy shapes the political activity of social classes which challenge the class interest of ruling classes. Thus class conflict is inevitable in capitalist system but that is determined by the major determining factors of ideology and political mobilization.[7] As per the Marxist theory, class struggle links the question of mobilization to state power. Here comes a very

5 Karl Deutsch (1961), 'Social Mobilization and Political Development', *American Political Science Review*, Vol. 55, No. 3, pp. 493-514.

6 Charles Tilly (1977), *From Mobilization to Revolution*, Michigan: University of Michigan, pp. 10-11.

7 Hal Draper (1978), *Karl Marx's Theory of Revolution*, Vol. 2, New York & London: Monthly Review Press, pp. 113-115.

vital part to be played by the proletariat in organizing mobilization for class struggles. This is a process which Marx theorize of a proletariat class evolves from a "class in itself" to a "class for itself". As he wrote in The Poverty of Philosophy: "Economic conditions had first transformed the mass of the people of the country into workers. The combination of capital has created for this mass a common situation, common interest. This mass is thus already a class as against capital, but not yet for itself. In the struggle . . . this mass becomes united, and constitutes itself as a class for itself".[8]

2. UNDERSTANDING SOCIAL MOVEMENT

Indian Scholar Shah (2002) notes in the introductory pages of his book, *Social Movements and the State*, states that "there is no precise definition of the term 'social movement' accepted by scholars of all disciplines or even scholars belonging to the same discipline."[9] Rudolf Heberle's (1951) made first serious attempt to theorize social movements. According to him, social movements arise from institutional deficiencies in a given society and those un-institutionalized needs would ultimately lead into organising of the masses which collectively challenge the powers that be. This way social movement generate and "aims to bring about fundamental changes in the social order, especially in the basic institutions of property and labour relationships."[10]

The early social movement research had been greatly influenced by psychological behaviourism that permeated in social sciences research. Among them, the theory of relative deprivation

8 Op. cit., Karl Marx (1955), p. 150.

9 Ghanshyam Shah (2002) (ed.), *Social Movements and State: Readings in Indian Government and Politics*, New Delhi: Sage Publications, p.15.

10 Rudolf Heberle (1951), *Social Movements: An Introduction to Political Sociology*, New York: Appleton-Century-Crofts, p. 6.

primarily worked out by Robert Merton (1950) and Walter Runciman (1966) are notable. Following this line of thought, Gurr (1970) argues that situation of relative deprivation by itself would not engender a social movement. Social movement erupt because of organised discontent. He emphasized on the causal significance of psychological frustration that arises from various kinds of deprivation i.e. social, economic, and political.[11]

Social movements can be defined as those movements which have an objective of bringing political and social change in a particular society by mobilizing people in an organized way. Wilkinson (1971) defines a social movement as, "...deliberate collective endeavour to promote change in any direction and by any means, not excluding violence, illegality, revolution or withdrawal into 'utopian' community... A social movement must evince a minimal degree of organization, through this may range from a loose, informal or partial level of organization to the highly institutionalized and bureaucratized movement and the corporate group..."[12]

Looking at only discontents of masses and their means for expressing it in the process of mobilization is not enough to understand the dynamics of social movements which are aimed at social change. Such a process must be firmly based on a relation to the ideological content of the movement as well as the specific social situations of its participants. Contextualizing this argument, Hobsbawm (1959) has studied a number of primitive forms of social movements and agitation by peasantry in the context i.e. of western and southern Europe of the nineteenth and early twentieth century what he calls "archaic movements", in which diffuse protest did not unite into organized demands for

11 Ted Robert Gurr (1970), *Why Men Rebel?,* Princeton: Princeton University Press, pp. 8-10.

12 Paul Wilkinson (1971), *Social movements*, London: Pall Mall, p. 27.

social and political transformation of society. He notes that they lacked a uniting ideological content or an organization through which one can embark on a program of specific demands, tactics, and strategy. These movements took many forms of: "banditry of the Robinhood type, rural secret societies, various peasant revolutionary movements of the millenarian sort, pre-industrial urban 'mobs' and their riots, some labour religious sects and the use of ritual in early labour and revolutionary organisations".[13]

While defining a social movement in the Indian context, Oommen (1990) notes that social movements are mobilizations against the status-quo. According to him, social movements should be studied by taking into account its historicity, salient aspects of the existing social structure as well as the future vision of society which they encapsulate and articulate. In this way, this has to be a study of the dialectical relation between historicity (past experiences), social structure (present existential conditions) and the aspiration for a better future (human creativity).[14]

3. CONTEXTUALISING PEOPLE'S WAR IN SOCIAL MOVEMENT FRAMEWORK

From the above discussion on the various frameworks of social movement, it can be argued that social movement could be and could not be a mobilization against the state and political system. But do social movements really challenge the status-quo and make efforts to change it? Or do they inadvertently strengthen the status-quo which in a parliamentary system gives a term of five years for opposition bourgeois parties to rule without ever doing

13 Erich J. Hobsbawm (1965 [1959]), *Primitive Rebels: Studies in Archaic Forms of Social Movement in the Nineteenth and Twentieth Centuries*, New York: W. W. Norton and Company, pp. 1-2.

14 T. K. Oommen (1990), *Protest and Change: Studies in Social Movements*, New Delhi: Sage Publications, p. 30.

away with the existing socio-political relations or dismantling the exploitative state structure. The social movement framework when applied to the People's War of Nepal brings out a complex case of political mobilisation. An examination of my field data of Thabang village shows that many strands of social movements existed in Nepal before emergence of the Maoist movement.[15] For instance, the national referendum conducted by monarchy in 1980 was boycotted by entire Thabang village. This was a clear example of a social movement which does not demand some rights and plead for justice from the ruling classes but decisively rejects the *Panchayat* regime in favour of the *Bahudal* (multi-party democracy). This anti-*Panchayat* movement was a result of countrywide peasant's mobilizations and students movement.

The anti-*Panchayat* political mobilization done by peasant youths of ordinary village went beyond the rubric of social movement framework. In sociological imagination of peasantry of Thabang, multi-party democracy was a new form of system opposed to the *Panchayat* system. It is a basic reason of their defying of despotic *Panchayat* government which resulted in a massive state repression through the deployment of the Royal Nepal Army. The security forces carried out a combing operation there in October, 1981. Some may argue that *Thabangi* masses were not treated by the state as Nepali nationals or citizens and therefore the country's army was sent in to suppress these 'anti-nationals'. But to follow this line of argument is to be already trapped in the logic of the state, because in reality, the masses had rebelled against the idea of nation by defying the monarchical state and the notion of nationhood as defined. This defiance of the monarchy by peasantry of Thabang itself reflects the initial murmuring of seizure of state power and an urge to dismantle it.

15 For a brief overview of revolts, rebellion and social movement, see, in Table VII & VIII included in Appendix-I.

Or for that matter the Anti-untouchability movement led by the Dalit Liberation Front in early 1990s in Nepal. As a key leader of the movement, Dhan Bahadur Nepali has argued that though the Anti-untouchability movement can be seen as an instance of social movements because it demanded ending of caste discrimination. But it was much more than a social movement because it held that until the existing political system did not altered, caste-based discrimination would be continued in one form or another. In this way the Dalit Liberation Front raised the crucial issue of capturing state power for the annihilation of the caste system. This Anti-untouchability movement continued after the initiation of the People's War.

The People's War (1996-2006) makes the socio-political mobilization in Thabang more in-line with much beyond to any social movement. While facing organised state terror of *Operation Romeo* on activities of the *Samyunta Janmorcha* (SJM), a series of cultural campaigns were mobilized over many years in between 1991 to 1995. The main objective of these mobilisations was to serve and to heighten their political consciousness in order to prepare the grounds for revolutionary armed struggle. These socio-cultural and political mobilisations just after the introduction of multi-party system were aimed at exposing the inept and corrupt state administration of the Nepali Congress Government led by Girija Prasad Koirala. At the same time, these social movements built struggles against untouchability, polygyny, patriarchy, alcoholism and orthodox cultural practices without touching religious sentiments of the masses.

It is evident here that the questions raised by various events of social movements in Thabang existed in different forms even before the beginning of People's War in Nepal. These set of mobilizations go beyond the limited scope of a social movement by aspiring for the seizure of state power. This is why these struggles later culminated in the establishment of the *Jansatta* (Peoples' Power) in villages like Thabang, which the social movement framework alone can never envision.

4. PEOPLE'S WAR IN NEPAL AS A POLITICAL MOVEMENT

It is therefore clear from the above discussion that the existing social movement framework cannot fully deal with the questions of state power as decade-old People's War in Nepal raise. It is therefore necessary to visualize a new framework which precisely accommodates the question of state power. We have already pointed out in the previous section the limitations of terming Nepal's People's War as a social movement. Frank and Fuetens (1987) have rightly argued by making a distinction between social and political movements. According to them, most of the social movements do not strive for state power. Rather they "seek more autonomy rather than state power" while a political movement is located in the state alone. They write further that "...this statement is a truism since *not* seeking –let alone wielding –state power is a sine qua non of a social movement, and state power would negate the very essence and purpose of most social movements".[16]

Therefore, following Pratt (2003), a movement such as People's War in Nepal which is geared towards seizure of political power (state power) is called a political movement. Political movements can take different forms: (1) Protracted People's War, (2) Mass Movement, (3) National Liberation Movement. Under political movement we can include a wide-ranging repertoire of political actions, be it demonstrations, tax strikes, workplace strikes,

16 Andre Gunder Frank and Marta Fuetens (2002 [1987]), 'Nine Theses on Social Movements', in Ghanshyam Shah (ed.), *Social Movements and State: Readings in Indian Government and Politics*, New Delhi: Sage Publications, p. 45.

sabotage, seizure of land/factories or a part of territory of a country, general strikes, burning tax records, guerrilla warfare and armed insurrection.[17]

Moreover, the Nepali People's War is also an *antisystemic* movement which draws its legacy from 1789's French revolution raised the famous slogan of "liberty, equality, fraternity"[18]. Many social movements are indeed *antisystemic* in the sense that the movements and their participants combat or otherwise challenge the system or aspects thereof. However, very few social movements remain *antisystemic* till the end in their attempt to alter political system and replace it by a new one. In the context of Latin America, Petras and Veltmeyer (2005) have concluded that all social movements in countries of Argentina, Brazil, Bolivia and Ecuador have failed to challenge the state power but rather they succumb to imperialism by taking electoral path.[19]

It should be noted here that a political movement of a nature of *antisystemic* & anti-imperialism was not new in global fights against ruling classes. The People's War as a form of political movement has been applied successfully in different countries in the past. Not only movement based on Marxist theory but many non communist forces of the last twentieth century applied theory of People's War in different countries. The important examples are

---

17 Jeff Pratt (2003), *Class, Nation and Identity: The Anthropology of Political Movements*, London: Pluto Press, p. 9.

18 Immanuel Wallerstein (1990), 'Antisystemic Movements: History and Dilemmas', in Samir Amin, Giovanni Arrighi, Andre Gunder Frank and Immanuel Wallerstein (eds.), *Transforming the Revolution: Social Movements and The World System*, New York: Monthly Review Press, pp. 13-14.

19 James Petras and Henry Veltmeyer (2005), *Social Movement and State Power: Argentina, Brazil, Bolivia, Ecuador*, London: Pluto Press, p. 235.

from the Pancho Villa in Mexico to that of the IRA in Ireland, Iran and from Palestinian's Fatah to the Cypriot EOKA.

But, it became the principal instrument of carrying out national liberation movements as well as revolutionary movements to capture state power following triumph of Chinese Revolution in 1949. The Vietnamese Communist successfully deployed this strategy first against the French colonialists in 1954 and later against American imperialism in 1960s. In doing so, the Vietnamese were careful to maintain a broad-based united front and a firm alliance with the peasantry. A similar strategy with a variation of guerrilla movement was advocated by Che Guevara and Fidel Castro during the Cuban revolution.[20] The Algerian people fought a well-organized guerrilla war against French colonists from 1954 to 1962. Similarly, the Sandinista revolutionaries of Nicaragua followed the doctrine of People's War successfully for two decades until a direct military intervention by American imperialism in the late 1980s crushed it. The American imperialism had deployed a counter-insurgency campaign through vigilante groups called the Contras while applying the same guerrilla strategy in reverse. The decade of 1960-80s saw similar instances of guerrilla wars which were fought by various Communist forces in Mexico, Guatemala, Venezuela, Columbia, Peru, and Bolivia of Latin America. In recent years, the Communist led People's War registered its presence in Malaysia, Philippines and India.

From the above discussion, it can be concluded that a wide variety of political movements exist in today's world. In this sense, Nepali People's War is understood as an agrarian armed struggle for the seizure of state power by revolutionary violence. Its goal was to overthrow Hindu monarchy rule and establish a Socialist state. Besides, case of Nepal points to an understanding of not

20 Walter Laquerur (1977), *Guerrilla: A Historical and Critical Study*, London: Weidenfeld and Nicolsen.

waiting for the final overthrow of the state for seizure of power but to simultaneously build the revolutionary state machinery in form of the *Jansatta* (People's Power) as an alternative system to the existing state machinery.

5. PEASANTRY AS A MOTIVE FORCE OF PEOPLE'S WAR

Political mobilization steered by peasantry are a great academic interest when seen as a distinctive examples of collective action from the economically, politically, and culturally underprivileged groups, as an attempt to improve their livelihoods by contesting against the power of the existing state machinery. This fact can be seen very clearly from the reading of social history of peasant rebellion of country. However, without having a proper definitional usage of the term peasant, it is very difficult while delineating classes among peasants set on agrarian society of Nepal where political movement of People's War was primarily mobilized by peasantries in the leadership of the CPN (M) based on their agrarian program.

"Peasantry is the majority of mankind"[21], but in spite of their numbers, they have been poorly understood. The Peasants are always the central force for capital production in a society primarily dominated by the agrarian background. In contrast, the landlord stood as the intermediate of relationship as a bloodsucking and parasitic community that controlled whole means of production. In a highly stratified society, they have not been regarded even playing a minor role but only to face continual oppression on the hands of ruling class whichever they be, but in spite of that too, they remained dominant force.

---

21 Teodor Shanin (1971) (ed.), 'Peasantry as a Political Factor', in *Peasants and Peasant Societies: Selected Readings*, New York: Penguin Books, p. 238.

Silverman (1979) notes in his survey of American Anthropological literature that Robert Redfield begun to popularise the concept of peasant. Although Redfield prefer to use the term "folk life" to the concept of peasant in his study of the peasant class of Mexico in 1926. It was not until 1950s the concept of peasant became distinct to folk life, both were understood as synonymous category.[22] Redfield (1956) opines that agrarian society is functionally part of a larger society and the term of peasant is defined in relation to the city. Without the city, according to him, there is no peasant, and if the society is entirely urbanized than there is no peasant either. According to him, the peasants are "...those rural people who control and cultivate their land for subsistence and as a part of a traditional way of life and who look to and are influenced by gentry or towns people whose way of life is like theirs but in a more civilized form."[23]

Wolf (1966) defined peasants as a rural cultivator who takes part in the actual work of production on the land and is very close to it.[24] Beteille (1974) argued that category of peasant often includes the characteristics of groups, classes and communities which otherwise cannot be regarded as peasants. To him, the term 'peasantry' has a variety of references and it should be regarded as "a more or less homogenous and undifferentiated community of families characterized by small holdings operated mainly by family labour."[25] According to Shanin (1971), peasants are small

---

22 Sydel Silverman (1979), 'The Peasant Concept in Anthropology', *The Journal of Peasant Studies,* Vol. 7, No. 1, (October issue), pp. 49-69.

23 Robert Redfield (1956), *Peasant Society and Culture: An Anthropological Approach to Civilization*, Chicago & London: The University of Chicago Press, p. 31.

24 Eric R. Wolf (1966), *Peasants*, Englewood Cliffs, N.J.: Prentice-Hall, p. 1.

25 Andre Beteille (1974), *Studies in Agrarian Structures*, Delhi: Oxford University Press, p. 24.

agricultural producer who with the help of a single equipment and labour of their families, produce mainly for their own consumption, while abiding by the holders of political and economic power.[26]

This way, it can be seen that there are different perspectives from which the question concerning peasantry has been treated. The first tradition stress on cultural aspect of peasantry and second one includes dealing of peasantry in structural institutional terms. The third tradition includes Marxists one which sees peasantry essentially as a suppressed and exploited segment of pre-capitalist society.[27]

Byres (1986) present a lucid survey by summarizing various Marxist perspectives on peasantry. According to him, the agrarian question at the end of nineteenth century was basically peasant question and it was inextricably linked with "political concern". The early Marxists "...were preoccupied with the problem of how to capture political power in European countries in which capitalism was developing apace and where large number of peasantries existed."[28] Marx's thesis on peasantry is complex and sometimes even more so because of its diverse usage into different contexts. Marx considered them as an ally of the working class in their struggle against the bourgeoisie to overthrow capitalism. But he also critiqued peasantry as "petty bourgeois" and termed them as a "sack of potatoes" after their reactionary role during

26 Op. cit., Teodor Shanin (1971), p. 240.

27 Virginius Xaxa (1989), 'Some Problems in Defining Peasants', in M. N. Karna (ed.), Peasant and Peasant Protest in India, New Delhi: Intellectual Publishing House, p. 23.

28 T. J. Byres (1986), 'Foreword: The Agrarian Question and Differentiation of The Peasantry', in Atiur Rahman (1986), *Peasants and Classes: A Study in Differentiation in Bangladesh*, London: Zed Books., p. xi.

1848 revolution in France.[29] He pointed out the political apathy of the French small holding peasants and their failure to pursue "class-for-itself" activity. But, in spite of such criticism of the French peasantry in particular, Marx believed in the revolutionary potential of peasants in general as an ally of the working class.

The early Marxist notions on peasantry were reformulated after successful revolutions in Russia and China in the twentieth century. In two large and populous nations of Russia and China, ideology of Marxism had harnessed revolutionary energies of the vast section of peasantry to overthrow old regime and radically refashion agrarian relations, laying the basis for a re-ordering of the entire gamut of social relations.

Following on these trajectories, Lenin (1964) first put the theory of working class-peasant's alliance in first successful state takeover of the *October Revolution* in Russia. Lenin's analysis of the dynamics of agrarian change involved a continuous theoretical engagement with the influential Russian Narodniks (i.e. populist) views. By his work, Lenin made a thorough critique of the statistics offered by the Narodniks on dynamic changes taking place in Russian agrarian economy and thereby reaching out with radically different conclusions. He divided the peasant community into three groups – poor peasant, middle peasant and rich peasant. Lenin's poor peasant is characterized by the existing pressure of fierce competitions, impoverishment and inextricable indebtedness which drove them to sell labour power on a regular basis to ensure their survival. The middle peasants were distinguished from poor peasants and the peasant bourgeoisie and their place in the agrarian social structure was most unstable. The process of de-peasantization resulted from capitalist investment in agriculture, swept away the middle peasant category and

29 Karl Marx (1977), *The Eighteenth Brumaire of Louis Bonaparte*, Moscow: Progress Publishers, p. 106.

reinforced the polarization between peasant bourgeoisie and rural proletariat.[30]

Based on the leading role of peasantry in Chinese revolution, Mao Tse-Tung (1967) lauded revolutionary prospective of the peasantry. According to him, without the poor peasant, the revolution would have been impossible and overthrow of feudal regime in China. The poor peasants not only formed foremost part of communist party activists while rich peasants, argued Mao, are at best inactive where struggle is underway; middle peasants are likely to be vacillating force.[31]

Formulating revolutionary course of anti-colonial political movement in a French colony of Algeria, Frantz Fanon went to the extent of observing that "In colonial countries the peasants alone are revolutionary, for they have nothing to lose and everything to gain…."[32] The anti-colonial revolutions occurred in decades of 1960s in Algeria, Cuba, Mexico, and Vietnam particularly depicts revolutionary role played by peasantries.

Following the above formulations delineated from different course of political movement led by peasantry, an important issue come in relation to autonomy of peasantry as a revolutionary class. In this context, Alavi (1965) proposed a thesis of "middle peasant". On the basis of his three case studies of peasant mobilizations, i.e., in pre-revolution Russia, mid-1920s China's Hunan movement,

---

30 Vladimir. I. Lenin (1964), *Development of Capitalism in Russia, Collected Works of Lenin, Vol-3*, Moscow: Progress Publisher, pp. 71-80.

31 Mao Tse-Tung (1967), *Selected Works of Mao Tse-Tung,* Peking: Foreign Language Press, p. 33.

32 Franz Fanon (1971 [1961]), *The Wretched of the Earth*, Middlesex: Penguin Books, p. 47.

and Telengana & Tebhaga movements of pre-independent India, he maintained that middle peasants were "the most militant elements of the peasantry."[33] This thesis, however, departs from the Marxist argument that it was the poor peasants who were the main revolutionary forces and revolutionary potential of middle peasants has been discounted. Though, this formulation sees middle peasants closer to poor peasants owing to their socio-economic conditions, but believed the political orientation of the middle peasants remains petty-bourgeois in character.

6. ISSUES OF CLASS, CASTE, ETHNICITY AND GENDER IN NEPAL

In the context of Nepal, peasantry includes a vast body of the socially deprived communities scattered in ethnic groups (i.e., Janjatis), dalits, religious minorities, and women. Besides, it also represents the economically marginalized, namely small cultivators, *Sukumbasi* (landless squatters) of the Tarai region, and agricultural labourers. With land constituting the predominant source of income, land ownership determines status and power in Nepal's dominant agrarian production relations. Consequently, it is the principle determinant for analyzing classes in the Nepali society. Due to various state-led land grants, unequal socio-economic relations and growing population density, little 'free' land is available today, and large numbers of Nepalese people are close to being landless, without access to sufficient productive land to provide for their own livelihood.

The concentration of land in the hands of few elite families and severe exploitation of peasantry through excessive labour expropriation has been a characteristic of the Nepalese political

33 Hamza Alavi (1979 [1965]), 'Peasants and Revolution', in A. R. Desai (ed.), *Peasant Struggles in India*, Bombay: Oxford University Press, p. 715.

economy throughout its history from before the centralized state formation came into existence. King Prithivi Narayan Shah, the man responsible for the conquest of land of Nepal had a good idea of the potential of the peasantry and he got basically peasant support in the project of conquest with the promise of land. The prevalent unequal land distribution was the root of this landlessness and agricultural underdevelopment. Those who are squeezed out of this relationship are often indebted and forced to sell whatever land they have and enter into bonded servitude with the landowner. Political movements such as the decade-long People's War in Nepal must therefore be understood in terms of disparities in land ownership and exploitative production relations.

Nepal not only faced extreme class-based inequalities but socio-cultural inequality based on caste, ethnicity, region, religion, language and gender too prevailed to a great extent. The history of Nepal's development as a nation-state is generally understood through the process of a process called *Hinduization*. Nepal is ethnically, linguistically and religiously diverse, being influenced by racial, cultural and religious features of the neighboring regions of India and China. It has been argued by many scholars that Nepal is a country of minorities which "forged in migration"[34] across many centuries. The Mongoloid groups who migrated from the north and east and Caucasoid groups migrating from the south and west (one of the factors being the Muslim invasion of North India), are dominant though even the single largest ethnic/caste groups make up barely 16 % of the total population.[35] The Dravidian and Proto-Australoid population is nominal and confined to some districts in the eastern Tarai region.

---

34 David N. Gellner (2007), 'Caste, Ethnicity and Inequality in Nepal', *Economic and Political Weekly,* Vol. XLII, No. 20, pp. 1823-1827.

35 Pitambar Sharma (2008), *Unravelling the Mosaic*: *Spatial Aspects of Ethnicity in Nepal*, Kathmandu: Social Science Baha, p. 3.

The Caucasoid population group is divided into *Varna* system, with differentiation into various regional and linguistic formations. It is important to note that the caste system in Nepal is distinct from the Hindu caste system in India, with only "three *Varna*" as opposed to the "four *Varna*" system; the Brahman, Kshatriya and Shudra. The category of the Vaisya is notably visible by its absence. The Nepali-speaking hill Hindu or Parbatiyas, form three social groups with distinct ethnic identities namely Bahun, Chhetris/Thakuris and Dalits. The Dalits remain the most oppressed and exploited class due to their status as *Achut/Sano jat* (Untouchable) in the Hindu caste hierarchy; Bahuns being the highest, followed by Thakuri/Chhetri, who have controlled the Nepali polity for nearly two and half centuries and continue to do so.

In Nepali language, the terms *jati* and *jat* are used interchangeably. In Nepal, *jat* denotes caste status of population groups of the Caucasoid extraction with strict hierarchical Hindu *Varna* system. The term *jati,* in contrast indicates population groups outside the *Varna* system of Mongoloid, Dravidian and Proto-Australoid extraction, the later have their own language, culture and native region. In recent denotation the term of *jati* are called as "Adivasi-Janjatis"[36] and do not originally belong to Hindu social hierarchy. The Census of 2001 identified 43 *Janjatis* and they have been loosely classified as *Matwali* by following *Muluki Ain* of 1854. [37] According to Bista (1991), though, Nepali model

36 The term of *Adivasi-Janjati* is of recent origin particularly after introduction of multi-party democracy in country since 1990s. The term of *Adivasi* is a Sanskrit term meaning 'first settlers' or 'earlier settlers'.

37 The 2001 census of Nepal had identified 43 Janjatis. Out of those 43 *Janjatis*, 5 are from mountain region, 20 from the Hills, 18 from Tarai region. Among the top ten most populous ethnic groups, Magar is the third, Tharu the fourth, Tamang the fifth, Newar the sixth and Rai the tenth.

of caste system is greatly influenced by Hindu customary ancient law of *Manu Smritis* but it "...does not exist in its original form anywhere in Nepal. It has been unorthodox and permeable from the beginning. The *Bahun* are the Nepali Brahmans, the Chhetri, the Kshatriya, and the *Matwali*, the Vaishya and Shurda."[38] Among the top ten most populous caste groups, Chhetri/Thakuri is the first, Bahun second, Kami the eighth and Yadav the ninth. The downtrodden caste is Shudra, called as *Dalit*.[39]

The Hindu caste groups living in the Tarai/*Madhes* region, who have been historically marginalised socio politically, are divided on the basis of many languages (*Maithili*-speakers of eastern Tarai, *Bhojpuri*-speakers of Central Tarai, and *Avadhi*-speakers of Western Terai). Though hill Hindu castes and Hindus of Terai region share the same religion and both have migrated from the Indian plains, but their marginalisation by successive regimes makes them different and its manifestations are seen in their practice of religion in terms of customs and tradition. According the census of 2001, Nepal has 103 caste/ethnic groups and religious communities and linguistic groups. It claims that 80.6% Hindus and 19.4% people believing in other religions exist, with 8 listed religions—Hinduism, Buddhism, Islam, Kiranti, Christianity, Jainism, Sikhism and the Bahai faith. Though outside this list, people believing in religious faith like Animism and Bon also exist. The 2001 census lists 92 languages and depicted that Nepali language was spoken by 48.61% of the total population.[40]

---

38 Dor Bahadur Bista (2008 [1991]), *Fatalism and Development: Nepal's Struggle for Modernization*, Kolkata: Orient Longman, p. 42.

39 The 2001 census has listed 15 Dalit castes of which 5 are hill Dalits-Badi, Damai, Gaine, Kami, Sarki, and 10 are Tarai/Madhesi Dalits-Bantar, Chamar, Chidimar, Dhobi, Dom, Dusadh, Halkhor, Khatwe, Musahar and Tatma.

40 There are 21 major spoken languages as following: (a) Indo-

While Nepal is essentially a country of minorities comprising more than sixty ethnic groups and castes, the *Tagadhari* (twice born) caste which includes –Bahun, Chhetri, Thakuri and Newar– were economically and politically dominant. This disparity is rooted in the political economy of the power structure and state formation since Gorkhali conquest to until recently. The royal land grants given to above mentioned ruling elite consolidated their political power. The Hindu high caste *Tagadhari* groups have had better access to material resources while the Dalit, Janjati, and various Madheshi castes and Muslims were generally excluded from the power structure. Within all groups, women generally faced gendered discrimination but with specifically gender based-inequality higher among Hindu upper castes and Muslims. Dalits in Nepal have been traditionally treated as untouchable by the high caste groups and their place was most vulnerable in the society.

The institution of the caste system was introduced much before the Gorkha conquest of Nepal. In petty kingdom of the *Chaubise* and *Baise* region, the Hindu social order operated loosely from many centuries and superiority of high-caste Hindu values and practices predominated. However, for many social groups the state-supported, high-caste Hindu regime of value remains only partially constitutive of their own values and beliefs. This high-caste hill region hegemony also articulates the latent class divisions in the Nepal society, since the values of high-caste Hindus are associated with high class and 'good breeding'. The discrimination based on class, caste, and ethnicity combines together with all important issue of gender based discrimination.

European languages such as *Nepali, Maithili, Bhojpuri, Tharu, Awadhi, Rajbanshi, Hindi*, and *Urdu*; (b) Sino-Tibetan as *Tamang, Newar, Magar, Rai/Kirant, Gurung, Limbu, Bhote/Sherpa, Sunuwar, Danuwar*, and *Thakali*; (c) Austro-Asiatic as *Satar* and *Santhali*; and (d) Dravidian.

And within every community, women are the most oppressed and marginalised. Traditionally, women are backbone of the subsistence rural economy, accounting for the bulk of agricultural work and animal husbandry, but they have no legal right over property. As per Nepali civil code, the daughter has no claim to parental property unless she remains unmarried till 35 years of age and only then she claims her share. But she has to forfeit it, if she marries. The Nepali women in general faced religiously sanctified exclusions right from the household level all the way up to the state level and which cover political, economic and cultural domains. Citizenship is through the male line. Socio-cultural practices detailed in the *Muluki Ain* of 1854 was built have enshrined oppressive patriarchal structures subjugating the Hindu women in particular. However, women from the *Matwali* communities like the Magar, Gurung, Tamang, and Rai have fewer religious cultural restrictions. A recent study of the Maoist movement argued that women from the poor peasantry and particularly the Janjatis and untouchable communities were most active in joining the People's War. There was around 70% of the women in the People's War were from the ethnic groups of various Janjatis and Dalit communities.[41]

The CPN (M) had recognised the plights of these oppressed sections of marginalised Janjatis, Dalits and women. By identifying and recognising the relations of exploitation in the Nepali society, the Maoists in the subsequent period of mass political mobilisation during the People's War aimed at attacking and destroying the basis of these unequal relations. In their "Forty Point demands" to the then government on 4 February 1996 while before initiating armed struggle, they had stated,

41 Shoba Gautam, Amrita Banskota and Rita Manchanda (2003), 'Where There Are No Men: Women in the Maoist Insurgency', in Deepak Thapa (ed.), *Understanding the Maoist Movement of Nepal*, Kathmandu: Martin Chautari, pp. 93-124.

> *Patriarchal exploitation and discrimination against women should be stopped. Daughters should be allowed access to parental property....All racial exploitation and suppression should be stopped. Where ethnic communities are in majority, they should be allowed to form their own autonomous governments....Discrimination against downtrodden and backward people should be stopped. The system of untouchability should be eliminated. All languages and dialects should be given equal opportunities to prosper....Regional discrimination between the hills and the Terai should be eliminated. Backward areas should be given regional autonomy.*[42]

7. LITERATURE REVIEW

The speed and intensity with which decade-old People's War expanded in a short time in Nepal inspired an abundant and growing literature that has investigated the root causes from various perspectives.[43] After reviewing with a bird eye view, some foremost points could be raised. The most important one was popular disillusionment with the then Nepali state to deliver expected democratization in power structure after restoration of multi-party democracy following a people's movement in 1990. Secondly, continuing poverty and a widening gap between rural and urban quality of life. Furthermore, major focus in such works has been on underdevelopment, state repression, ethnic conflicts, and external intervention in the politics of Nepal. The early

---

42 See, "Forty Points Demand" in Appendix.

43 Only a selected literature has been reviewed in this section since the subject have been covered from a number discipline from political science to policy & security studies, journalism, sociology, history and a vast body of reports produced by national and international NGOs.

writings of Nepali journalists Thapa and Sijapati (2003) covered above encompassing aspects but lack analytical depth.[44] They present historical background, initiation, and growth of Maoist movement in subsequent years and state's suppressive response to it from 1996 onwards. These works explain that the Maoist emergence had weaken the then Nepali state and it was effectively non-existent in districts of Western Nepal. The state's presence was largely confined to the district headquarters which were heavily fortified by the Royal Nepal Army.

A very few works have dealt with the dynamics of political mobilization of Nepali Maoism with historical grounded analysis. The edited volumes by Thapa (2003), Hutt (2004) and Karki and Seddon (2003) look at Maoist movement from an ethnographically informed perspective.[45] Mishra (2004) made effort to look political movement of People's War by showing it as a product of social and political context while also linking its ambiguous relations with Indian state which effectively controlled key of power in Nepal.[46]

The literature dealing Maoist's governance as mobilized by the CPN (M) at village level provide a useful reference for this work. The study by Sales (2003) is significant in this context which is based on Maoist mobilization among Kham Magars community

44 Deepak Thapa and Bandita Sijapati (2003), *A Kingdom under Siege: Nepal's Maoist Rebellion*, London: Zed Books.

45 See, Deepak Thapa (2003) (ed.), Understanding the Maoist Movement of Nepal, Kathmandu: Martin Chautari; Michael Hutt (2004) (ed.), *Himalayan 'People's War': Nepal's Maoist Rebellion*, London: Hurst & Company; Arjun Karki and David Seddon (2003) (eds.), *The People's War in Nepal: Left Perspectives*, Delhi: Adroit Publishers.

46 Chaitanya Mishra (2004), 'Locating the 'Causes' of the Maoist Struggle', *Studies in Nepali History and Society*, Vol. 9, No. 1, (June isse), pp. 3-56.

living in Rolpa & Rukum districts, which is locus of my research. The Maoists were able to mobilize the Magar ethnic group from very initial phase to the extent that this region has come to be known as Maoist heartland.[47] She traced history of radical communism among the Kham Magars and analyses their self representation to explain the attraction Maoism held for them. A perception that the Magar community should see themselves as subjugated warriors whose indigenous forms of autonomy are at stake grew stronger with the rise of the various ethnic movements in the post-1990s era. It proved fortuitous for the Maoists who found that the Kham Magars were ideal for political mobilization while waging their People's War.

Studies by Schneiderman and Turin (2004), Shah (2008), Onesto (2005), and Ogura (2007, 2008) are based on peasantry's testimonies of different regions where different forms of people's government operated. The writings elaborate reasons behind the emergence of the Maoist government in different parts of country and it's unleashing of socio-political- economic-cultural transformation in its wake.

Based on content analysis of newspaper reports from 1998 to 2001 with ethnographic inputs, Schneiderman and Turin (2004) have explained process of establishment of district level Maoist government in Dolakha district of central-eastern Nepal.[48] Their

47 Anne De Sales (2003), 'The Kham Magar Country, Nepal between Ethnic Claims and Maoism', in Deepak Thapa (ed.), Understanding the Maoist Movement of Nepal, Kathmandu: Martin Chautari, pp. 59-88.

48 Sara Schneiderman and Mark Turin (2004), '"The Path to *Jansarkaar",* in Dolakha District: Towards an Ethnography of the Maoist Movement', in Michael Hutt (ed.), *Himalayan 'People's War': Nepal's Maoist Rebellion'*, London: Hurst & Company, pp. 79-111.

work explains that amid the background of demonization of the Maoists as a terrorist in government discourse, the peasant's imagination of Maoist was a political and sympathetic one. While Shah (2008) has explored the relation between culture and resistance by taking a selective case study of a rural women uprising against the Maoist run village peoples' government of Dullu in Dailekh district in 2004. Based on ethnography of displaced families of village, he argued that villagers comprehended setting up of village Maoist government in a contrast to government run VDC committee. But when lived experience of the people contradicted both the normative claims of the Maoist government and monarchical government, the popular reaction against them articulated in spontaneous grassroots uprising.[49]

The work of American journalist Onesto (2005) based on extensive travelling in the Maoist controlled areas in 1999 and provide useful insights into expansion of People's War in countryside. She informs that a policy of destruction with construction was taken up by the CPN (M) while setting up village government to work out development program in their influenced area after defeating security forces.[50] In an another significant work, a Japanese journalist Ogura (2007, 2008) examined root causes of the People's War and the mobilization of people's power in different villages of Rolpa and Rukum districts.[51] Using mainly

---

49 Saubhagya Shah (2008), 'Revolution and Reaction in the Himalayas: Cultural Resistance and the Maoist "New Regime" in Western Nepal', *American Ethnologist*, Vol. 35, No. 3, pp. 481–499.

50 Li Onesto (2005), *Dispatches from People's War in Nepal,* London: Pluto Press.

51 Kiyoko Ogura (2007), 'Maoist, People, and the State as Seen-from Rolpa and Rukum', in H. Ishi, D. Gellner and K. Nawa (ed.), *Political and Social Transformation in North India, Social Dynamics in Northern South Asia*, Vol.2, Delhi: Manohar, pp. 435-475; Also

oral narratives of grass roots Maoist activist, she argues that anti-state feeling created by the suppressive measures of the state security forces since of the *Panchayat* times made a ground for the Maoist mobilization. She argues that these people's governments were functioning successfully "like a state" and were involved in the overall developmental activities such as construction of infrastructure and delivery of justice through people's court with a primary orientation of making the people aware of Maoist politics. She describes about functioning of people's court judicial roles were performed by district level people's governments.

8. RELEVANCE AND OBJECTIVE OF STUDY

However, the studies mentioned above do not deal extensively with the manner in which the Maoist village government created a democratic space for the oppressed population in their daily lives. Moreover, what was the reason which made people to get mobilized behind the PLA and Maoist party organisation in a large manner if not of their hope of altering the existing exploitative and oppressed power relation of Nepali state and society. This is main lacuna of these studies which my research would try to address. It is important to study this sociological transformation in daily life of peasantry who now from a group of obedient, mute subjects were becoming assertive and confident participants of People's War. This becomes all the more significant as the Maoist dismantled structure of popular assertion and organs of village people's government after entering in Parliamentary road of

---

see, Kiyoko Ogura (2008), 'Maoist People's Governments, 2001-05: The Power in Wartime', in D.N. Gellner and K. Hachhethu (ed.), *Local Democracy in South Asia: Micro Process of Democratization in Nepal and its Neighbours,* New Delhi: Sage Publications, pp. 175-231.

bourgeois democracy in 2006. These are following question which my study tries to do investigate:

1. Has People's War as a form of political mobilization been a necessity of the people of Nepal? If so, what is the political, economic and social rationale of such a mobilization?
2. What is *Jansatta* (People's Power)? How has it emerged as a concept and also as a form of political mobilization? What is the necessary dialectical relation between political mobilization and people's power? Can one exist without the other? Where does one locate People's War in the political mobilization towards people's power?
3. What have been the symbols of people's power? How far these symbols transformed the lives of people economically, culturally and socially? How far has the emerging scenario of Democratic Federal Republic of Nepal contributed to this dynamic?

9. METHOD, EMPIRICAL SITE AND THE RATIONALE OF THE STUDY

This is an ethnographic attempt based on primarily relying of participant observation of Thabang village in various phases starting from 2010 to early 2012. This village is located in a mid-western district of Rolpa. The data has been collected by recording in-depth interviews in an informal setting and recording life histories and oral historical narratives encompassing ordinary villagers to political activists and members of the PLA located in various cantonments in Nepal. In addition, pamphlets, newspaper reports and documentary films and various Maoist documents been widely used.

Map: Geography of Nepal[52]

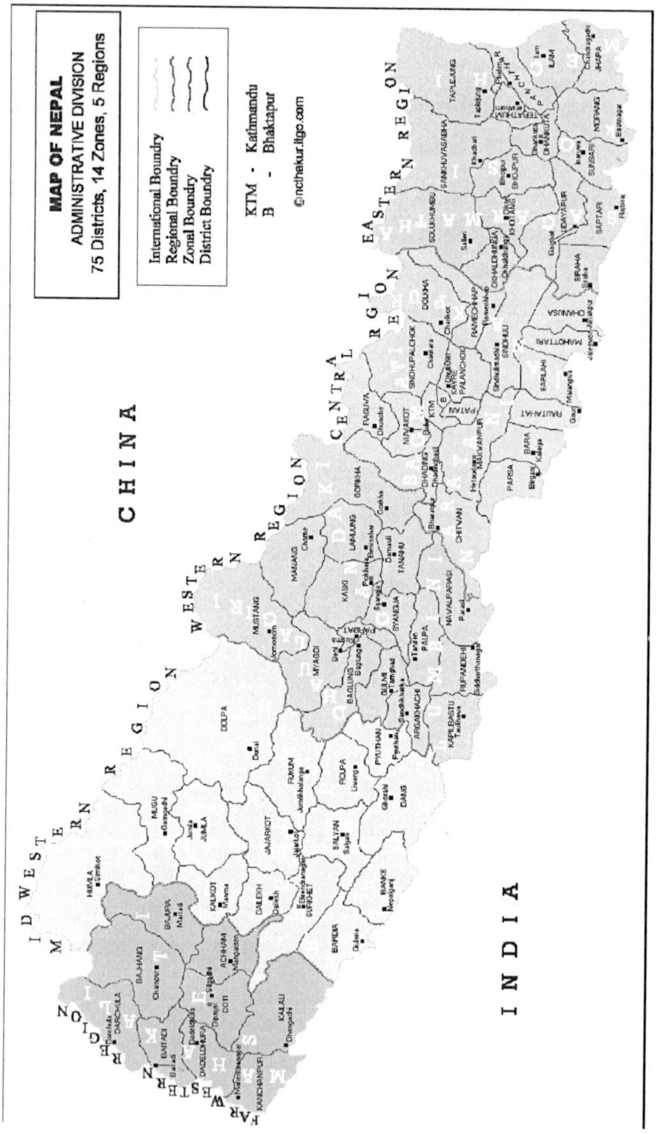

52 Source: www.ncthakur.itgo.com

The selection of Thabang village as a field site was specifically done since it was a key location of Nepali People's War. The people here provided logistic, recruitment, shelter and other kinds of support for various battles fought in different stages of development of the Maoist movement. It was the first village in entire country where local people's government was formed by the end of 1997. At various phases of development of the Maoist movement, hundreds of political activists from Thabang were sent by the CPN (M) to propagate Maoism in country. This was the same village which was declared a *Bishes Jilla* (Special District) and capital of Magarant Autonomous Regional People's Government in 2004.[53] This way the selection of site for field work is based on above grounds and if we have to look at what happened with a revolutionary process that was organised during the Maoist movement as well as its objective, a complete picture could only be grasped by studying Thabang at various phases of People's War along with its past.

10. REFLECTIONS FROM THE FIELDWORK

First of all, I want to clarify some key issues which are essentially linked with this study. My understanding of sociology is deeply rooted in my political activism in solidarity with Maoist politics in Nepal.[54] This was the reason that I took up such a topic

53 The Magarant Autonomous Region includes 14 districts of Western Nepal. These are Rolpa, Rukum, Pyuthan, Salyan, Dang (only northern part), Baglung, Gulmi, Arghakhanchi, Myagdi, Syangja, Palpa, Nawalparasi (only mountain side), and Tanuhan (only half region).

54 My political journey began with AISA, a left student organization while studying in University of Allahabad. Here, I came into contact with the Maoist movement in Nepal since 1999. Subsequently, while studying at Delhi's Jawaharlal Nehru University, I came in contact with the CPN (M)'s migrant organisation. I have been

for my research. Therefore, my understanding and interest of state and society in Nepal in general has been influenced by long standing people's aspiration to establish Socialism in Nepal. My understanding of field site therefore is multiple and it is more than just selecting a field site and limiting my study solely within that.

While taking fieldwork for this study, I have been to Nepal for several times. My first Nepal visit was done soon after the 19 days April movement in 2006 which eventually resulted in the downfall of monarchy. This was a time when peace negotiations between the CPN (M) and Nepal government had begun after signing various point agreements. As per the agreement, the Maoist had disbanded their village governments and their PLA was kept in cantonments under the supervision of the UNMIN. These political developments opened up many questions worldwide especially on the fate of Maoist's movement. At this period, Nepali media reports were full of news about how the Maoists had not actually disbanded their local people's government. The Maoist leaders assured the well wishers of Nepali revolution that they were preparing for an insurrection for final seizure of power. In this context, election of Constituent Assembly was held in 2008 and I too participated as an election observer by leading a team of activists, journalists and scholars from progressive sections of India.

My activist concern with politics of Nepal has helped me select the site of Thabang. I was more concerned with the transformations that took place after the base area was established and *Jansatta* began to function at village level. I decided to take up this study of Thabang to clear my doubts amid reports by Maoist aligned journals worldwide that a "sea change" has taken place in

---

one of organizer of the India-Nepal People's Solidarity Forum to oppose Indian hegemony in Nepali politics. I resigned from my organizational responsibilities in early 2010 after realizing that the Nepali Maoist has taken a wrong direction.

their controlled area and they were on right track of completing revolution in Nepal. Although, abolishment of monarchy was indeed a positive development but even after the Maoist-led government was formed and resigned shortly made me convinced that "semi-feudal and semi-colonial" character of the whole state machinery remained intact. The peace process was going on but final goal of seizure of state power did not happen which the ultimate goal of the People's war in Nepal as was assured by the Maoists. These developments raised the key question worldwide whether the fundamental transformation of Nepali state and society has taken place as claimed by the Maoists. The mainstream media was full of narrations that the Maoists are not committed to the peaceful path and still aspire for seizure of state power by military means, and they are still exercising local people's government in the countryside. The Maoist leaders' speeches were full of rhetoric of final seizure of power. However, after the eventual fall of the Prachanda-led government it was proved that the character of Nepali ruling classes and the State has not changed even a little.

In this context, I carried out my fieldwork for the present research in four phases from May 2010 to June 2012. During first phase, I stayed for a month in Thabang village. I had read that transportation in hill region is very poor and it takes hours for one to reach a destination. But real experience began when I passed through those rugged mountains. I travelled with a group comprising a PLA couple of Thabang VDC and Journalist from America. For a local resident coming from Kathmandu by bus, it takes a whole day to reach Thabang after getting down at Sulichaur market. But, since we were new traveller, so it took 2 days to reach Thabang. Whereas the root from district headquarters of Libang to Thabang was rougher compared from Sulichaur market and also considered unsafe since by passing through a vast forest. In early morning, our group took route of Sulichaur market to Thabang which was under construction then by the GTZ, a German developmental agency. We reached Phuliban village of Jaimakasla VDC in the evening by an overcrowded jeep and spent night in a local hotel. It was next day in late evening that we were able to reach Thabang by a torturous walk.

It was a festival season in village. I observed the Bhume festival and participated in dance processions. My identity as a political activist helped me to make initial rapport with local activists who helped me in arranging my stay in commune in Rachibang village. I conducted around eleven un-structured interviews from some activists and villagers. But I lacked a camera therefore I could not take photographs of documents related to personal records of activists. The foremost realization of first phase was that my understanding of the rural setting will be insufficient unless I could communicate in Nepali language. Till this period, having Hindi as my primary language, I could read Nepali since both the languages have an identical *Devanagri* script. But I could barely understand their Nepali dialect while communicating to villagers.[55] Though, listening to BBC Nepali radio service since 2005 was most helpful to grasp elementary Nepali but I faced difficulty in comprehending Nepali in colloquial setting. It did take a lot of time for me to speak Nepali and understand the nuanced meanings of everyday life. The lesson of Nepali elementary text such as *Teach Yourself Nepali*, which is popular among western tourists, was of no use for me.[56]

From the Maoist magazines and interaction with activists, I was informed that after initiation of People's War, many socio-political and cultural transformations had taken place in the society of Thabang. The caste discrimination against Dalits had

55 My personal interaction with activists of migrant Nepali labour organizations based in India was mainly through Hindi.

56 This was also a reason that I did not consider myself as "foreigner" while in Nepal as opposed to tourists from western countries.

ceased to exist and assertion of women's rights have took place. I was told that it was police who fear people of Thabang as opposed to police terror anywhere else in Nepal or in my country, India. Therefore, after being in Thabang for the first time, I took these "claims" at face value and could not understand the complicated dynamics behind it. My understanding of the situation however developed and improved when I took second phase of fieldwork.

I spend some three and half months from mid September 2010 to end of the year. My primary objective at this phase of field work was to situate myself not in a particular location but to visit the entire region of Thabang VDC. Secondly, I had decided to make conscious efforts in communicating in Nepali language and de-class myself by accepting whatever food the villagers offer. My aims were quite different from first phase as I had stayed then mainly interacted with a selective group of people and I was largely treated as "special"[57] guest and had offered me *Dal-Bhat* (pulse and rice). On a very limited number only, they offered me *Dhindo*, a staple food made of maize floor and meat of pork & buffalo which is the main diet in the Kham Magar region.

Only at this period of fieldwork, I could feel that how an average villager of Thabang thinks about government sitting in Kathmandu. A deep rooted hatred exists in their mind against Nepali state. These responses came while I was interacting with people in general. Many women made a straightforward question on many occasions as to why I was there and they wanted to know

57 It was because of my identity as Indian and also a supporter of Nepali revolution. I was often seen with linking to Indian radical formation of different Marxist-Leninist streams adhering Marxism-Leninism-Maoism. At the same time, my location at JNU was taken as equivalent to political-ideological level of the Maoist leader Dr. Baburam Bhattarai who was an alumnus of this university. In Nepal, JNU is known as a "socialist university".

whether I was a pimp in disguise of a student who had come to lure young girls. It gave me idea that it is important to record these historical narratives and life histories of ordinary people of both men and women who have grown up and were organized under the banner of People's War to assert against state repression and patriarchy.

It has been reported by academic writing[58] that women of Thabang are less oppressed and have greater share in managing household. While doing informal interviews, I have realized that this is not the objective reality, as my work depicts dominant practice of polygyny which was regarded as a socially accepted tradition before commencement of Maoist movement. It is commonly said almost by every woman I interacted that during People's War, sexual violence was controlled by the village *Jansatta* committee. The practice of child marriage in guise of 'love marriage' once discouraged is again re-emerging. I found also re-emergence of the practice of *Jari* by which man takes another's wife by paying money to him as a penalty since he took his property. Most unfortunate event was suicide by some young married women.[59] Many such narrations were recorded which speak about the male domination in Thabang.

While beginning of second phase of fieldwork, I arrived at a conclusion that not accepting food (i.e., meat of pork, buffalo and cow) when people offered me while visiting them leads into unwillingness and lack of opening up reflecting on research

58 Augusta Molnar (1981), *The Kham Magar Women of Thabang*, Kathmandu: CEDA.

59 3 such cases took place during this phase of study. In two such cases, reason of their suicide was their pregnancy while husband is in foreign and in one case was due to husband's abusive behavior coupled with his heavy drinking behaviour and threat of marrying another woman.

objectives and answering my specific points. Most of village household had offered me *jand-raksi* (homemade liquor and beer) at various occasions which I had declined. Following these insights, I made conscious effort to overcome my disliking of food they offered me. I situated myself at the hostel of Thabang High school which turned out to be helpful since I could arrange for transcription of field notes and move easily. I returned to hostel after 3 to 7 days after visiting a village. This particular decision made fruitful results. I was able to speak Nepali relatively more fluently and could also develop a taste of local food. But this decision also had bad repercussion on my health.[60]

The methodology of participant observation teaches that unless a researcher attach with people in their everyday life by making oneself like one among them, this kind of study is not possible. The training as a sociologist helped me to understand how ethnicity dominated society of Kham Magar was different from caste based Hindu society. This was a pertinent question which was also linked with class analysis of the Kham Magar society. The most downtrodden households comprised of poor

60 Soon after returning to India, I was diagnosed Tuberculosis (TB) in April, 2011. I have to complete a 6 months course of TB treatment in a New Delhi based Dots centre from mid-April to first week of October, 2011. The major reason of TB was that I did not had a staple diet since of habit of eating very early morning / evening which was quite opposite for me as I was used to food three times a day breakfast in morning, lunch in afternoon and dinner in night. In Thabang, there is no concept of breakfast in morning except of afternoon by eating fried maize/ millet with potato. After eating in early morning before 8 am, for whole day I felt hungry most of times. The other reason was also because of my smoking habit. Though, I have found smoking cigarette also helped me make a good relationship especially interviewing older generation people.

peasantry and daily wage labourer mostly represented by Dalit community. At the same time, to the century's long process of state formation based on national code of 1854 had an impact in the social stratification in Thabang by making sub division within Dalit community. Living in this society I could grasp the patron-client relationships of Jajmani system in India and a Dalit's relationship with other community. While cooking food dish either in commune hotel or in family households the people could become attached to me without treating me as a mere guest or foreign tourist. While living with them in their houses and eating with them in different households, I could extract those insights of grasping class and caste based inequality in Thabang. While eating in a rich/middle peasant family house and eating in a family of poor peasantry, I found a great difference. Everybody owns land in Thabang but measurement of land in quantity does not make much sense unless its location, size and fertility are taken into account. The rich households eat rice and *roti* (bread) quite often. Whereas, cooking of these dishes in poor household was like celebrating festivals and they cooked *Dhindo* almost every day.

The interviews were recorded at various locations while travelling with villagers from one village to another. I conducted the interviews in their leisure time, especially at the time of breakfast during afternoon and amid drinking beer in the evening. Beside this, recording of interviews were done by visiting them and helping them ploughing their fields and staying in farm huts. I observed festivals of *Dasain*, *Tihar, Bhume* and various family rituals of marriage, birth and death rites as a participant in these events.

The third phase of field work was to visit PLA combatants of Thabang residing in mainly different divisions of various camps located in different parts of country. It was completed by taking two trips from September to October, 2011 in a short interval by visiting

Shaktikhor cantonment located in Nawalparasi. It was followed by another field investigation between February to March in 2012 to visit cantonments located in Dahban and Jhyaltungdanda. Though, I met many PLA combatants in Thabang but I wanted to get a field insight while being in cantonments waiting to be integrated in the Nepal Army now called the National Army.[61]

I revisited the field site from April to June, 2012 for around 3 months. This was last phase of field work and I undertook a particular visit of Pyuthan and Dang district along with visiting Thabang. There I met some veteran communist activists who had played leading roles in founding of primary school in Thabang. Three particular life histories were also recorded at this phase which is included in this work. After transcription of field data, I found that interview with high ranking leaders of village *Jansatta* were not based on nuanced understanding and hence not fruitful. The leadership refused to share with me the sensitive issues especially on specific problems and contradiction of the Maoist governance of Thabang Special District and its dealing with everyday life of peasantry. These ideas were a result of my reading of Maoist documents and gaining insights from transcription of a PLA brigade commander's life history. Therefore, I had conducted some more life histories with new insights which included life histories of a Dalit activist and peasant women included in this study.

I solely relied on my English transcription from Nepali. At initial phases, it was very time consuming to transcribe even a 30 minutes recording that took entire day but gradually my efficiency

61 The erstwhile "Royal Nepal Army" is called now "Nepal Army", after the success of April People's Movement of 2006, and subsequent re-instatement of parliament removed the "royal" suffix from every institution of Nepali State. Now onwards, the "His Majesty Government" was removed by "Nepal Government".

developed whereas transcription of leaflets and documents in Nepali was relatively easy.

11. LIMITATIONS OF WORK

It is very important to do a rigorous sociological analysis of People's War of Nepal which has so far been studied dominantly by with a stick of security-centric policy framework i.e., 'counter-insurgency 'or 'terrorism'. However, no attempt has been made to see it a coherent way that it was a political movement that fundamentally asserted until the present state power is not abolished then any kind of social transformation would be impossible. Therefore, once security frameworks are applied to analyse such a process, then it leaves no scope for a rigorous sociological and political analysis. Most studies of Nepal portray ideology of Maoism as rhetoric and not as an ideology by using their 'objective' framework. Another dominant trend is the glorification of Nepal as the pristine land and peace loving Hindu Kingdom. The portrayal of the People's War in Nepal also appears in their writing as ethnic assertion without linking it with the history of the peasantry's political mobilization against the oppressive and exploitative state. For these scholars, class differentiation among peasantry and hardship of village Nepal hardly make any sense and they consider ethnic identity as of sole importance.

Generally, Indian scholarships look at the political movement of People's War from a counter-insurgency and security perspective which once posed threats to security of Indian state. Indian scholars are also deeply embedded in a sociological imagination of treating Nepal either as *Asal* (pure) Hindu state or as an 'unofficial state/province' of India, reflected in their 'big brotherly' attitude towards Nepal. It is a sorry situation following of the so called 'post-colonial' studies. This is the reason why no studies have been done to understand the political economic reality of Nepal by Indian sociologists, other than from a security framework by abundant 'Nepal experts'. Thus, my study is a modest attempt to challenge the dominant academic discourse on Nepal.

Following this it can be said that being as a researcher from India was my major political and cultural limitation and sometimes as challenge. This was reflected at various phases of conducting field work. For example, the villagers recounted to me their past experiences of the activities of Indian businessmen in the region to involve in trafficking of young girls to sell in Indian brothels. This caused various questions while interacting with women especially those of the younger generation. Secondly, rural population often perceived me as a probable 'agent' of Indian Intelligence Agency called the Research and Analysis Wing (RAW). It is generally believed that domination of India in Nepali politics existed since the times of British Raj. The reason could also be one that I conducted my fieldwork particularly after fall of Prachanda government but one can easily observe the influence of the Indian hegemony on every aspects of Nepal, from economy to culture.

The strength of study was my identity as political activist which had positive effect because I was easily accepted in rank and file of Maoist party organisation. However, this also implied negative points. While meeting with displaced families of Thabang and leaders of other political parties my political identity became liability and hindrance to get their perspective.

12. CHAPTER PLAN OF BOOK

This book has been organized in 6 chapters.

The chapter-1 is introductory one which also sets the analytical framework to study of People's War in Nepal. It is argued that People's War was political movement which aimed to alter power structure by mobilizing peasant population. The chapter also sets ethnographic sites, methodological issues and sociological reflection gained during fieldwork.

The chapter-2 examines the nature of state and society of Nepali agrarian scenario. This is based on two parts. First part deals with political economy of state formation after the Gorkhali conquest of Nepal in 1769 to until recent of 1990s. The remaining part deals with ideology behind state formation that polity was based on *Hinduization*.

The chapter-3 explains ideology and practice of the CPN (M). It describes further different components of the Maoist's program and its remedy after theorizing of a thesis of "semi-feudal, semi-colonial" Nepal. This made the Maoist to apply a political military strategy of People's War to carry out a New Democratic revolution in Nepal.

The chapter-4 is based on ethnographic study of Thabang VDC. It is divided into two parts by dealing two exclusive periods of history of communist movement of this village. The first part explain rebellious conditions which gave birth of communist seeds in the village which made peasantry turn against the *Panchayat* regime in spite of facing state terror. The second section portray scenario after beginning and expansion of guerrilla war since 1996. The Maoist's model of governance was organised here by making Thabang a Special District is explained further.

The chapter-5 is continuation of earlier chapters. Here, I have made thread of narratives based on six life histories. The first one is in this series put voice of a Magar peasant woman while the other five are representatives of various ranks of Maoist activists representing Maoist army, Dalit community, village government and party organisation. The objective of these presentations of life histories is to portray the historical setting of Thabang which made their early life cycle of childhood, education to adulthood and attain at a political believe. Their lives in this sense were a reproduction of a larger reality of political churning of Nepali society which emerged in form of People's War.

The chapter-6 deals the main findings of this book. It locates the ideological revision of the CPN (M) which ultimately produced a thesis of 'Cash Maoism' in Nepal.

CHAPTER 2 State and Society in Agrarian Nepal

> *...But if everyone is alert, this will be a true Hindusthan of the four jats, greater and lesser, with the thirty-six classes. Do not leave your ancient religion. Don't forsake the salt of the king.*[1]
>
> **— Prithvi Narayan Shah in *Dibya Upadesh***

In this chapter, an attempt has been done to look at state formation of Nepal in various phases after its emergence in present boundaries. This is underlined fact of state formation and its impact on Nepali society which is primarily rooted in political history of Gorkha conquest which was called as unification. This is important to note here that this unification project made further attempts by being embodiment of landed *Tagadhari* caste Hindu patrimonial state by extracting taxes from a vast majority of peasantry. The majority of this peasantry came from various non-Hindu tribal communities of *Janjatis*. Further, it looks into the period of internal crisis and adjustment within Hindu ruling elites during the British rule in India. It was a marking period in agrarian economy of Nepal which institutionalized dimensions of economic underdevelopment and external migration. This was a period Nepal turned up as a semi-

1 This excerpt is based upon two commentaries based on original text of *Dibya Upadesh*. See, L. F. Stiller (1989 [1968]), *Prithwinarayan Shah in the Light of Dibya Upadesh*, Kathmandu: Himalayan Book Centre, pp. 42-44; Baburam Acharya and Yogi Narharinath (2061 [2010 VS]) (ed.), *Rashtrapita Badamaharajadhiraj Shi 5 Prithvinarayan Shahko Dibya Upadesh*, Antarashtriya Manch Chhapakhana, pp. 45-51.

colonial state of British India by allowing recruitment of warriors from its hill for its imperial project.

Moreover, how the Nepali society forgone in changes by locating it in political economy of Nepali state which ultimately was responsible to devise ideology firmly rooted in Hindu polity. After Indian independence, because of external power balance, the Rana rulers lost their British alley which made in resulted emergence of monarchy again to establish its *Panchayat* regime after a short stint of multi-party democratic exercise. Over the many decades progressed, country's economy was to be added with a heavy dependence on remittance economy of Nepali labour in India, Gulf region to others destinations worldwide. It was further assisted by propagating development rhetoric by politics of foreign aid and by assimilation project of non-Hindu social groups in name of the Nepali Nationalism that was an extension of original project of making Nepal a real land of Hindus.

In this way, my understanding of state and society of agrarian Nepal constitutes two dimensions of political economy, and ideology of state formation. However, before going further, it is important to present a short but concise discussion on state formation.

1. CONCEPTUALIZING STATE FORMATION

The state have the power over vast territories populated by millions of people and it control people's actions everywhere. The state is the institution which has authority to raise armies and maintain police power to supervise law and order of civilian life. It has powers to declare war against another state; print currency; collect taxes; arrest, imprison people and impose death sentence. It exercises a vast network of bureaucratic officialdom to govern and regulate society. It is why for this reason that the state, regardless of government is both infuse awe and reared in lives of its citizens of a particular society.

However, state has not existed of eternal times. In Human civilization, there are many illustrations of societies that did not have this institution called state. It came into exist at a certain stage of development of society "... which was necessarily bound up with the split of society into classes, the state became a necessity..."[2] In Marxist framework, the institution of state is regarded as a devise to maintain and defend class domination and exploitation. The state emerged out of struggle between two antagonistic classes of exploiters and exploited. The emergence of state was paralleled by the appearance of these opposed classes. The originators of this institution were wealthy and prosperous by exploiting a vast majority of population where they constituted an insignificant minority. Therefore, in order to protect its wealth, the exploiting minority needed a special force and special instrument of power. In sum, this is called the state. In his seminal work on state, Lenin argued that;

> *The state is, therefore, by no means a power forced on society from without;... Rather it is a product of society at a certain stage of development; it is the admission that this society has become entangled in an insoluble contradiction with itself, that it has split into irreconcilable antagonisms which it is powerless to dispel. But in order that these antagonisms, these classes with conflicting economic interests might not consume themselves and society in fruitless struggle, it became necessary to have a power, seemingly standing above society, that would alleviate the conflict and keep it within the bounds of 'order'; and this power, arisen out of society but placing itself above it, and alienating itself more and more from it, is the state.*[3]

---

2 F. Engels (1977), *The Origin of the Family, Private Property and the State: In the Light of the Researches of Lewis H. Morgan*, Moscow: Progress Publishers, p. 170.

3 V.I. Lenin (1968), 'The State And Revolution' in Selected Works of

Following above definition it can be argued that the dominant ruling class use and controls state as its instrument to put their interest by portraying it as common people interest. This leads the rival classes and groups to confront for power from ruling class. In their course of struggle, nonetheless, the legality of state is rarely questioned except its authority face question during crisis time when the state become unsuccessful to make a way out the basic question linked to social, political and economic aspects. This lead to decline of legitimacy of state and its ruling classes occurred through by manifestation of class conflict which gets manifest in forms of resistance.

It is argued in this work that the analysis of the state formation of Nepal is possible in terms of an approach which can identify the underlying structures of political economic relation with which they developed over time. Only with such approach, based on construction of an independent conceptual tools, it is possible to explain both underlying political- economic relations and ideology behind it, and to reveal the specific features of the former which generate and reproduce the apparent dominance of the latter.

2. POLITICAL ECONOMY OF AGRARIAN NEPAL

The agrarian society of Nepal was originally tribal in organization and ruled by tribal heads by customary laws. The population had a communal mode of production generally characterized by pastoral and shifting cultivation.[4] The early social history can be traced only with the advent of 'hunting nomads' of Mongoloid stock (i.e., Kirat) from south-east and pastoral nomads of Caucasoid stock (i.e., Khas) from the north- west to meet at Nepal valley (today's Kathmandu valley) around first millennium B.C. Whereas the evolutionary dynamics took its own slow course to varying forms

---

Lenin, Moscow: Progress Publishers, p. 266.

4 Dor Bahadur Bista (2008 [1991]), *Fatalism and Development: Nepal's Struggle for Modernization*, Kolkata: Orient Longman, p.16.

of tribal communal formations in other parts of territory, it was Kathmandu valley with its excellent agro-climatic advantage for stabilized agriculture and primitive entrepôt status for trade between Indian plains and Tibetan plateau that became the citadel of early civilization in line with the Greek city states. The property relations were characterized by the system of communal land ownership known as *Kipat* and *Raibandi* that was not only equitable but was based on a number of considerations such as family needs, collective responsibility, mutual respect and welfare. Under this system all resources including lands and forest were controlled communally by law and distributed in accordance with family requirements. The pre-Hindu-states before the Gorkha conquest were organized on the basis of kinship. Instead of subordinating people by excluding them from the rights in the land, these states included groups of people within an expanding kinship organization.

At first the, monarchy was established in Kathmandu. By Third century, Nepal Valley (i.e. Kathmandu Valley) under a pre-Hindu kingdom known as Lichhavis dynasty, a class society was developing that was based on differentiation of social division of labour and diversified agricultural and craft production. Except for the neighboring hilly areas of the vicinity of the Kathmandu valley which must have been affected by the social process of Kathmandu valley, the other areas of country seem to have followed their own dynamics to embryonic proto-class formations out of the tribal communal society till the early tenth century. However, after the 11th century there was a great influx of high caste Rajput Hindu migrants from Indian plains fleeing from Muslim invasions of northern Indian kingdoms. The gradual encroachment by the Hindu refugees succeeded to establish petty Hindu kingdoms throughout hills since then. These immigrants who brought with them the superior war technology and skills, could, in course of time overcome the tribal communities who followed animistic religious faith and become their masters.

The establishment of petty Hindu principalities meant a significant development in technology and in the division of labor in society, and emergence of class structure and emergence of state structure in the larger parts of the territory of Nepal. As Blaikie et al. (1980) notes that the;

> *...nobility as well as the courtiers, clients, officials, and generals of these petty states, tended to be 'High caste' Hindus (Bahun and Chhetris) of Indo-Aryan extraction while the subject classes, who were taxed and obliged to serve as soldiers in order to maintain the state and the ruling classes, Included the majority of the Indigc nous Mongoloid populations (whose tribal structures and small chiefdoms had been only partly destroyed by the establishment of these Hindu Kingdoms), and also the 'low caste' artisans (e.g. blacksmiths, leatherworkers and tailors) and small farmers who accompanied the warrior leaders in their gradual migration into and within the Nepalese hills.*[5]

The new technology of warfare enabled them to establish Hindu petty kingdoms and new technology of production enabled them to destroy the communal mode of production. Whenever a new petty state were formed, therefore, they were associated with a significant development of the productive forces in agriculture, warfare technology and in coercive and extractive capacity of the state.

3. THE RISE OF GORKHALI STATE

> *On Chandragiri's top I asked, "Which is Nepal?" They showed me, saying, "That is Bhadgaon, that is Patan, and there lies Kathmandu." The thought came to my heart that if I might be king of these three cities, why, let it be so. At this time these two astrologers said to me.*

---

5 Piers Blaikie, John Cameron and David Seddon (2005 [1980]), *Nepal in Crisis: Growth and Stagnation at the Periphery*, New Delhi: Adroit Publishers, p. 24.

"O King, your heart is melting with desire." I was struck with wonder. How did they know my inmost thoughts and so speak to me? "At the moment your gaze rested on Nepal [Nepalma] you stroked your moustache and in your heart you longed to be king of Nepal, as it seemed to us." "Will this come to pass?" I asked. "You, O Prince, have held at all times great respect for cows, Brahmins, guests, holy men, the gods and goddesses. Also in our hand lies the blessing of Saraswati. You will one day be king of Nepal."

- Prithvi Narayan Shah, *Dibya Updesh.*[6]

The inhabitants of the surrounding hills, plains and mountains refer to the valley as Nepal even though they lived within political frontiers of the then kingdom of Nepal. The Nepali historiography describes the present state of Nepal as a brainchild of king Prithvi Narayan Shah. He is solely been offered an expression as 'father of nation' in school text books to public discourse. His invasion of Nepal valley is presented as such that through such act Nepali nationality came into existence out of many disparate feudal Hindu petty states and peoples of the region.

Thus, it is pertinent to illustrate those facts of history which lead to Prithvi Narayan Shah to invade the land which was popularly called unification of Nepal. In the mid-18th century, the Nepali state had been stretched over the period of six centuries of the petty Hindu kingdoms. These included estate administration of the *Chaubisi rajya* (24 states) in the Gandaki region and *Baisi rajya* (22 states) in Karnali region. These petty states were embodied with caste Hindu caste social order and were kin organised states. This was a period that a steady fall down of the Mughal Empire in the northern India was paving a way for emergence of European commercial and military onslaught in the region. Thus, under the cumulative imperatives of the need to reorganise the society to

6 Cited in op. cit., L. F. Stiller S.J. (1989 [1968]), p. 39.

meet the increased revenue demands of the state and proliferating non-labouring classes rallying around it and the threat of suction separately into the rising East India Company (or British empire) in the south, led to Gorkhali campaign for larger, unified state of Nepal in the latter half of the 18th century.[7]

Eventually shifting his capital in Kathmandu[8], the Gorkhali state extended its sovereignty over all along the foot hills of the Himalayan from the Teesta River in east to the Sutlej River of the west. The present state boundary consisting of the hill tract between the Mechi in east and the Mahakali in west with a narrow strip of plains in the south was defined when the expansionary drives of the Nepali state came to halt with defeat at the hands of the East India Company. In a remarkable study on implication of Gorkha conquest, Pradhan (1991) tend to argue that:

> *Historians of Nepal tend to describe the polity before the conquest of Prathvinarayan Shah as the state of 'political fragmentation' before 'national unification'. However, 'fragmentation' implies a breaking or separation into pieces of a pre-existent whole; and national unity connotes the change, a conscious one, from the chaos of national disintegration to a state of cohesion. Such a description also presupposes the presence of various factors contributing to the sense of national unity among a people with aspiration towards a separate national identity. Herein lies the debate- was Nepal ever a nation before Gorkha forged it into one and did it ever have a physical shape comparable to the present one to merit such description?*[9]

7 Stephen Lawrence Mikesell (1999), *Class, State, and Struggle in Nepal: Writings 1989-1995*, Delhi: Manohar, p. 89.

8 Gorkha was the capital of Prithvi Narayan Shah before conquest of Kathmandu valley.

9 Kumar Pradhan (1991), *The Gorkha Conquests: The Process and Consequences of the Unification of Nepal, with Particular Reference to Eastern Nepal*, Calcutta: Oxford University Press, p. 2.

Thus the agrarian state of Nepal was built by conquering and certainly it was not a comprehension of some intrinsic national spirit and national unity.

4. PEASANT LANDLORD RELATIONSHIP

From the Lichhavi period until before the emergence of Gorkhali state in mid 18th century, land was vested in the state. The rulers of these petty kingdoms had divided it into three categories: a) lands directly under Royal family, b) land under *Birta, Guthi, Jagir*, and c) land under public property. It could be said that throughout the course of making petty Hindu states, the direct producers enjoyed only the right to cultivate but ownership of lands as formally vested in the state itself. This enhanced the society into ruling class and subject class in significant way and made inequalities more acute between them. During the course of state expansion, the main aims of *Gorkhali* rulers were to strengthen military power for controlling the conquered areas and extracts revenues directly or indirectly to further the objective of territorial expansion. One can maintain that political unification did not affect the basic structure of the society even though change took place in the fortunes of many persons, families, castes and ethnic groups.

With land being the main source to strengthen military power and revenue collection, the rulers deputed Hindu high caste men to administer throughout the country. The lands were distributed among them under different forms which were exempted from taxes from initial periods to encourage new settlement in conquered territories. At this period the ruling class consisted of those petty Hindu states before the Gorkha conquest which the new empire superseded and incorporated, predominantly of Thakuris under Shah Kings, with Chhetri-Bahun as *Bhardars* (courtiers). Now it is clear that the land grant and assignment policy followed by the Gorkha rulers favoured particular sections of Nepalese society by excluding others. Those given the land tended for the most part to be Bahuns, Thakuris, and Chhetris whose social and political status corresponded to that of the ruling class itself. The tribal communities mainly Gurungs, Magars, Tamangs and other non-Hindu groups like Limbus (except Newar) rarely reserved such favours from state. On the contrary they tended to suffer a progressive encroachment of the lands they either occupied by tradition or owned by virtue of previous land grants.

The Newars were given space to hold high positions after three Hindu high castes (i.e. Brahmin, Kshatriya, and Vaishya) in central administration of Nepal. During the campaign for state expansion the Gorkhali rulers had recognized communal *Kipat* tenure to allow "internal autonomy" for Limbus. This autonomy was eroded after high caste Hindu officials began to encroach on Kipat lands. Consequently a large number of Limbus migrated to the adjoining areas of India and Sikkim. The Gorkha rulers of Kathmandu then confiscated the *Kipat* lands of fugitive Limbus and granted them to non-Limbu settlers under *Raikar* and *Birta* tenure.[10]

After the establishment of sovereignty of Nepal the ultimate ownership of all the went to the sovereign as embodiment of the state. As a result, the system of state landlordism named *Raikar* was started throughout the kingdom except in some areas of east and west regions where strong collective feelings prevailed.[11] The rent receiving class consisted of the Bahuns, members of royal family,

10 Mahesh Chandra Regmi (1971), *A Study in Nepali Economic History, 1768-1846*, New Delhi: Manjushri Publishing House, pp. 50-51.

11 It was the collective ownership on the means of very important production (i.e. land) and it was clear form of system of exploration to the indigenous cultivators comprising mainly Magars, Tamangs and Gurungs. See, Mahesh C. Regmi, (1978), *Thatched Huts and Stucco Palaces: Peasants and Landlords in the 19th Century Nepal*, New Delhi: Vikas Publishing House, p. 17.

nobility, government officials, priests and other persons of non-agricultural class who did not cultivate their lands themselves. However, this privileged class did not pay regular taxes to central administration. Consequently, the administrative burden of state was rested primarily on peasantry, craftsmen and merchants. Because the energies of the government concentrated primarily to the collection of revenue to finance its growing military and administrative expenditure, concern for the well being of the people seldom found a reflection through the disbursement of public funds. The overall economic situation of Nepal was rural, agricultural and subsistent; which resulted in uniformity with respect to land tenure also. After the Gorkha conquest, the petty rulers of subjugated principalities were replaced by a *Subba* or a regional administrative head. These principalities were not brought under direct control under the center and their feudatory chiefs had the same status as equivalent to administrative head. These chief were given internal autonomy as a tributary state.

It may be argued that the only changes brought about by the conquest of the Gorkha, was the establishment of a centralized state and unitary feudal authority. The *Subbas* conducted theirs affairs as before, and the *Gorkhalis* adopted a policy of minimum change in the administration of the expanded kingdom. Therefore there was no single law regulated in the whole new empire after Gorkha conquest of Nepal. By the end of the 18th century virtually the entire area that is now Nepal had been incorporated into a loosely articulated hegemony as an administrative unit only.

Figure-I: Land tenure system in agrarian Nepal[12]

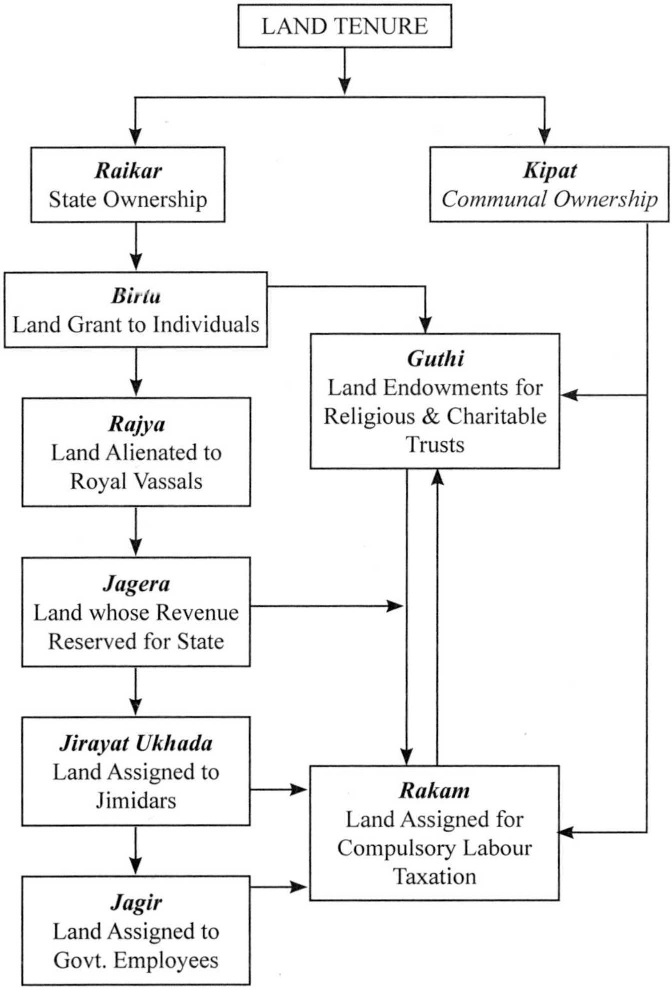

12 **Source:** Baburam Bhattarai (2003), *The Nature of Underdevelopment and Regional Structure of Nepal: A Marxist Analysis*, New Delhi: Adroit Publishers, p. 70.

As the Gorkha conquest did not bring about any economic changes, it could make some believe that the peasantry and the humble folk of the lower orders remained untouched by political turmoil. However, this was not the case. The *Gorkhali* conquest accelerated many other existing processes which had begun much earlier which had occurred in economic field. The necessities of the military campaigns made them to resort to economic practices that had far-reaching implications.

The usual mode of defraying the expenses of the military establishments and paying the army was by assignments of land as *Jagir*. The *Birta* grants were made to the eminent commanders and *Kus birtas* to Brahmans for their various religious/ritual services. Higher ranks in the army tended to be filled from among the Chhetris (including the Rajput or Thakuri). Others at the most rose up to the rank of captains. Up to the middle of the nineteenth century, armies were raised when needed and disbanded when not required. In general, only members of the higher castes were retained in service during peace time. Hence they monopolized the *Jagirs*.

The Gorkha conquest needed more land in order to satiate more appetite which subsequently led to the inevitable increase in the number and extent of *Jagir* holdings. The old *Birta* grants were confirmed when their holders readily submitted to the Gorkhalis and new ones were granted to potential defectors, eminent military leaders and scheming Brahmans; besides, the defeated rulers had also to be placated. It is true that at times attempts were made by king Ranabahadur Shah and other successors of Prathivinarayan Shah to confiscate *Birta* grants. However, the built-in socio-political system was such that nothing much could be achieved. Moreover, such actions were dictated not by any principles but by personal idiosyncrasy or political expediency. Therefore, the land grants like *Birta* and *Jagir* cultivated by the peasant population had no direct relationship with the state and;

> *...the government exercised no direct control. Police and judicial functions were discharged by the Birta owners. As long as Birta owners were politically loyal and were not excessively oppressive, the government had no direct concern with the peasantry. Vested with the proprietorship of an estate, the Birta owners enjoyed a miscellany of conventionally rights and the proceeds of numerous personal servitudes and exactions. Secure from the interference of local officials in the exercise of their rights, they owed allegiance only to the king, an allegiance occasionally manifested when a new king was crowned or the royal princesses were married, or during war and other emergencies.*[13]

The *Jagirs* were assigned for a fixed period of time. Since the assignee employed in active military/civil service seldom lived on his *Jagir* land, he left the cultivation to the cultivator. Such absentee *Jagirdars* sold '*tirjas*' (authority to collect taxes) to brokers called '*dhokres*'. These agents profited by collecting more than their investments and as a result, the cultivators were oppressed. Similar system existed even in *Raikar* and other lands also. Though, Prithivi Narayan Shah had advised that taxes be collected by government officials for effectiveness, the *Gorkhali* administration had to depend on agents called *Ijaradars*. These *Ijaradars* collected as much as they could, paid a fixed periodic sum to the government and appropriated the excess collected. In many places the *Subedars* and military commanders acted as *Ijaradars*.

The land grants of *Birta* implied the divesture of the ownership right by the state to private individuals, but it was not always total and unconditional. The *Birtawals* were obligated to supply troops and materials. Their lands were often cultivated by the *Adhiyars*, who, as the very name suggests, paid half the produce to their landlords, retaining the other half for themselves. In these cases,

---

13 Op. cit., Mahesh Chandra Regmi (1971), p. 44.

shares fluctuated according to the amount produced. To keep their income steady the *Birtawals* later replaced *Adhiya* with their *kut* system under which cultivator paid a fixed quantity of their produce and other commodities or else a cash amount. The quantity fixed was bound to be higher than that of *Adhiya*. In fact the change was made for this very purpose. The peasant now bore all costs and risks of marketing. To tide over the difficulties the peasant had to take loans. Rural indebtedness became a common feature and conditions favoured the rich landlords, mostly Brahmans, who now took up on a large scale money lending and other speculative functions. The *Jagir* and the *Birta* holders always saw to it that they got more than what they would have otherwise got from the land.

The Nepali peasants did not enjoy any tenurial security; they could be evicted according to the will of the landlords. This occurred when they failed to pay the stipulated amount of produce or the cash in lieu; landlords then made settlements with others who agreed to pay higher amounts. Besides these risks, peasants under heavy form of tenure bore many other burdens. The miserable life of peasants does not stop by paying his land tax to state. They also had to pay *Jhara*, a type of unpaid labour obligation specially organized during war or rebellion. It was in another form, however, a tax only. The practice of *Jhara* was utilized for the construction, repair, and maintenance of Royal court, supply military appliances and construction of road, canal, fortification and temple etc. The peasant populations of all caste/ethnic groups have to perform this practice. However, as per the Gorkhali regime's order, only Bahun among the upper caste Hindu Tagadhari were exempted from this labour provision. Regmi (1971) gives an illustration of this provision by quoting a government order issued in 1815 during Nepal- British war.

> *Join Bhardars at Makwanpur in fulfillment of your Jhara obligation and work according to their orders.*

> *Persons who can bear arms shall come along with their shields, swords, bows, arrows and guns. Other shall bring spades and axes. Those who work sincerely for us shall be granted honors, rewards and expenses according to their services. Anybody who does not work on Jhara basis according to our order shall be severely punished.*[14]

The demands for *Jhara* could be extremely onerous on the small cultivators who were not exempted and often took away from their fields for appreciate period of time. Not only that they have to provide their labour, but also their tools and rations for duration of the task set to them and this pushed the general peasantry and poor people to direction of poverty and exploitation. Rent hiked on them and the rate sometimes was about 75 percent and that obliged the peasantry to get credit. Due to high rate of interest, land rent, government taxes and *Jhara* system, the conditions of peasantry became so weak that most of them compelled to leave their village too. These men could not go away and lived as bondage labourers or slaves to overlords. These situations of producing bondage labourers or slaves were created by the excesses of government and bureaucracy.

The Gorkha rulers made an official decree of legalizing slavery system in 1803, but the high caste hill *Tagadhari* Hindus were protected not to make slave. Slaves used to be sold officially. Debtor often became bonded labourers. Thus a person could be mortgaged like a piece of property. Children were sold as slaves to settle loans and powerful persons in the village often enslaved the poor. Pradhan (1991) notes about state of slavery at this period in this manner;

> *An Englishman named Raper, who visited Garhwal in 1808, describes the sale of slaves at a Gorkhali post in a pass leading to Ha-Ka-Pir, where 'slaves were brought*

14 Ibid., p. 106.

> *down from the hills and exposed for sale'. 'Many hundreds of these poor wretched', he wrote, 'of both sexes, from three to thirty years of age, are annually disposed of in the way of traffic. These slaves were brought down from all parts of the interiors of the hills and sold at Hardwar at from ten to one hundred and fifty rupees each'.*[15]

The expansion of the state apparatus and of conspicuous consumption of imported luxury goods by the nobility was considerable during the 19th century; the surplus required increased accordingly. Land grants were made in increasing numbers throughout the century, particularly in *Tarai,* so as to promote irrigation, settlement and opening of virgin land for cultivation. During the first decade of 19th century, however, the state came up against the limits to grow on the basis of territorial expansion, in the form of the Sikh to the west and East India Company (British India Empire) to the south. But the most important thing was that at the culmination of the Gorkha conquests to until early 19th century, Nepal had became a unified kingdom but not a unified society and its Gorkha rulers also did not like to do so.

5. NEPAL BECOMES PROTECTORATE OF BRITISH INDIA EMPIRE

Ambitions of further territorial expansion by the Shah rulers came up against the imperial ambitions of the East India Company and ended with Nepal's defeat and signing the Treaty of Sagauli in 1816. Territorially, Nepal lost the whole of the area west of the Mahakali River, Terai, and area east of Mechi River. The treaty of Sagauli accorded Nepal a protectorate status which was politically and economically subordinate to British India Empire but formally independent state. Nepal was obliged to accept the

15 Op. cit., Kumar Pradhan, (1991), p. 178.

appointment of a British Resident in Kathmandu, and to forbid the direct communication with any western power except Great Britain. Nepal was obliged to accept also the arbitrary of British government if raised any dispute with Sikkim. It was not until 1923 that this treaty was modified and the independence of Nepal was recognised by the British government.

The preceding discussion documents that what was the historical trajectories that led to economic underdevelopment of agrarian Nepal under Gorkhali rulers. Various historical accounts suggests that Nepal, before Sagauli treaty was though not an industrial nation but was a self sufficient in many aspects. The Nepali countryside had a well developed small scale local manufacturing industries producing textiles, iron, and copper. It is suggested by Regmi (1971) that after Gorkhali conquest, the State used to export metal goods to Tibet and used to import salt, yak, raw wool, musk, borax and woollen cloths.[16] The reason behind this idea of Nepal being self sufficient and self supporting was its isolated geographical and socio-economic position that led its people to develop a mechanism to fulfil their requirement. It was why that "such forced isolation and self reliance made people industrious and content with whatever they had or whatever they could produce to meet all their few simple needs of daily life".[17]

In this context it is important to note that after Sagauli Treaty, the British India wanted to make Nepal and Tibet its own market. The trade of south began to dominate since 1816 and increased three times within fourteen years. The Indian merchants could move into inner parts of Nepal. This brought an end to its

16 Op. cit., Mahesh Chandra Regmi (1971), pp. 24-25.

17 B.P. Shrestha (1967), cited in Nandra Raj. Shrestha (1982), *The Process of Rural-To-Urban Migration in the Agrarian Economy of Nepal*, Unpublished Ph.D Dissertation submitted to Department of Geography, Indiana University, p. 105.

territorial expansion- to the middle of the 19th century was a time of internecine conflict between the growing empire of the East India Company and the Nepali rulers for sovereignty over the region. After the defeat of Nepal and signing of Sugauli treaty in 1816, the British India Empire began enrolling thousands of Nepali captives in colonial Indian army. They are called world renowned the brave *Gurkhali* soldiers and their tradition of supplying man power fighting others wars still continue as India and British government recruits them in their respective *Gurkha Regiments*.

Nepal's fate of becoming a virtually a protectorate to British India become prominent after a bloody event of 1846. Unable any longer to expand their territorial estates by external conquest due to the superior military power of the East India Company, the leading families of Nepal's ruling class called as *Thar-ghar*[18] fought amongst themselves for control of the government and intensified their exploitation of the direct producers on the land. The Kunwar brothers, in leadership of Jang Bahadur Rana acquired power through a massacre of the competing families of the *Bhardars* (landed aristocratic ruling class). Through event like *Kot* massacre in the middle of the 19th century, Jang Bahadur Rana emerged as a sole ruler and this marks the commencement of the -104 years of Rana oligarchy from 1846 and the capture of Prime Ministry and the subordination of the monarchy to itself. Mikesell (1999) observes on aftermath developments of takeover by Rana regime. According to him;

> *"... the toiling people of the country, who in previous century had joined in the project of national conquest*

18 It literally means 'houses with the names'. Here it is meant as follow; group of 6 families traditionally associated with the Shah dynasty in Gorkha principality namely the Pande, Aryal, Panta, Rana, Khanal and Bohra. These families had helped the rise of the principality of Gorkha. These constituted inner circle of *Gorkhali* ruling elite.

> *by the Gorkha rulers in anticipation of being set up as independent farmers on their own plots of land, found themselves thrown into worse penury, poverty and suffering than ever before. Increasingly unable to make a living as farmers, they were driven in growing numbers into mercenary labour in the colonial Indian army. This history of mercenary labour, long presented by colonial ethnographers and military historians as expressing the essentially military glorification of character of Nepali culture ... became increasingly amplified through all kind of migratory labour from agricultural and industrial labour to large-scale sex labour.*[19]

6. EMERGENCE OF PATRIMONIAL STATE

The British Imperialist preserved Nepal with its entire antique but never merged it as a colony of Empire. Now the Gorkhali state turned up in early nineteenth century as a "patrimonial state or semi-feudal"[20] which has deep roots in agrarian power structure. Thus began a period of emergence of patrimonial state of Nepal which under the contingency of landed elites (notably Rana clan) has interest of fulfilling administrative and military purposes of British imperialism. It was, in essence, as Shrestha (2001) argue, "... an embodiment of landed elites who have historically prepared and supplied the whole echelon of state bureaucrats: from the lowest to the highest level".[21] It was controlled by devising a system where annually an overall review of performance of all level of bureaucrats appointed by state.

---

19 Op. cit., Stephen Lawrence Mikesell (1999), p. 90.

20 David Seddon, P. Blaikie and J. Cameron, (1979), Peasants and Workers in Nepal, New Delhi: Vikas Publishing House, p. 28.

21 Nanda R. Shrestha (2001), *The Political Economy of Land, Landlessness and Migration in Nepal*, New Delhi: Nirala Publications, p. 152.

The Rana rulers gave over control of their foreign diplomacy and conceded any ambitions for additional territory in exchange for recognition of their regime, non-interference in their internal affairs-including monopoly control over internal trade (a concession subsequently begrudged but never taken back) and many forms of exploitation of their indigenous peoples and resources-and collusion in supporting all forms of dissent. The British did not go so far, however, as recognizing the Jang Bahadur's attempts to claim the Royal title, '*Sri Paanch*' - five times honoured- leaving him and his descendents to satisfy with the lesser '*Sri Tin*' (three times honoured) and thereby preserving doubts in their claims to legitimacy."[22] Thus, the event of the *Kot* massacre made the Shah monarchs lost their *de facto* power over state of Nepal and finally they became recorded as mere *de jure* kings.

Administration under this patrimonial state had two main purposes: the collection of revenues and the maintenance of law and order, the latter primarily in order to facilitate the former. The revenues of the state were not distinguished from those of the *Ranas* and treasury surpluses were regarded generally as their personal income; and that between 25 % and 50% of total state revenue was appropriated personally to the *Rana* prime minister. The state departments such as public revenues were treated as part of the ruler's private purse, so senior appointments in the bureaucracy, including the important post of district governor. This entire system was called *Pajni* and was monitored and conferred personally by the Prime Minister. Districts were graded (A, B and C) according to such factors as distance from the capital, population and revenue potential, and the prime minister's closest kinsmen and most loyal followers were retained in Kathmandu or sent to govern the more important or turbulent districts, while those of lesser status, or whose presence in the capital was not

22 Op. cit., Stephen Lawrence Mikesell (1999), p. 91.

desired, were assigned to the least sought-after post in districts of C grade.[23]

The function of bureaucracy were primarily extractive and repressive, rather than productive, in the sense that it was concerned with the collection of revenue and the maintenance of law and order rather than with increasing productivity and improving the country's economic base. In many respect the structure of the administration under the *Ranas* in Nepal resembled that of the *Mughals* in India.

Despite the lack of interests in the productive base demonstrated by the state bureaucracy, there is many evidences that revenue to the state increased slowly throughout the 19th century and early part of the 20th century, mostly as a direct result of the increasing agricultural production. The then British official in Nepal named Hodgson estimated that trade between Nepal and India, worth around 3 million rupees in 1831, had grown to over 30 million by 1891.[24] Around the turn of the century it appears that rice accounted for nearly 40% of Nepal's export to India, with mustard oil seed providing a further 20%; from India Nepal imported a massive quantity of cotton clothes and yarn- nearly 60% of all imports- as well as other manufactured goods. A substantial portion of the profit accruing from increased foreign trade (in which it must be noted the balance favoured Nepal) was pocketed by the Ranas who had established monopolies over the trade in important commodities, either directly or else through contracted agents.

The new relationship between British imperial power and the then Rana prime minister, Jang Bahadur became more manifest

---

23 S. Kumar, (1967), *Rana Polity in Nepal: Origin and Growth*, Bombay: Asia Publishing House, p. 37.

24 P. C. Rawat (1974), *Indo-Nepal Economic Relations*, New Delhi: National Publishing House, p. 67.

during 1850s when he paid a visit to Europe. To make believe to the imperial government Jang Bahadur had abolished the *Sati* system, opened the forest of Nepal-*Tarai* for British enterprises, managed to sale the timber to India and he himself led the many Nepali regiments to suppress the India's War of Independence in 1857. The same year, he also gave formal consent for recruitment of Nepali *Gurkhas* for two *Gurkhas Regiments* in British Indian army. In 1858, the British government transferred to Nepal "in full sovereignty territories in the far western Tarai region, which had been taken from Nepal by Sugauli treaty of 1816." This was done in "recognition of the eminent services rendered to the British government by the state of Nepal...during the mutiny of native army in 1857..."[25] British power in India thereafter became virtually unchallenged and many Indian princely states were integrated into British ruling system as member of imperial power. Nepal, however, was not a member of that 'order', but formally an 'independent' state but virtually a semi-colonial status with the prerogatives attributable to sovereignty and the British Indian government treated it as such for all practical purposes.

Later successors of Rana regime such as Bir Shamsher had done legal treaty with British India of sending Nepali in the British India army in 1885 and hence allowed it unhindered access to Nepali labour power of its choice. Moreover, he actively encouraged it and even accepted the British Empire request not to recruit tribal communities of Gurungs and Magars in domestic Nepali royal army. Locating hindrance to capitalist development and Nepal's remaining as underdevelopment economy under a patrimonial and a semi-colonial state; Nepali Sociologist Mishra (2007) observes,

---

25 C. V. Aitchison (1863), cited in S. R. Tamang, (2000), *Nepal in Feudal Order*, Kathmandu: Sangam Publication, pp.18-19.

> *The breeding ground for Gurkha labour power, which had first been limited to a few locations in Himanchal Pradesh and had later spread to now known as Uttar Pradesh, Bihar, Bengal and Assam, now covered the territory of independent Nepal. The Gurungs, Magars, Rais and Limbus were in the prime list of the British not only because most of them were non-Hindu, but also because they were available in increasingly in large numbers, in large measure due to the (by now) fast paced weakening of the communal organization of resource use and the consequent immiserization of a substantial proportion of the households in the central and the eastern hills. ... More than 27,000 soldiers were hired between 1886 and 1904. Roughly 200,000 – 20 percent of the adult male population in the country –were drawn to India during the first inter-capitalist global war (better known as First World War). Approximately, the same number participated in the second global war. The exodus considerably hurt agriculture and food supply in rural areas of Nepal. It also hurt the collection of land revenues. Beginning 1919 the British started compensating this loss of revenue to the comprador state class of Ranas by making an annual present of one million rupees. The amount, expectedly, was doubled after the Second World War. In addition, the Rana Prime Minister Judha Shamsher was awarded a gift of 1,750,000 sterling pounds for his help.*[26]

Nepal was a valuable concern for British Empire so that they could exploit mercenary *Gurkha* soldiers' recruitment open. This whole thing resulted in marginalization of peasantry and mass migration from Nepali hill region. The hill region saw a five time increase from late 1890s to early 1930s in mass migration of Nepalese from hills to Sikkim, Assam and tea plantations of

26 Chaitanya Mishra (2006), *Essays on the Sociology of Nepal*, Kathmandu: Fine Prints, p. 61,

Darjeeling and Jalpaiguri. These evidences of political history of Nepal noted above support that under the Ranas, patrimonial state of Nepal had developed over as a "Semi-Colony". The ruling landed class was happy enough since of receiving a very large sum of remittance money in exchange of the *Gurkha* recruitment and incessant migration of poor peasant of the *Bahadurs*.

The forest clearance in Tarai region of Nepal made expanded cultivated land. This made to increase cultivation of cash crop by Nepali peasantry. These crops included opium, jute, tobacco and sugarcane and were heavily promoted by British Indian rulers in northern Indian region. This made Nepal to import these products to Indian market. This made also to promote a consumption of luxuries among ruling landed class in Nepali hills. This trade figure between British India and Nepal shows this precisely. For instance, from 1879-80 business figure of Rs. 9.8 million raised to Rs. 87.9 million in 1920-21.[27] The introduction of British Indian railway network in the last decade of the Nineteenth and Twentieth century across Nepali border paved the way to development a capitalist market in Nepal. However, it was landed ruling class of patrimonial state that made profit out of construction of railway line. As Seddon (1979) argues that "the railway connecting the Nepalese tarai to the great markets of north India ensured that the revenue from forest and other land granted to the members of the nobility by the rulers of Nepal was far greater than it could possibly have been in earlier periods. It is no coincidence that Rana palaces were constructed around the turn of the century on a far grander scale than any before, or that luxury imports from Europe came during this period to dominate the consumption of the nobility."[28]

Therefore it was why; the patrimonial state was uninterested to development of homegrown domestic craft and artisans.

27 Ibid., pp. 62-63.

28 Op. cit., David Seddon, P. Blaikie and J. Cameron (1979), p. 25.

So imports from north India was promoted for everyday consumption commodities on large scales. The conventional rural society grown craft and cottage industries of hills were badly hit in particular by the flow of foreign cotton goods and metal ware. More particularly, the farming of cotton extensively cultivated in almost all parts of Nepali hills lost to cheaper machine-produced cloth. This led mass of villagers to search means of livelihood as a seasonal or permanent migration to India.

Though changing economic imperative over more political one was symbolized with the signing of treaty with British-India government in 1923 which recognized Nepal's political sovereignty but ushered in the concept of economic 'common market'. This finally paved the way to damage remaining base of domestic craft industries in Nepal. All through the economic exploitation from without took mercantile form, as there was nothing in Nepal which could offer higher profits to industrial capital than was provided in India. However, Nepal's formally recognized diplomatic relationship by British Empire helped to acceleration of trade between two sides. It obviously helped to Nepal's dependence of mass manufactured commodities on Indian capitalists and to be further exploited without any restriction after 1923 treaty. This set the basis which over the years firmly establishes the virtual absence of local industries. It is why industrial capitalism in Nepal could not make any significant headway. The patrimonial state too was not keen to remove Nepal's dependent character of its economy. Seddon et al. (1979) argue succinctly on whereabouts of this bitter fact by noting that; "This dependence for trade and transit on India virtually to the exclusion of any other country, serves to reinforce India's monopoly position in the Nepalese market and her ability to perpetuate that monopoly through international trade agreements which Nepal has little choice but to accept."[29] The mercantile forms of economic articulation continued to dominate Nepal relation to British India.

29 Ibid., p. 32.

It was why patrimonial state of Nepal remained a semi-colonial in nature when the British Imperialism left India in 1947.

7. THE *PANCHAYAT* REGIME: *BIKAS* BY FOREIGN AID

The Rana rule was overthrown following Indian independence in 1951. It was done after a tripartite arrangement organized by Nehru government by which now the *de jure* Shah monarchy with help of Nepali Congress replaced the Ranas Prime Ministers by becoming *de facto* ruling class of state. This entire event is popularly known as the revolution of 1951 but it made hardly any change in the lives of peasantry. The whole structure of class relations and the patrimonial system of administrative apparatus remained intact. The agrarian state of Nepali society remained in place exploitative which was a cumulative of Gorkhali (i.e. Shah) and Rana regime's policies respectively.

Though, Nepal remained a sovereign and independent country but its economic wellbeing was depended on capitalist economy of British India. Being a protectorate state of British Empire, Nepal remained a poorest country. Inequality was firmly rooted in the Nepali village society in which land played the most important role. A large majority of the population suffered from chronic poverty, unemployment and socio-economic inequality. Though some got employment by getting recruited as Gurkha soldiers to serve interest of British Raj, but it was not helping Nepali peasant society. Moreover, a sorry state of Nepali economy made people from hills to migrate in large numbers to Indian cities.

The advent of revolution of 1951 suddenly wake up from a centuries old sleep that Nepal is an 'underdeveloped' country. Since then the concept of *Bikas* (development) gained currency in Nepal. Gradually ruling class erected a line of demarcation between development and underdevelopment. Since then scores of diplomatic missions and bilateral development aid agencies began to enter Nepal. Therefore, the ruling class opened its doors for the first time to large scale foreign aid. So on January 23, 1951, the United States Operations Mission and Nepal Government signed an agreement for technical Cooperation. This is also presented that on this year, Nepal formally entered into the development and modernization process. It was announced by the then newly elected president of the United States Harry Truman on January 20, 1949. Though a small amount of 22,000 Nepali Rupees as a first cheque of American aid, it was directly related to Truman policy of Communist threat based on cold war politics.[30] This was part of the larger American mission in the 'underdeveloped areas' of Third World to save peasantry from the communist movement. This was also a time that a Communist Revolution triumphed in China and making waves in Asia, Africa to Latin America.

Alongside of the foreign aid, a short stint of multi-party democracy was also introduced in Nepal. The Nepali Congress party, who had a Socialist orientation, came to power after winning first general elections. The new Prime Minister BP Koirala, despite being from propertied class tried to invoke land reform measures through first democratically elected government. This caused mounting pressure from the old regime of landlords who were ruling over countryside. Though, Nepali Congress had won election since it got popular role in anti-Rana rebellion but its social base was landowning elite. A Socialist oriented party had come into power but it had not challenged the traditional ruling elite residing in rural region. The top to lower level of bureaucrats and royal army officers were drawn from this elite class. This class was seldom interested any type of land reform as a harm to their conventional privileges. This led King Mahendra to organize *coup d'état* in December 1960 by dissolving elected parliament and arrested all its members including Prime Minister. Joshi and Rose (1966) had written about the landowning elite's mood which

30 Nanda R. Shrestha (1999), *In the Name of Development: A Reflection from Nepal*, Kathmandu: Educational Enterprises, p. 67.

led to king's apprehension that the Socialist Nepali Congress was planning abolition of Hindu monarchy.

> *A large majority of the landowning and commercial interests in Nepal, for instance, were unalterably opposed to the Nepali Congress government's land and taxation policy. The moderate character of the economic legislation enacted by the Koirala Cabinet did not diminish their apprehensions, since these measures were considered to be merely the first in a series of gradually more drastic changes in the land and taxation system. These vested interest groups, with their close ties to various cliques in the palace, had long since concluded that the King was the last effective barrier to the imposition of fundamental economic reforms, and this attitude was crucial in determining their response to the December coup.*[31]

This whole episode of suppressing democratic elected government by usurping power made Hindu monarchy depended on foreign aid. The step taken by King Mahendra was after all learnt from the policy intervention of Truman agenda. In fact, financial help through foreign aid was playing a regressive role. Observing aid from four biggest nations namely America, Soviet Union, China and India, Gaige (1975) commented in early 1970s;

> *The financial support of the four major aid-giving nations has been accompanied by the rhetoric of change. However, their aid had assisted the monarchy both directly and indirectly to create a better-equipped and better-trained army and to put a large number of potentially restive young men on the bureaucratic payrolls. It is true that aid-giving agencies of several nations have pressed the king for reforms, but aid programs have been maintained*

31 Bhuwan Lal Joshi and Leo E. Rose (1966), *Democratic Innovations in Nepal: A Case Study of Political Acculturation*, Berkeley: University of California Press, p. 388.

> *despite the confirmed absence of significant reforms because for these nations change had a lower priority than maintenance of status quo, which they all found to their advantage for different reasons. Thus, in the short run at any rate, foreign assistance has enhanced the monarchy's chances of survival and has inhibited the growth of pressures for fundamental change.*[32]

It is also crucial to mention that geographical position of Nepal between two giant but politically antagonistic nations (i.e., China and India) also made chance to survival for despotic monarchy despite its regressive step. The Ranas to Shah Rulers had exploited this geographical terrain to maintain their rule in past. However, after especially Communist takeover in China and its subsequent takeover of Tibet in 1950 gave ruling landowning class free hand to exploit Nepal to their advantages. Indian government considered that a 'special' social-cultural and historical relation with Nepal would be the best way to counter Communist propaganda in Nepal.

The geo-political tension between India and China made Nepal a bargaining chip further. This made enterprise of foreign aid very large since from India to China and others gave impetus which eventually made Nepal in the state of external dependency. The aid provided by India and China, though, had intended for a modernization effort of a pristine society still ruled by a medieval Hindu King. The aid by Nepal's immediate neighbor India had their strategic interests which clearly got mentioned in the Treaty of 1950s soon after overthrowing of Rana regime. Indian focus was on road infrastructure followed by air connectivity domestically. Prior to 1950s, there was no motor-able road outside the Kathmandu valley. The hilly region connectivity was so slow and painful that the Nepali villagers usually took Indian route to

32 Frederick H. Gaige (1975), *Regionalism and National Unity in Nepal*, Delhi: Vikas Publishing House, p. 200.

reach their respective destination. The open border with India had an immense significance for development of Nepali society and its agrarian economy. In early 1952, India government provided financial help by linking hill region (i.e., Kathmandu) to Tarai part of Nepal (i.e., Raxaul) with a major highway called the *Tribhuvan Rajpath* named after King Tribhuwan. The early Chinese financial aid was also following Indian strategic effort of building infrastructure. The Arnoko highway was to connect national capital Kathmandu to Chinese border Kodari.[33] Therefore, it can be argued that economic development was not their central objective rather to thwart each other influence by maintaining Himalayan kingdom of Nepal a 'buffer state' of their rivalries. Soon, the train of foreign aid made Nepali ruling elite in its grip. The counties like America, Britain, India, China, and Soviet Union joined major aid countries to Nepal. The list later accommodated others European countries with others.

While a democratically elected government was put in prison and officially the monarchy did not also hold absolute power. To siphon foreign aid money in name of modernization and development of Nepal, an illusion of legitimacy was created. Thus a 'democratic' constitution was proclaimed by from landowning elite class in 1962. By devising an administrative apparatus called the *Panchayat* was established from top to bottom (i.e., village, district, regional and national) levels. The king absolutely controlled these representatives of party less 'democracy' called the *Pancha*.

The *Panchayat* regime toyed lofty vision of development discourse called rural development. Here came American financial aid, so the *Panchayat* regime could rescue peasants by designing a program like the Village Development Project. The

33 Op. cit., Piers Blaikie, John Cameron and David Seddon (2005 [1980]), p. 66.

American aid was set to experiment its mission in a "development laboratory like Nepal". The reason for American modernization and developmental mission was that Nepal was a "blank state" or "textbook opportunity". For this, a community development school was opened in July 1952 in Kathmandu to train development workers. This was followed by opening up of such training centers as many around dozen in various locations of hills to Tarai's region of Nepal in 1950s.[34] The aim of American mission with its agencies like USAID and Ford Foundation was to produce a developmental worker who was trained in "...community motivation and self-help programs, receiving basic technical information on agriculture, health, malaria control, sanitation, and literacy." Therefore these workers could serve villagers effectively as a "stimulator, catalyst, and spark plug" for development of agrarian society.[35]

8. THE FARCE OF LAND REFORM

Amid these multiple developmental schemes to uplift poverty ridden rural life, a very little was done. Though, these schemes delivered many promises of community development in rural society but without tangible results. Realizing its limitation, and policy level pressure created by major aid countries, the *Panchayat* regime gave an impression of land reform.

The below tables make this picture clear politics of land reform in Nepal.

---

34 These were based in following places: Biratnagar, Pokhara, Hetauda, Butwal, Ilam, Rapti Valley, Nepalganj, Gaur and Janakpur.

35 Tatsuro Fujikura (1996), 'Technologies of Improvement, Locations of Culture: American Discourses of Democracy and 'Community Development' in Nepal', *Studies in Nepali History and Society*, Vol. 1, No. 2, pp. 271-311.

Table-III: Land tenure distribution before 1950[36]

No.	Land Tenure	Area (in ha.)	Total area (in %)
1.	Raikar	963,500	50.0
2.	Birtha	700,080	36.3
3.	Guthi	40,000	2.0
4.	Kipat	77,090	4.0
4.	Raijya, Jagir, Raikam	146,330	7.7
	Total	1,927,000	100

The land reform act of 1964 did relatively little to uproot landowning elite's position in village society. The objectives of land reform legislation were not to make Nepali agrarian society an egalitarian one. The *Panchayat* regime made it sure for interest of landed class by making them aware so they could disguise Nepali state. Thereby land reform diluted its essence while landowning class kept land holding (granted as *Birta, Guthi* to *Jagir* etc) in names of brothers, sons, domestic servants, and even in some cases of animals like dogs too. Therefore, by paying bribes to land reform offices, it was effectively made sure that no individual held large portion of land. Brown (1996) summarizes impact of land reform that its results; "…were 'modest'. The amount of land acquired and redistributed was minimal and the number of beneficiaries was small. Consequently, there was no major change in the disparity of holdings. Serious handicaps hindered the implementation of land reform. There was no proper cadastral survey and, therefore, it was left to the goodwill of landowners to declare the extent of their holdings."[37]

36 Source: M.A. Zaman, (1973), cited in Op. cit., Baburam Bhattarai (2003), p. 69.

37 T. Louise Brown (1996), *The Challenge to Democracy: A Political History*, London: Routledge, p. 59.

Table-IV: Land tenure distribution after land reform of 1964[38]

Land Tenure	Percentage of Households: Total HH	Percentage of Households: HH with Land-Holding	% of Cultivated Area	Average Size of Holding (hectare)
I: With Land-holding	92.2	100.00	100.00	—
1. Landlords				
2. Owner-Cultivators	1.8		26.91	
3. Owner-cum-Tenants	62.0	3.31	49.11	18.33
4. Tenants Cultivators	19.1	65.22	15.36	1.67
II: Landless (including non-agricultural population)	2.3	20.70	8.62	1.64
	19.1			
	2.3	10.77	—	1.74
	7.8	—	—	—
Total	100.00		100.00	100.00

The campaign was based on a carbon copy of Chinese Cultural Revolution. The *Panchayat* regime circulated a "Mahendra Thought Book" on the lines of Chairman Mao's famous Red Book. They also issued button picturing Mahendra following a copy of Mao's pictures. It was made mandatory for officials and members of the *Panchayat* hierarchy to wear this button picturing the King. The outline of campaign got no clear mission to uproot poverty

38 Source: M. A. Zaman (1973), cited in op. cit., Baburam Bhattarai (2003), p. 134.

ridden unequal village society. Rather its "…plans sounded less like a public-work program than a religious crusade. There were no quotas of well to be dug, tress to be planted, or roads to built. Instead, there were admonitions about eschewing pomp and luxury, corruption and class consciousness."[39]

Development of the nation became the sole justification for the *Panchayat* rule. To be more precise, "to break open the fountain of development" (*bikasko mul phutaunu*) was the sole motto of King's rule.[40] The king and the state officials spoke about this in every speech and conventions. Many Songs and plays were written and played in radio programs including a state sponsored feature film called *Parivartan* (change) was made and promoted. However, state seldom thought over agrarian distress in everyday lives of the village Nepal.

In early 1960s to late 1970s, Nepal was categorized as one of the world's Least Developed Countries. It received foreign assistance from more than twenty donor agencies representing the Socialist to Capitalists block. While comparing with Panchayat government annual budget, the sum amount of aid received by Nepal was huge one. It was reported that three-quarter of the state's development expenditure was funded by foreign aid money. By the late 1980s, proportion for foreign aid amounted 15.4 percent of Nepal government's Gross National Product (GNP). Developmental experts from around the world were called in to 'modernize' village society. To design programs, various foreign governments with their donor agencies and United Nation agencies opened their shining offices in national capital Kathmandu. Their office staff included a huge bureaucratic set up to monitor their developmental program. This was followed by others including the international Non-Government Organizations (INGOs) too to process the foreign aid money freely. This whole cycle though

39 Ibid.

40 Kamal R. Adhikary (1996), 'Naming Ceremonies as Rituals of Development', *Studies in Nepali History and Society*, Vol.1, No.2, pp. 345-364.

produced a mushrooming growth of a bureaucratic ruling class. Mikesell (1999) notes by putting a profound remark on socio-cultural impact on landowning class that the aid became now their "...new wealth to purchase properties and build houses in the prime urban locations, especially in capital Kathmandu, and furnish itself with all the associated appliances of convenience and accoutrements of status from automobiles to refrigerators to Johnny Walker whisky (proudly displayed next to Barbie dolls in the glass cabinets of middle class homes)".[41] The real crisis of Nepali agrarian society that was exploitation and inequality yet been addressed. This was known fact that vast mass of peasantry were living on a brink of subsistence or either poor and owned little land.

Based on these above discussion, it can be argued that the *Panchayat* government rarely gave a thought on providing livelihood to its population. Though, it was reminded again and again in government and developmental agency's voluminous reports that agriculture plays a central role. But it is an important fact of village society that rural livelihood have never been completely dependent on agriculture.

9. DEVELOPMENT THROUGH REMITTANCE (VIA LABOUR MIGRATION)

The Nepali society has a long history of foreign labour migration. First it was set in early nineteenth century when some Nepali warrior went Lahore to serve in army of the Sikh Maharaja Ranjit Singh. Thus in this way, people sending remittance by working abroad (i.e. India) were given a nickname of "*Lahure*".

Traditionally, Nepali society experienced two types of external migration in search of livelihood. Though, these two also bear marks of political history of Nepal. First fact, it was the Treaty of Sugauli in 1816 that increased migratory stream from Nepali hills. Soon

41 Op. cit., Stephen Lawrence Mikesell (1999), p. 97.

after the 1816's Sugauli Treaty, from 3 Gurkha Regiment, the British increased it to 51 Regiments till World War II. The British policy thirst to maintain 'independent status of Nepal' depended on the Gurkha recruitment. Secondly another kind of migration has been recurrent aftermath of the 1850s and majority of villagers consisted of slaves and debtors. The oppressive land and labour policies of the Gorkhali & Rana regime led to a consequential widespread agrarian indebtedness in rural society. The question for peasantry was for survival and this prompted many people to migrate away from their villages. Caplan (1970) has observed with reference to Darjeeling that by 1891, half of population consisted of the Nepalese migrants. Moreover, he notes by citing 1941 census of British India that "Nepal provided 45 percent of the foreign immigrants into India... there are 3 million people of the Nepalese origin regularly resident in north Bengal and north Assam alone. Another estimate that 2 million Nepalese live in India, Sikkim and Bhutan."[42]

India, traditionally, has been a favourite destination of different communities of hill population. Other than in Indian army recruitment and Public Sector Companies, the large majority worked in informal sector. The nature of these jobs has been either low-skill jobs either as in construction, or watchmen and industrial works. All most all working in informal sector come and return their homes being employed as seasonal and semi-permanent migrant labour force. But seasonal migration remained a regular feature of rural economy since long. An American developmental agency had found in its survey conducted in late 1950s that around 87 per cent male population of hilly districts looked for seasonal employment. Since late 1980s, while the *Panchayat* regime was in decline, the Gulf region emerged new places of employment for Nepali working class. The Gulf countries included Saudi Arabia, Qatar, the United Arab

42 Lionel Caplan (2007 [1970]), *Land and Social Change in East Nepal: A study of Hindu-Tribal relations*, Lalitpur: Himal Books, p. 6.

Emirates, Bahrain, Oman and Kuwait. Moreover, countries of East Asian region like Malaysia, Brunei, Hong Kong, Saipan and South Korea were also regarded popular destinations.

According to a government official estimation based on national census of 1991, it was said that 400,000 Nepali worked abroad in 1980s. This number rose in 1991 to 660,000. The large majority of this number (i.e. 89 percent) worked as a seasonal labour in India. But a considerable number of 71,000 people consisting 11 percent worked in other than India.[43] In another study it was reported that in the early 1990s, India contributed around 40 per cent of remittance while 3 per cent constituted foreign overseas countries from the Gulf to East Asian region (see, Table).

Table-V: Share of remittance in Nepali economy in late 1980s[44]

Sources	Number of Remittances	Value of Remittances
India	40 %	33 %
Foreign Countries	3 %	22 %
Urban Nepal	25 %	32 %
Rural Nepal	33 %	12 %

Though the greater part of migrant labour force was men, considerable amounts of remittance also send by women. These women migrants labour were traditionally employed in the loosely defined area of 'personal and community services'. Now other than India, the Gulf and East Asian region also becoming hotspot for women migrant workers in names of employment

43 David Seddon, with Jagannath Adhikari and Ganesh Gurung (2001), *The New Lahures: Foreign Employment and Remittance Economy of Nepal*, Kathmandu: Nepal Institute of Development Studies (NIDS), p. 45.

44 Ibid., p. 4.

abroad. Basically it was a destination of working in sex industry that was so prevalent in Indian cities. In the late 1980s, though number is debatable that 200,000 women were found working in brothels in Mumbai, Madras, Bangolore, Kanpur, Varanasi, Lucknow, Calcutta, Delhi and other cities in India.[45]

At the decline of the *Panchayat* regime, the share of agriculture was decreasing in the agrarian sector. Its contribution to Nepal's Gross Domestic Product (GDP) was accounted around 50 percent in 1980s. But it fell to 45 per cent in 1991. Therefore as labour force working in agriculture also fell. Gradually, the semi to long term labour migration became a regular and necessary feature of the rural livelihood.

10. THE BAHUDAL REGIME: DEMOCRACY WITH NEO-LIBERALISM

The early 1990s appear in Nepal as the restoration of multiparty democracy after a political movement led by the Nepali Congress and the Left parties. This uprising led to the overthrow of the 30 year old *Panchayat* system by replacing a multi-party democracy with Constitutional Monarchy. While the political change of 1990 led to the emergence of people's demands for greater involvement of the state for a welfare measures from area of service provisions to deal widespread economic inequalities and social discrimination. Ironically, this was a period of intensification of Structural Adjustment Programs in Nepal with a continuation of the despotic *Panchayati* state. However, it must be noted that much before arrival of a multi-party democracy, the Nepali state had accepted the World Bank dictated neo-liberal model of development in 1984. The multi-party system accepted the same neo-liberal course without giving a second thought. Now the 'new'

45 David Seddon (1995), 'Aids in Nepal: Issues for Consideration', *Himalayan Research Bulletin*, Vol. 15, No.2, pp. 2-11.

Bahudal state has a single task of redefining the role of state away from being a direct provider of public goods to the intermediary of rules in the market forces.

The foreign aid continued to remain a panacea to uproot underdeveloped Nepal. In 1990-1991, the total foreign aid was 286.5 million Dollars and it amounted 40 per cent of the government of Nepal's expenditures. Nepal received foreign aid from nearly all countries of Western world. When the west's policies got changed, a focus of Nepal's developmental was also re-arranged accordingly. Adams (1998) explains further about arrival of neo-liberal model in Nepal:

> *The shift in developmental policy towards privatization at the end of the United States' Reagan years, the effect of World Bank IMF structural adjustment programs which shifted emphasis to "user groups" and self-financing schemes for rural development and health care institutions, and the increasing stress on a "people-centred, grass root" model for development in metropole agendas led to an enormous growth of in-country NGO's working under bilateral, multilateral, and international grants and loans. In 1994 it was reported that there were 6,000 local NGOs in Nepal, handling Rs. 2 billion (%400 million), or roughly one-twentieth of the amount of the operating budget of the government for 1994-1995, all with the goal of "development."*[46]

In developmental discourse, Nepal still be considered as a "least-developed country" and ranked one of the poorest five countries of world with a per capita income of 200 Dollar. It remained "...a super mountainous country which makes an idea

46 Vincanne Adams (1998), *Doctors for Democracy: Health Professionals in the Nepali Revolution*, Cambridge: Cambridge University Press, p. 50.

backdrop for documentaries on television".[47] Now the country's poverty & economic inequality was seen as a product of excessive population of Nepal. The unequal distribution of resources like land was considered negligible by the multi-party democratic government. Nepal's agrarian present-the villagers had any relation from the 'progress' outlined by the multi-party democracy. In terms of employment, majority of country populace directly depended on agrarian sector. Whereas, farming constituted governing component of agriculture, elements like forestry, fishery, livestock plus seasonal migration were also included essential to rural economy.

But gradually, the remittance by Nepali migrants labour became an easy way to come out from whole year's painful investment in agriculture. According to the Nepal Living Standards Survey of 1995/1996, some 24 per cent rural household received regular remittances. More than 43 per cent of all remittances to rural Nepal came from Nepali migrant labour employed in foreign countries of the India to the Gulf to East/South East & Europe. Based on government & developmental agencies reports of early 1990s, Seddon et al. (2001) had estimated roughly 350,000 Nepali employed in foreign employment. However, this assessment as showed in below table does not categorically give numbers of Nepali working in informal sector. And the major proportion of these workers employed in the British/Indian *Gurkha* brigades and Indian government owned public sector enterprises. Further they argue that the value of remittance send to Nepal by labour force from abroad consisted "between 13 % of GDP and 25 % of GDP."[48]

47 Op. cit., Nanda R. Shrestha (1999), p. 8.

48 Op. cit., David Seddon, with Jagannath Adhikari and Ganesh Gurung (2001), p. 43.

Table-VI: Nepali migrant workers in foreign employment & remittances they send home[49]

Region	Workers (estimated)	Remittances (estimated)	Workers (possible)	Remittance (possible)
The West	15,000	4.4 billion	—	—
The Gulf	40,000	1.5 billion	—	—
East/ South East Asia	44,000	23 billion	—	—
India	250,000	6 billion	1,000,000	40 billion
Others	1,000	—	—	—
Total	350,000	35 billion	1,100,000	60 billion

Along with foreign aid, the remittances of Nepali peasants became major sources of income for Nepali ruling class. The value of these two surpassed 50 per cent of government annual budget. However, the peasant life did seldom saw any positive transformation of multi-party government rhetoric of 'progress' and 'development'. Instead, the village got cosmetic changes. Soon after, the regime changes in 1990s, the laws of local government were also subsequently rewritten according to an idiom of the multi-party democratic of the constitution. During in *Panchayat* days, the lowest units of village to top national assembly were known as *Panchayat*. Now after 1990, the village unit of the *Panchayat* was called as Village Development Committee (VDC) according to a government directive. Mikesell (1999) notes down the crisis facing by rural social world of Nepali peasantry;

> *The villagers—90 percent of the population –[are] ambivalent because they had seen no change except that life continues to grow precipitously more difficult: agricultural development schemes leave them more in debt than ever, urban speculators take their lands, the commons continued to be encroached upon,*

49 Ibid., p. 51.

> *their daughters are abducted to foreign brothels, and lists goes on. The individual of political parties who mobilized them with their slogan during election and promises disappear when they get into parliament of Kathmandu.*[50]

Sadly this, 'restoration' of democracy in the 1990s failed to undermine the deeply engrained relation between exploitative production relations on the ground and the power structures of Gorkhali and Rana legacy. The political change in 1990 had opened the space for transformative politics in a limited sense. Issues of inequality, discrimination and marginalization began to come to public visibility through conscious actions of peoples and organizations located in different social spaces. This juxtaposed uneasily the neoliberal public policies adopted by Nepali Congress and the Left fronts governments. Within neoliberal public policies, despite the great promises that have been held out for multi-party democracy for the last thirty years since the king's dissolution of parliament, multi-party democracy could not allow the common people to actually propose their own representatives or start to govern themselves. The multi-party democracy saw around dozen regimes within less than a ten year. Indeed, most of the abuses of the *Panchayat* regime were continued.

11. IDEOLOGY OF STATE FORMATION: *ASAL HINDUSTHAN*

It is been noted above in section discussing political economy of state formation that how the Rajput's military conquest of Nepal from India was already in progress after Muslim invasion of northern Indian plains. The sole purpose of the warrior Hindu upper caste Rajput arrival to a tribal land of Nepal was to capture state power. Gradually, the process of *Hinduization*

50 Op. cit., Stephen Lawrence Mikesell (1999), p. 113.

was made possible by the political and economic domination of the *Tagadhari* Varna of Hindu upper caste Rajput and Brahmin. The consolidation of the caste organization was done under state jurisdiction. The ideology of *Hinduization* can be defined as a way that the *Varna* relationships are inserted into societies that was not Hindu. It can start with a few high caste settlers moving into an area and gradually displacing and subordinating existing population.

In the *Dibya Upadesh*, Prithivinarayan Shah has defined his kingdom as a land of original Hindus, an *Asal Hindusthan* (pure *Hindusthan*) as opposed to India which had already been 'polluted' by Mughals and later by their British successors. He was the first to use word *Mughlan* (land of the Mughals) for the then India.[51] The ruling class of the Gorkhali state consisted predominantly of *Thakuris* under *Shah* Kings, with Brahmins as *Bhardars* (courtiers). So the concept of national integration (as a nation-state) had a single meaning which can be explained in terms of *Hinduization*. In reality the *Hinduization* of Nepal was actually an imposition of the culture of the *'Parbatiya'*, most significantly their language, Nepali (originally known as *Khas kura*), and religion, Hinduism, on an indigenous tribal population. Before the Gorkha conquest, Nepal had a sizeable Buddhist population which the new Hindu rulers could not afford to overtly offend. In many cases the religious endowments of the Buddhists were confirmed, but there was always a strong preference for Hindu rituals and practices.

The Gorkhali state's penal code was based on the Hindu ancient scriptures. The essential tenets of Hindu law were preserved and state institution practised it. Those who defied it were degraded to a low caste. It was called also *panchakhat* which according to the Hindu scriptures of *Manu Smriti* code included five kind of severe

51 Op. cit., L. F. Stiller (1989 [1968]), p. 46.

punishments. This was as following; confiscation of property, the degradation to a low caste, banishment, mutilation and death. All of these penal measures and also enslavements were applied in case of non-conformity by the non-Hindu tribal communities. According to Pradhan (1991);

> *This form of punishment prevailed in India during the early eighteenth century, but it was a penal action inflicted by the state power in Nepal and sometimes used to punish the enemies of Gorkha. The chiefs of Palpa who offered stiff resistance to Gorkha in 1762 were put to death and their children 'were delivered to the most vile and abominable tribe (Sarki) to be educated in their odious profession, as outcastes'. What a judge of the chief court of Nepal once told British Resident is revealing, 'Below (in plains of India) the Sastras (are) things to talk of; here, they are acted up to'.*[52]

The process of *Hinduization*, initiated by the Shahs speeded up by the emergence of the Ranas in the power. Jung Bahadur Kunwar seized power in 1846 and established the heredity rule of his family. The Ranas effectively ruled the country until 1951 while the reducing the monarchy to the role of a religious figurehead. Following Nepal's defeat in 1816, the era of Gorkhali conquest ended, and consolidation required a more 'unified' kingdom in which ideology of *Hinduization* took a major leap. In 1854, Jung Bahadur promulgated a set of law throughout the kingdom which became constitutional code to regulate state and society of Nepal. This code of *Muluki Ain* was largely based upon the ancient Hindu texts. By this code, it was clearly demarcated that how the *Tagadhari* landowning elite want to nurture and what the state and society of Nepal stand for them. Jung Bahadur Rana wrote in 1854,

52 Op. cit., Kumar Pradhan (1991), p. 162.

> *[It is] a Hindu Kingdom the law of whose court maintains that killings of cow, women and Brahmans shall not be allowed. [It is] a sacred land of the Himavatkhanda, of the holy shrines [dedicated] to Vasuki, the effulgent phallus of Pasupati and Guhyesvari...It is the only Hindu Kingdom in the Kali Age...*[53]

The *Muluki Ain* of 1854 situated all communities of land of Nepal in a "national" hierarchical manner under the following given categories.

Figure-II: Caste hierarchy according to the *Muluki Ain*[54]

* = the position (status) of the castes within the caste group is not precisely determined

E = ethnic group

1. **Caste group of the "Wearer of the holy cord" (*tagadhari*)**

   Upadhyaya Brahman

   Rajput (Thakuri) ("warrior")

   Jaisi Brahman

   Chetri (Ksatri) ("warrior")

   Dew Bhaju (Newar Brahmins) E

   Indian Brahmin

   Ascetic sects (Sannyasi, etc)

   "Lower" Jaisi

   Various Newar castes* E

   .....

53 Prayag Raj Sharma (2004), 'Introduction' in Andras Hofer, (2004 [1979]), *The Caste Hierarchy and the State in Nepal: A study of the Muluki Ain of 1854*, Lalitpur: Himal Publication, p. Xvi.

54 Source: Op. cit,. Andras Hofer (2004 [1979]), p. 9.

2. **Caste group of the 'Non-enslavable Alcohol-Drinkers' (*namasinya matwali*)**

   Magar* E

   Gurung* E

   Sunuwar* E

   Some other Newar castes* E

   .....

3. **Caste group of the 'Enslavable Alcohol-Drinkers' (*masinya matwali*)**

   Bhote* E ("Tibetanids" and some "Tibetanoids")

   Cepang* E

   Kumal* E (potters)

   Hayu* E

   Tharu* E

   Gharti* E (descendants of the freed slaves)

   .....

4. **Impure, but 'touchable' caste (*pani nacalnya choi chito halnunaparnya*)**

   Kasai (Newar butchers) E

   Kusle (Newar musicians) E

   Hindu Dhobi (Newar Washermen) E

   Kulu (Newar tanners) E

   Musulman*

   Mleccha* (European)

   .....

5. **Untouchable castes (*pani nacalnya choi chito halnuparnya*)**

   Kami (blacksmiths) equal status

   Sarki (tanners, shoemakers)

   Kadara (stemming from unions between Kami and Sarki)

Damai (tailors and musicians)
Gaine (minstrels)
Badi (musicians)
Pore (Newar skinners and fishermen) E
Cyame (Newar scavengers) E

Though all groups within these broad five categories were not 'castes', the *Muluki Ain* prescribed caste status for them based on Hindu notions of purity and pollution in many domains of social life, such as inter-caste community of boiled rice, acceptance of water, and sexual relations. The code also prescribed certain practices, such as consumption of Beef, which was not taboo among many ethnic groups.

The *Muluki Ain* besides allowing some degree of autonomy in some areas was also neutral as far as Muslims, Buddhists or other religions was concerned, neither encouraging nor prohibiting their practice of faith. Although the *Muluki Ain* recognized and accepted some degree of cultural diversity, it translated cultural differences into 'hierarchical' caste categories. The ethnic groups that consumed alcohol were categorized as *Matwali* and rated lower than most of the '*Parbatiyas*'. Punishment for infringing laws, especially conceiving inter-caste relation, was more severe for them than for the wearers of the holy thread. Since the *Muluki Ain* had structured the social universe into a broad caste based classification, there was a lot of pressure on non-Hindus to conform to Hindu norms, at least in their public behaviour and inter-caste relations. Gurung (1997) observed about nature of this state:

> *The polity and society of Nepal was indeed devised in the image of a Hindustan. To begin with, the etymology of the place-name Gorkha itself was rationalized as goraksha (cow protection), symbolic of the sanctity of the cow for Hindus. The Cow played a special role in the process of defining Hindu identity and the extent*

> *of centralized power. The ban on cow slaughter was probably first enforced in the whole kingdom in 1805. Its subsequent incorporation as a proviso in the Muluki Ain represented consolidation of the regime including the periphery of beef-eating people.*[55]

The Rana rulers through their rein sought to sustain values that had underpinned the Nepalese state since its creation. In the first place, they projected themselves as the guardians of the Hindu social order enshrined in Nepali's legal system and on the other hand preserved the discrimination against those at the bottom of the hierarchy. The ruling class also sought to project themselves and their regime as natural champions of the 'Parbatiyas', particularly of the Thakuri-Chhetri caste to which they themselves belonged. This was probably a major reason behind the 1905 decision to allow only Nepali-language documents to be permitted as evidence in court and behind their attempt to portray opposition as Newar-inspired. Pride in the conquest of the Newar kingdoms was still reflected in the national anthem which before 1967 referred to the maintenance of the *Gorkhali* rule over Nepal. Yet at the same time the Ranas tried to foster a 'unified' Nepal centred round their regime. The official adaptation by 1930s of the name Nepal for the whole kingdom and of Nepali for its principal language, replacing '*Gorkha*' and '*Gorkhali*' was probably part of this strategy.

12. LEGACY OF HINDUIZATION CONTINUED IN PANCHAYAT AND BAHUDAL

The scholars like Onta (1996a) have observed that during the reign of the *Panchayat* rule, the Nepali language, Hinduism

55 Harka Gurung (2008 [1997]), 'State and Society in Nepal', in David N. Gellner, Joanna Pfaff-Czarnecka with John Whelpton (eds.), *Nationalism and Ethnicity in Nepal*, Kathmandu: Vajra Publications, p. 504.

and monarchy constituted "...the triumvirate of official Nepali nationalism".[56] Since the time of Gorkhali conquest, every government attempted to promote Nepali as the national language and the sole medium of instruction in schools. In 1955, a landmark report by the first National Education Planning Commission went so far as to argue that Nepal as a basic language would gradually disappear other languages of ethnic communities if children are taught from very childhood. Onta (1996a) explained further about intentions of state;

> *Making the Nepali language its medium, this national culture was propagated through state-owned print and radio media and most forcefully, through the standardization of school-level educational textbooks since the early 1960s. The aim of this national culture was to "implant a vigorous and forceful patriotism among the youth". It is this national culture which is said to have misrepresented at its best and wiped out at its worst, the cultural identities of many ethnic groups.*[57]

The Hindu ruling elite tried to show the numerical dominance of Hindus in Nepal by classifying even non-Hindus ethnic groups as Hindus. From the point of view of the rulers, the plurality of Nepalese society was conceived of within a uniform socio-political framework: diverse castes and ethnic categories were incorporated into a holistic framework of a 'national caste hierarchy'. Along with this *Panchayat* regime appropriated the *Bir Itihas* (brave history) of Nepal as one of the central themes of Nepali ruling class culture. Backed by the state apparatus, this culture was both elaborated and disseminated through print, radio and visual media as well

56 Pratyoush Onta, (1996a), 'Creating a Brave Nepali Nation in British India: The Rhetoric of *Jati* Improvement, Rediscovery of Bhanunhakta and the Writing of *Bir* History', *Studies in Nepali History and Society*, Vol.1, No. 1, (June issue), p. 38.

57 Ibid.

as educational resource materials. As Onta (1996b) notes that Nepali state created a sensibility of a shared history which he calls *Rastriya Itihas* (national history) –among the inhabitants of Nepal. The writing of national history and its teaching in schools through standardized textbooks –a key means of its dissemination –were at the centre of the state-sponsored effort to make students into citizens socialized and loyal to a particular image of nationhood of *Bir* (brave) to *Bikas* (development).[58] The *Panchayat* period witnessed a concerted effort to implement the ideals of a unified nation-state, that is, to forcibly evolve a 'nation' with a common culture and language. The so called unity of nation was expressed in a *Panchayati* slogan of "*ek bhasha, ek bhesh, ek desh*" (one language, one dress, one country). To achieve this end, there was a move towards greater centralization of politics and administration, with an emphasis on transportation and communication as a step towards modernization and development.

At the beginning of the *Panchayat* era, due to the dynamics of domestic politics and the perceived need to join the rest of the world, the state sought to replace the hierarchical social order based on the caste system by recognizing cultural diversity and equality of all citizens' before the law. Caste and ethnicity were no longer significant legal categories although they continued to remain socially valid. The caste system, though not explicitly abolished, was absent from the new *Muluki Ain* introduced in 1963 by King Mahendra. The *Muluki Ain* of 1854 was to remain into effect along with it. This new code though not explicitly abolishing caste hierarchy does not approve of it.[59] Despite the egalitarian rhetoric, cleavages persisted: the caste system was not

58 Pratyoush Onta, (1996 b), 'Ambivalence Denied: The Making of *Rastriya Itihas* in Panchayat Era Textbooks', *Contributions to Nepalese Studies*, Vol. 23, No. 1, pp. 213-254.

59 Op. cit., Andras Hofer (2004 [1979]), pp. 1-2.

abolished, and caste/ethnic distinctions were reinforced by the fact that ethnic groups largely lacked networks giving access to high positions, and displayed cultural modes differing strongly from those prevailing among the elites in the centre.

Ethnic communities as legal categories disappeared from the legal discourse, but they did resurface to some extent in the census as linguistic and religious categories. Demographic classification in the census remained discriminatory, since it recorded a large number of people who practiced other faiths as Hindus. Linguistic classification of the population provided only rough, and perhaps misleading data on the ethnic communities because many of them had given up their mother tongues or were bilingual, leading to their classification as Nepali-speakers. The law as well as the census thus attempted to 'erase' caste and ethnic identities of the population to bring about a more egalitarian society as well as to wipe away cultural differentiation that existed in diverse land.

Though, people's movement of the 1990s brought a fresh breath of air to the downtrodden and oppressed communities and generated a ray of hope among the people who has been marginalized socio-culturally by the despotic *Panchayat* regime. A reformed constitution of the Kingdom of Nepal 1990 accepted Nepal as a "multi-ethnic, multi-lingual...Hindu and Constitutional Monarchical Kingdom".[60] The phrase of "Hindu Kingdom" remained unchanged throughout the constitution but king's authority was narrow down by its position of "Constitutional Monarchy". But, the validity of divine authority of the Hindu monarch has been seldom questioned. The centuries old past legacy of national code of 1854's *Muluki Ain* (including King Mahendra updated version of 1963 code) had an enduring impact

60 Rajendra Pradhan (2002), 'Ethnicity, Caste and a Plural Society', in Kanak Mani Dixit and Shastri Ramachandaran (eds.), State of Nepal, Kathmandu: Himal Books, p. 13.

on the people. Though 1990s constitutional reform, the *Muluki* Ain was declared invalid. Thus the multi-party state tried to show officially that it does not perpetuate discrimination based on caste and ethnicity. But the hierarchical social order built on Varna system remained valid. Moreover, it was re-affirmed by the constitution of Nepal promulgated after introduction of the multi-party democracy that defined the country as a Hindu kingdom. The census of 1991 declared 80.6 per cent of population as Hindu.[61] The data of census was questioned by many because it was difficult for people to identify others religious faiths (i.e., Buddhism, Animism, Islam and Christianity etc) other than Hinduism. Thus the idea of Nepal- *Asal Hinduthan* - as pure land of Hindus was unchallenged by multi-party democratic state.

After elucidating the process of state formation, it becomes clear that at one side the political economy of state formation was based on unequal agrarian relations and on the other, its exclusive ideology of Hindu polity. This coming together of these two processes forced people to organise many rebellions since the Gorkhali conquest of Nepal. The rise of the Maoist movement in Nepal was an organised result of all this, which consolidated different oppressed communities under one umbrella.

61 Op. cit., Harka Gurung (2008 [1997]), p. 520.

CHAPTER 3

Ideology and Practice of the CPN (M)

War is the continuation of politics by other [i.e. violent] means.

— Carl von Clausewitz, *Prussian General* **(1780-1831)**[1]

In this chapter, an effort has been made to elucidate the ideology and practice of the People's War. The chapter is subdivided into two subsections; first deals with basic elements of Maoist ideology and secondly deals with an overall view of their practice in Nepal. Through a particular set of ideological interpretation, the CPN (M) made an analysis of the society and the state which made a basis for them to initiate armed struggle in Nepal. It is also describe here that how they devised specific plans based on their practice in Nepal in different phases of People's War –strategic defense, strategic equilibrium & strategic offensive. Before going in to detail, however, it is necessary to discuss the meaning of ideology & practice as the Maoists comprehended it in material condition of Nepal.

1. IDEOLOGY & PRACTICE IN COMMUNIST DISCOURSE

The concept of ideology is a highly debated and contentious subject both in its theorization and also in its application. McLellan (1986) confer, that "Ideology is the most elusive concept

1 Bernard Semmel (1981), *Marxism and the Science of War*, London: Oxford University Press, p. 46.

in the whole of social science."[2] In general usage, ideology has been defined as a set of ideas and beliefs that constitutes a perspective or worldview through which social, economic and political realities are interpreted. Ideology is used either in a pejorative or a value-neutral sense. But when it is used in political sense then often contains political connotations. Ideology therefore is a set of ideas accompanied by political goals, intents, interests, and commitments. While a worldview need not necessarily subsume a political outlook, an ideology always contains political perspective. The main purpose of an ideology is to affect change in society guided by a normative thought process which gets reflected in practice. The practice of any particular ideology in public matters makes it central to politics.

Ideology as a concept got wider currency from the works of Karl Marx and Friedrich Engels. The best known Marxist understanding of ideology is expounded in *The German Ideology* written jointly by Marx and Engels in 1840s. According to them;

> *The ideas of the ruling class are in every epoch the ruling ideas, i. e. the class which is the material force of society, is at the same time its ruling intellectual force. The class which has the means of material production at its disposal has control at the same time over the means of mental production.*[3]

Through this work, they critiqued Feuerbach's understanding of religion and Hegelian political philosophy. They argued that it is mistaken to start from human consciousness and to proceed from this to an investigation of material reality. According to them,

2 David McLellan (1986), *Ideology*, Milton Keynes: Open University Press, p. 1.

3 Karl Marx and Friedrich Engels (1974), *The German Ideology*, London: Lawrence and Wishart, p. 64.

social existence determines consciousness, and not the other way round. Marx and Engels thus adopted a materialist conception of history, in which economic forces rather than great personalities or ideas lead to progress in society. Based on his study of Marxist literature on ideology, Williams (1977) attaches three variations of meaning to it:

1. A system of beliefs characteristic of a particular class or group;
2. A system of illusory beliefs- false ideas or false consciousness–which can be contrasted with true or scientific knowledge;
3. The general process of the production of meanings and ideas.[4]

Thus, Marxist philosophy holds that any ideology has its corresponding material basis and represents various forces of production operating within the society in a particular epoch. The emergence of new forces of production also gives birth to its corresponding ideology which comes into contradiction with the existing production relations and the ideology that supports it. Therefore, while the emergence of the capitalist class engendered bourgeois ideology, the proletarian class gave birth to ideology of communism, which stands opposed to all hitherto existing ideologies. However, the reliability of ideology gets tested in real life or through Practice.

The notion of Practice refers to action and activity. It is through Practice, that human being is basically differentiated from all other beings. In this sense, man is understood as a being of Practice. In Marxist sense in general, it is through a universal, free, creative and self-creative activity by which humans create, make, generate,

4 Raymond Williams (2016 [1977]), *Marxism and Literature*, New Delhi: Oxford University Press, p. 55.

produce, struggle, modify and change society and him. Practice is regarded a central concept in the Marxist theory of knowledge which in turn serves ideology by a persistent way of production and class struggle. Through, *Theses on Feuerbach*, Marx has propounded lucid meaning of dialectical-materialist understanding of relations between Ideology and Practice. In Marx's *Theses on Feuerbach*, the notion of Practice was placed centrally. Circumstances affect man but also man alters circumstances. It is this idea of transforming the immediate world that voiced through his critique of Feuerbach. The 8th *Theses* says: "Social life is essentially *practical.* All mysteries which mislead theory to mysticism find their rational solution in human practice and in the comprehension of this practice".[5]

These formulations were not mere talk but based on a real practice since Marx himself had participated in communist activities of his times. It is this organic relationship between Ideology and Practice which became a foundation stone for the Communist parties to attain goals of revolutionary political movements. It is why, he therefore declared more than a century ago that "The philosophers have only *interpreted* the world, in various ways; the point, however, is to *change* it."[6] Moreover, the Practice also assists Ideology when it is undertaken through application in ideological programmes by devising a set of strategies and tactics in specific society. Mao Tse-tung discussed this question while writing in his philosophical essays *On Practice* in 1937:

> *...ideas, theories, plans, or programmes are usually altered partially and sometimes even wholly, because of the discovery of unforeseen circumstances in the course of practice. That*

5 K. Marx (1976), 'Theses on Feuerbach', in K. Marx, F. Engels, V. Lenin, *On Historical Materialism: A Collection*, Moscow: Progress Publishers, p. 13.

6 Ibid.

> *is to say, it does happen that the original ideas, theories, plans or programmes fail to correspond with reality either in whole or in part and are wholly or partially incorrect. In many instances, failures have to be repeated many times before errors in knowledge can be corrected and correspondence with the laws of the objective process achieved... In a revolutionary period the situation changes very rapidly; if the knowledge of revolutionaries does not change rapidly in accordance with the changed situation, they will be unable to lead the revolution to victory.*[7]

2. CORE ELEMENTS OF MARXISM-LENINISM-MAOISM

Brought into existence by capitalism, the proletariat is considered by the Marxists as the last revolutionary and internationalist class in human history. In Europe, its emergence and struggle against capitalism paved the way for the founding of Marxism. Marx and Engels laid the foundations of the ideological world outlook of the proletariat – the dialectical and historical materialism and scientific socialism. Under the motto "Workers of the all countries, unite!" the first Communist International was founded with initiative and under the leadership of Marx and Engels. It spread the thoughts of *Communist Manifesto* among the workers and simultaneously fought against various opportunist trends appearing in the International Communist Movement of that time.[8] They analyzed the development of capitalism and the penetration and influence of capitalist commodity production not

7 Mao Tse-Tung, (1971a), 'On Practice', in *Selected Works of Mao Tse-Tung,* Peking: Foreign Language Press, pp. 78-79.

8 The *Communist Manifesto* was written between December 1847 and January 1848.

only in the capitalist countries but in all parts of the world. They wrote jointly in *Manifesto of the Communist Party*:

> *The bourgeoisie, by the rapid improvement of all instruments of production, by the immensely facilitated means of communication, draw all, even the most barbarians, nations into civilization. The cheap prices of its commodities are heavy artillery with which it batters down all Chinese walls, with which it forces the barbarians' intensely obstinate hatred of foreigners to capitulate. It compels all nations, on pain of extinction, to adopt the bourgeois mode of production; it compels them to introduce what it calls civilization into their midst, i.e., to become bourgeois themselves. In one word, it creates a world after its own image.*[9]

When the Communist Manifesto was written down, various struggles were fought by people in different region of the world which has been turned by capitalism as its colonies. It is in this context that in Paris, the proletariat, for the first time in history, seized state power through armed revolt. Known as the "Paris Commune" worldwide, this historical revolt affirmed the basic principles of Marxist ideology. Through lasting for a short period of only 72 days due to its inherent limitations, Marx and Engels declared that its experience would live forever.

By the end of the 19th century, capitalism developed into imperialism in few countries of Europe and it made far sight changes in not only in those imperialist countries but in rest of world divided in colonial states. It was Lenin, a Russian communist leader who analyzed this and showed its implications for the proletarian revolution worldwide. Examining the new features of capitalism in its imperialist stage, Lenin explained how it had become even more an international system of accumulation

---

9 Karl Marx and Frederick Engels (1977), *Manifesto of the Communist Party*, Peking: Foreign Language Press, pp. 34-38.

and based on exploitation. While colonialism was characterized economically by the export of goods and finished products, the imperialist era was defined by the export of capital itself, argued Lenin in his work *Imperialism, the Highest Stage of Capitalism*. Thus the process which Marx and Engels had described in the *Communist Manifesto* – the tendency for the introduction of commodities produced in the capitalist countries into backward areas of the world to transform these areas in the image of the capitalist countries – did not materialize in the era of imperialism. Lenin pointed out that with the advent of imperialism and the consequent changes in the nature of the relations between the capitalist countries and their colonies, colonial domination by imperialism tended to retard the development of capitalism in the colonies and kept them in an enforced state of backwardness.[10]

According to Lenin, in these colonies, the immediate struggle had to be waged against imperialism and feudalism. The forces that could be united were not only the proletariat, but also the broad sections of peasantry, the petty bourgeoisie in the urban areas and sections of bourgeoisie themselves, especially the patriotic section of the national bourgeoisie. Despite the fact that capitalist production relations were penetrated in urban areas of Russia which Lenin summarized as a stage of monopoly capitalism. The countryside, in contrast, where the grand majority of people lived was ruled by the feudal lords. Russia until February 1917 was continued to be ruled by the Tsarist autocracy. According to Lenin, the working class must fight to carry out through the democratic revolution with peasantry (i.e. poor peasants and rural proletariat) as its trustworthy collaborator. It was called the Bourgeois Democratic Revolution and then it would be followed by next stage of people's struggle to achieve the goal of the "Socialist

10 V. I. Lenin (1968a), 'Imperialism, The Highest Stage of Capitalism', in *Selected Works of Lenin*, Moscow: Progress Publishers, p. 172.

Revolution and the Dictatorship of the Proletariat". Lenin argued that achievement of democratic revolution was not an end in itself but a required stage in order to complete the Socialist goal.

> *The democratic revolution is bourgeois in nature. The slogan of a general redistribution, or "land and freedom" –that most widespread slogan of the peasant masses, downtrodden and ignorant, yet passionately yearning for light and happiness –is a bourgeois slogan. But we Marxist should know that there is not, nor can there be, any other path to real freedom for the proletariat and the peasantry, than the path of bourgeois freedom and bourgeois progress. We must not forget that there is not, nor can there be at the present time, any other means of bringing socialism nearer, than complete political liberty, than a democratic republic, than the revolutionary-democratic dictatorship of the proletariat and the peasantry.*[11]

In the course of ferocious struggle against reformism and parliamentarism after the violent suppression of 1905 revolution in Russia, the Bolshevik Party developed the revolutionary struggle following Lenin's methodology by successfully completing revolutionary seizure of state power in 1917.

This marked the establishment of the first socialist state and made a huge impact worldwide. Now due to the changes brought out by imperialism and victory of Russian revolution, the national liberation struggles in colonial countries were no longer a part of the old bourgeois democratic movement but became a component part of the world proletarian socialist revolution. Following the victory of the October Revolution in Russia in 1917, Lenin and (later also significantly by Joseph Stalin) not only analyzed the

11 V. I. Lenin (1968b), 'Two Tactics of Social-Democracy in the Democratic Revolution', in *Selected Works of Lenin*, Moscow: Progress Publishers, p. 125.

changes in the general character to the colonial movements, but paid particular attention to the development of these colonial liberation movements of the East. The victory of the *October Revolution* had spread the Marxist ideology by developing it further and this is in sum called ideology of Leninism. The formation of communist parties now built on the Marxist-Leninist style throughout the world.

The *October Revolution* brought the salvos of Marxism-Leninism to countries like China, and opened broader prospects for proletarian-led revolution. During the Chinese revolution, Mao Tse-tung showed that in countries like China, although there are many survivals of pre-capitalist relations (widespread survivals of feudalism or semi-feudal relations particularly in villages), the revolution that is necessary to resolve the underlying contradictions of society and to liberate the people is not a bourgeois-democratic revolution leading to the rule of the bourgeoisie and the establishment of capitalism but a New-Democratic Revolution, led by the proletariat and transform the social system by eliminating the pre-capitalist economic and social relations, thereby opening the road to socialism. In 1927, Mao underlined in his work, "Report on an Investigation of the Peasant Movement in Hunan", the central role of the peasants in the Chinese revolution. He wrote:

> *...a revolution is not a dinner party, or writing an essay, or painting a picture, or doing embroidery; it cannot be so refined, so leisurely and gentle, kind, courteous, restrained and magnanimous. A revolution is an insurrection, an act of violence by which one class overthrows another. A rural revolution is a revolution by which the peasantry overthrows the power of the feudal landlord class. Without using the greatest forces, the peasants cannot possibly overthrow the*

> *deep-rooted authority of the landlords which has lasted for thousand years. The rural areas need a mighty revolutionary upsurge, for it alone can rouse the people in their millions to become a powerful force.*[12]

By giving central role to peasants to carry out agrarian revolution, he argued that the road to the seizure of power will pass through armed struggle in a state of semi-feudal and semi-colonial China. Here, the proletariat and its party by chiefly depending on the peasants had to be mobilized by waging a protracted nature of People's War in rural region by building a Base Areas. This eventually created a situation to encircle the cities and finally seize the cities. While evolving a Chinese road to the Communism, Mao Tse-tung also developed a military strategy for revolution in countries of the Third World dominated by imperialism and its auxiliary forces of ruling nexus of bourgeoisie to feudal warlords. This strategy was an outcome of a Chinese peculiar condition while Communist Party of China was leading mass resistance against Chiang Kai-shek and later Japanese imperialism in 1930s-1940s.

The correctness of this strategy formulated by Mao in light of Marxism-Leninism in the conditions of Chinese society was borne out by the success of Protracted People's War in completing the New Democratic Revolution in China. This experience was one of the main inspirations for CPN (M) in formulating their own ideology which they termed as Maoism.

3. HISTORICAL EVOLUTION OF NEPALI MAOISM

With the restoration of multi-party democracy in 1990, the position of different left parties on the question of using the parliament for furthering the revolutionary movement was strongly debated. Many left factions held a view that multiparty

12 Mao Tse-Tung (1971b), 'Report of an Investigation of the Peasant Movement in Hunan', in *Selected Works of Mao Tse-Tung,* Peking: Foreign Language Press, pp. 23-24.

democracy could be one of sub-stages to reach goal of Socialism. However, the recent success and shortcoming of 1990s movement of democracy was also a hotly debated subject among various Nepali left formations. The radical faction led by the CPN (M) upheld a view that "... the 1990s Revolution was, overwhelmingly, a revolution of middle class. Given the agrarian nature of the economy, and the consequent low level of urbanisation, the middle class was concentrated primarily in Kathmandu Valley and urban centres of the plains...The peasants of rural Nepal were, in general, bystanders in the process of political change... Nepal's Revolution of 1990 was, without question, an urban affair."[13]

The Maoists was then divided into many smaller radical communist factions. Two major streams existed within by these groups, first by a faction of CPN (Unity Centre) which later became the Maoist and secondly by the conglomeration of factions of Nirmal Lama and Mohan Bikram Singh's CPN (Masal) which later united into one called CPN (Unity Centre-Masal). Subsequently, they regrouped as the CPN (Ekta Kendra) or Unity Centre.

The foremost communist party was then CPN (United Marxist-Leninist) and be better known as UML. The UML was first communist party who rose up to power when its leaders Manmohan Adhikary became Nepal's Prime Minster in November 1994. Though, the UML government was short lived but it was historical significance since of recent demise of the Soviet Union in 1990s. Therefore, it was a party which was strongly criticized by the Unity Centre on their documents and writings. The Maoists had regarded the *Jhapali* peasant movement as a revolutionary one while pointing out its deviations.

> *... the armed struggle of 1972-73 in Jhapa with the political line of protracted people's war [rose] in rebellion*

---

13 T. Louise Brown (1996), *The Challenge to Democracy: A Political History*, London: Routledge pp. 117-118.

> *against right revisionism prevalent in the Communist movement... although there were deep shortcomings in the leadership in terms of petty-bourgeois mechanistic and 'leftist' adventurist tendencies, it was however an important far-reaching rebellion against the autocratic feudal rule of the king and against the rightist reformist tendencies that had entrenched deeply into the Nepalese Communist Movement.*[14]

In the 1970s the UML was widely known as the *Ma-Le* which had made efforts to organize a violent peasant uprising in Jhapa district of eastern Koshi region. Called as the *Jhapali*, they had formed All Nepal Revolutionary Coordination Committee (Marxist-Leninist) in 1971 in leadership of Man Mohan Adhikari. They had killed some landlords by following a political line to "annihilate landlord". The severe state repression and subsequent failure of the *Jhapali* uprising made its leadership to think over and review both strategy and tactics of the "Nepali road to Socialism".[15] Until 1980s, the *Jhapali* had re-oriented political mobilization in the cities by leaving work in rural areas and known as *Ma-Le* by unifying small communist factions in leadership of Madan Bhandari.

Thus, according to the Nepali Maoist, the UML had abandoned ideology of Maoist Thought and accepted Deng Xiaoping's rule in China as socialism. The collapse of Soviet Union and Eastern European countries led to further re-evaluation of its strategy since it was conceived that communism has failed as a system. In the early 1990s, as per the analysis of the Maoists, the UML went

---

14 CPN (M) (1997a), 'Strategy and Tactics of Armed Struggle in Nepal', in *The Worker, Organ of the Communist Party of Nepal (Maoist)*, No. 3, (February issue), pp. 20-21.

15 Stephen Lawrence Mikesell (1999), Class, State and Struggle in Nepal, *Writings 1989-1995,* New Delhi: Manohar Publications, pp. 99-100.

towards bourgeois parliamentarism. Instead of believing that the communist party should participate in such a parliamentary system by simply to expose it from within, the UML in contrast became committed enthusiastically to competitive multiparty democracy and took over all the values associated with bourgeois liberal democracy. In short, UML endorsed the bourgeois democracy by terming it with 'new' ideology of the *Jantako Bahudaliya Janbad* (multi-party popular democracy) from the *Naulo Janbad* (New Democracy) which was basically rhetoric in essence to enter in parliamentary democracy.[16]

From a Maoist perspective, this was evidently a revisionist deviation. They had cited the polemics of Lenin against Bernstein to oppose the UML's ideological deviation. Like Bernstein, the Maoists maintained, UML had abandoned the basics of Marxism including the belief that the state, regardless of its institutional arrangements, is always a dictatorship of the class that controls it. At the same time, they traced their deviation from pages of history of Nepalese Communist movement:

> *... Nepalese reformism has never raised the slogan of state power in revolutionary Marxist way. Here a tradition to talk strategically about democratic revolution but advocate the reactionary state power practically and tactically and struggle for it has been set. This disease has grown widespread ever since the then party general secretary Manmohan Adhikari told the king in 1955 that the party will only propagate peacefully about socialism and made the party legal to extent that it would support parliamentary system.*[17]

16 Stephen Mikesell (2007), 'Prajatantra', in Mery Des Chene and Pratyoush Onta (eds.), *Nepalko Sandarbhma Samajsastriya Chintan*, Lalitpur: Social Science Baha, p. 22.

17 Prachanda, (2004), 'The Problem of Ideological Deviation in the Nepalese People's Revolution', in *Problem & Prospects of*

Besides UML's parliamentary reformism, the Maoists uncovered the ideological line embraced by the Mohan Bikram Singh who was considered as father of Nepali Maoism. This radical faction of the Nepali Communists was influenced by China's Cultural Revolution and Pushpa Lal Shrestha, the founding father of the Nepali Communists was also part of this faction. This faction had argued Protracted People's war is the only way to conclude a successful New Democratic Revolution in Nepal. Mohan Bikram Singh adhering Mao Tse-tung thought believed that an "elected Constituent Assembly" would was minimum level to establish bourgeois democracy in Nepal while Pushpa Lal Shrestha's faction (who later known as CPN (Marxist)) had advocated for the "restoration of multi-party democracy". Singh's led faction was later culminated in the CPN (Fourth Convention/Congress) by holding a party Congress in September 1974 at Banaras in India. In early 1979, Nirmal Lama replaced Mohan Bikram Singh from party leadership for "initiating agrarian revolution" but it never begins and Lama's campaign ended with king Birendra's announcement of the national referendum in May 1979.[18]

As the *Panchayat* regime won the referendum by manipulating, this made a debate within the Fourth Congress. Nirmal Lama was in favour of taking parts *Panchayat* body's election while group led by Mohan Bikram preferred boycotting elections. At the same time around in 1981, death of Chairman Mao and subsequently political program taken by the new Chinese leadership caused major debate in the Fourth Congress. The faction led by Nirmal Lama acknowledged the new Chinese leadership under Deng

---

Revolution in Nepal: A Collection of Articles by Com. Prachanda and Other Leaders of the CPN (Maoist), Nepal: Jandisha Publications, pp. 22-23.

18 Deepak Thapa with Bandita Sijapati (2004), *A Kingdom Under Seige: Nepal's Maoist Insurgency, 1996 to 2004*, Kathmandu: The Printhouse, p. 25.

Hsiao Ping. While Mohan Bikram Singh led faction denounced it by calling new Chinese leadership as "counter-revolutionary" and adherence to Mao Tse-tung's thought and stand with Cultural Revolution. Finally, in 1983, Fourth Congress faced a major split in which Mohan Bikram set up his own party in November 1983 called as CPN (Mashal). While explaining reasons behind growth of Maoism in Nepal, Nickson (1992) notes by taking cognizance of this event as a turning point:

> *Mashal was quick to associate itself with an international regrouping of Maoist parties which took place in the wake of the overthrow of the 'Gang of Four' in China in 1976. In March 1984 Mashal delegates attended the second international conference of Maoist parties and organisation in London which formed the Revolutionary International Movement (RIM).*[19]

However, splits among radical faction continued. Following its Fifth Congress, CPN (Mashal) broke up in 1985 in two faction namely Singh led CPN (Masal) and CPN (Mashal) by Mohan Baidya, 'Kiran'. Both took suffix of the Masal and the Mashal with a slight difference of Nepali alphabet of "*Sa*" and "*Sha*". The meaning of both was "lighting torch" and was only differentiation of punctuation. Kiran led faction was known as the *Moto Mashal* which later culminated as CPN (Unity Centre) and Mohan Bikram Singh led fraction was known as the *Patlo Masal*. Both factions adhered to Mao's idea of People's War and had claims of "true follower of Maoist Thought". To overthrow the *Panchayati* state, the CPN (Mashal) attempted an urban insurrection in the national capital Kathmandu in 1989. Called as "Sector incident of 1989", Mashal activists blackened king Tribhuvan's statue and attacked police post

19 R. Andrew Nickson (2007 [1992]), 'Democratisation and the growth of Communism in Nepal: A Peruvian Scenario in the Making', in Deepak Thapa (ed.), Understanding the Maoist Movement in Nepal, Kathmandu: Martin Chautari, p. 8.

in Kathmandu. It got failed miserably amid state repression and was termed by party's central committee as a 'mistake'. Taking a moral responsibility, party's general sectary Kiran abdicated in favour of Prachanda. By summarizing this debate, Adhikari (2010) notes:

> *By terming their doctrine Maoism, the Nepali Maoist asserted that Mao's theoretical work was equivalent in stature and profundity to those of Marx and Lenin. Maoism, just as Marxism and Leninism in the past, was the scientific interpretation of society and provided the correct guide to action for communists in semi-feudal and semi-colonial countries. This being the case, a Mao-style protracted people's war was absolutely necessary if Nepali society was to be liberated and move towards socialism…Singh and the other believers in Mao-thought, on the other hand, denied the absolute validity of Maoist doctrine. They recognized the importance of Mao's contribution, but thought that the world had not essentially changed since Lenin's time. As such, the latter's tactics were still applicable to revolutionaries everywhere. An absolute focus on a prolonged armed insurgency against the state was misguided, especially in Nepal, where state was too powerful for the communist parties to take on by armed force. Until such a day when the "objective" and "subjective" conditions, became conducive for armed struggle, other political means such as street protests, organizations of the peasantry and proletariat and participation in elections should be used against the existing state.*[20]

---

20 Aditya Adhikari (2010), 'The Ideological Evolution of the Nepali Maoists', *Studies in Nepali History and Society*, Vol. 15, No. 2, pp. 230-231.

After political parties were again legalised in 1990, some 30 years after being outlawed by the *Panchayat* regime, various fringe Communist groups got united in changing times. In particular, some radical factions—notably the CPN (Fourth Convention) led by Nirmal Lama, the CPN (Mashal) led by Prachanda and a faction led by Dr. Baburam Bhattarai that had rebelled against the CPN (Masal)—formed the CPN (Unity Center). Based on its on-going pledge to armed revolutionary struggle, the Unity Center remained an underground organisation. Nevertheless they had an open political front, called the Samyukt *Jan Morcha, Nepal* or (SJM). Through this, they had participated in the 1991's general election and emerged the third largest party after the Nepali Congress and the *Ma-Le* faction by winning nine seats.

By late 1991, they held it's Unity Congress, where party lines eventually clashed and resulted in split again. The bone of contention was implementing military strategy of armed struggle in Nepal. The faction led by Prachanda supported a Chinese-styled Protracted People's War while the other, led by Nirmal Lama, favoured a Russian model of mass insurrection. Even after Prachand's document get was adopted at the Unity Congress by a majority vote, the intra-party debate continued. This eventually resulted in the break-away of Nirmal Lama's faction in mid-1994 from the Unity Centre. For about six months later, in early 1995 the majority faction led by Prachanda decided to change the name of Unity Centre to the Communist Party of Nepal (Maoist). The adoption of the adding "Maoist" in their party name was a result of their affiliation with the RIM (Revolutionary International Movement), and was oriented to strengthening the party's revolutionary image. Simultaneously, they also formally decided to quit parliamentary politics and began preparations of armed struggle amid police repressions in Western and Eastern region of Nepal where they had won parliamentary election in 1991.

Figure-III: Factionalism in Nepali Left and emergence of CPN (M)[21]

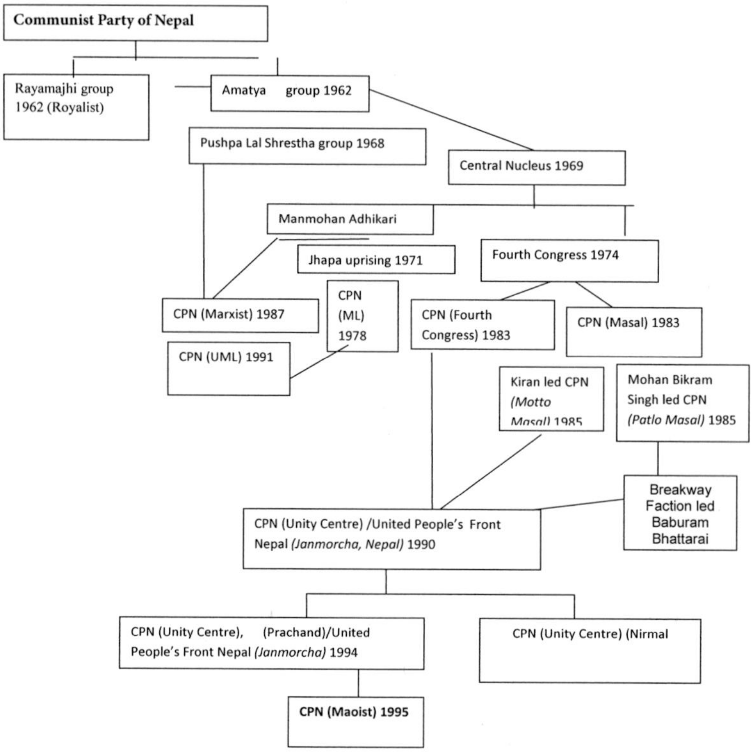

4. THE CPN (M) WORLDVIEW

The Nepali Maoists located itself in the practice of revolutionary Marxism in the political-social conditions of Nepal that intended to alter state and society. Their ideology, however, is not based merely on an interpretation of Nepali society and state but is also very much linked to an interpretation of world history and global and regional connections as a part of international communist movement. Guided by their ideology, they set a political program

21 **Source:** Martin Hoftun, W. Raeper and John Whelpton (1999), *People, Politics and ideology: Democracy and Social change in Nepal*, Kathmandu: Mandala Book Point, p. 392.

and formulated the strategy and tactics to achieve this. It was their political programme which set the tune of a particular analysis of key contradictions in the Nepali society that plagued political, economic and socio-cultural structures and impede social progress. At the same time, they gave prominence by formulating a pertinent worldview which would give them an edge to alter the existing order. They aligned their MLM (i.e., Marxism-Leninism-Maoism) ideology with their particular worldview which got reflected from its analysis of socio-cultural and politico-economic history, structures and processes of Nepali society and charted specific strategies which would help them to make a radical rupture from the present social order. To take this course, they had drawn from the worldwide MLM political practice and literature. By a leaflet that was issued on 13 February, 1996, they had pointed out this fact that their political movement was associated to worldwide political struggles for Socialism.

> *What... we are also conscious of and confident about it that this struggle will get support and help from the communist revolutionaries and struggling masses the world over and this will in turn assist all those revolutionaries. Because this struggle of ours will be a part and parcel of the world proletarian revolution undertaken with a view to end the exploitation and oppression of men by the men and to end forever the war itself. In this context, we would like to make a special mention of the ongoing people's revolution in Peru based on Marxism-Leninism-Maoism and the Revolutionary International Movement (RIM) and revolutionary movements the world over based on the same.*[22]

22 CPN (M) (2004a [1996]), 'Appeal of the CPN (Maoist) to the People', in *Some Important Documents of Communist Party of Nepal (Maoist)*, Nepal: Jandisha Prakashan, p. 31.

It is been noted above that a debate of waging an armed struggle by emulating Chinese revolution was running from many years within the predecessor of the Nepali Maoists. The CPN (Mashal) upheld a political line based on ideology of "Maoist Thought" since 1984, when it took membership of global body of the Maoist organisations. However, its leadership never took tactical steps towards starting agrarian revolution by showing a ruthless suppression by the *Panchayat* state machinery. Eventually, this had caused many splits organisationally since times of their party leadership of Mohan Bikram Singh. Stressing on the importance of an ideologically clear line, Maoist General Sectary Prachanda had argued in an interview to American journalist Li Onesto in year 2000 which appeared in the *A World To Win*, the organ of the RIM:

> *In Nepal, our first effort was to correctly grasp the science of Marxism-Leninism-Maoism. For this, we strove to link ourselves with the arduous and challenging ideological struggle waged by the genuine communist revolutionaries of the world against the Chinese counter-revolution after the death of Comrade Mao Tse-tung. Taking the synthesis of the Great Proletarian Cultural Revolution, the highest expression of conscious class struggle as our starting point, we delved into serious study. We made a particularly fervent study of the ideological struggle that erupted in the process of the development of the Communist Party of Peru, the Revolutionary Communist Party, USA and in other countries... Also, we made an attempt to draw lessons from the positive and negative aspects of the revolutionary and national movements of different countries, including India, the Philippines, Turkey, Iran, Sri Lanka and others...*[23]

23 Li Onesto (2001), 'Interview with Comrade Prachanda', *A World To Win*, 2001/27, pp. 38-39.

Through these political experiences of recent political movements, they eventually could commence Protracted People's War in Nepal.

5. THE SEMI-FEUDAL, SEMI-COLONIAL THESIS

A sociological analysis of People's War in Nepal has to take into account the CPN (Maoist) analysis of the Nepali state and society through which it identified the political forces that kept the country subjugated and underdeveloped through a low level of capitalist development. Based on its ideology, the Maoist interpreted Nepali society and state on their specific worldview which eventually provided the grounds for armed struggle in Nepal.

Most of the communist parties of Nepal which draw their legacy from the birth of the Communist Party of Nepal in Calcutta in 1951 characterize Nepali society as "semi-feudal, semi-colonial". Many Nepali left parties since Pushpalal Shrestha times to CPN (UML) and predecessor of the Maoist have maintained this characterization of Nepal. The CPN (Maoist) too held the institution of the Hindu monarchy and the Indian state as primarily responsible for the oppression of the Nepali people. It said that the monarchy stood at the helm of the "semi-feudal" order by giving various attractive slogans of development and prosperity in every Five Year Plans on the one hand, and the Indian ruling classes had forced Nepal to become its "semi-colony", on the other. Both exploited and extracted surplus from the vast majority of population and hindered the development of Nepali society from agrarian to a capitalist society.

Claiming to be guided by this Marxist-Leninist-Maoist framework, the Maoist offered a class analysis of state and society in Nepal. According to this, these six classes are; proletariat, farm workers, middle peasants, rich peasants, petty-bourgeois and national bourgeoisie. They regarded proletariat class as "fundamental motivating force" to complete New Democratic Revolution in Nepal but since its number is very small in Nepal because of low industrial development and centered in urban regions only. The farm workers and middle peasants were considered by them reliable force for their struggle. Among these classes, rich peasants were considered "a vacillating force". The class of national bourgeoisie consists of very tiny number in Nepal. In comparison to large section of people representing petty-bourgeois class, the CPN (M) comprehended it as an "auxiliary force". However, the classes of national-bourgeoisie and petty-bourgeoisie both were regarded having "contradictory character".[24] It was said that the peasantry as a revolutionary class to carry out agrarian revolution in Nepal. The Maoist adopted this specific policy formulation through their Third Expanded Meeting of central body meeting held in March 1995.

It is been noted earlier in Chapter-2, that how traditionally, the distribution of land was consisted among upper caste Hindus – Bahun, Thakuri/ Chhetri castes of courtier called as *Kazi*, *Bhardars*. This eventually led to the concentration of large tracts of land in hands of few families and land owning elite by *Guthi* to *Birta* grants. By a specific class analysis of nature of Nepali society, the Maoists regarded this in sum an exploitative process which had ramifications centuries later expressed in the form of People's War. It was agriculture sector only that made the majority of population to get employment while nearly half of the GDP came from this sector. But the state of Nepalese agriculture had been extremely uneven, backward and almost pre-capitalist in nature. By pointing out on the causes of People's War, the Maoist argued that,

> *70 per cent of poor peasants own about 25 per cent of land, 25 percent of middle peasants own around 45 per cent of the land and 5 percent of rich peasants and*

24 Op. cit., CPN (M) (1997), p. 25.

> *semi-feudal own 30 percent of the land. According to one early report, by a specialist from the FAO, who came to Nepal to evaluate the effects of the so called land reform of 1964, the structure of land ownership is even more unequal. According to this report, 8 percent of Nepali population was totally landless and of those who had some land, 65 per cent of poor peasants owned 25 per cent of the land, 25 per cent of middle peasants owned 25 per cent of the land and 10 per cent of rich peasants and semi-feudal owned 65 per cent of the land. In the Terai, those big landlords with more than 10 hectares each owned more than 50 percent of the total land, where in the hills, poor peasants constituted more than 80 per cent of the population…"*[25]

Therefore the majority rural proletariat and poor peasantry were forced to work the land of the rich under highly exploitative conditions in the hills to the low land of *Tarai* region of Nepal. The oppressive conditions in the ownership of land and relations of production in entire Nepal from the hills with tiny plots of land with very low productivity to the big plots of land in the fertile Tarai region, the role of moneylenders was always a helping hand to landowning elite class. In the hill region the number of owner-cultivators was relatively higher. As much as one half of their produce had to be surrendered by the tenants to the landlords. In addition the system of bonded agricultural labour was also widely prevalent.

According to the Maoist formulation, the gruesome exploitation that the peasantry faced from Nepali state historically to present times prevented it from investing in agriculture to a degree that would lead to a capitalist breakthrough. Over the last few decades, the exploitation by the landowning ruling class was intensified by the arrival of imperialist finance capital into

25 Baburam Bhattarai (2003), 'The Political Economy of the People's War', in Arjun Karki and David Seddon (eds.), *The People's War in Nepal: Left Perspectives*, Delhi: Adroit Publishers, p. 132.

the agricultural sector through state institutions like Agricultural Development Bank. Though the ruling landowning elite had realised that a transformation in Nepal's social and economic structure was required for modernization and growth, the attempted land reform in 1960s was doomed to miserable failure due to strong opposition from the same landed elite which has been the fundamental class base of the Hindu monarchy. This prompted them to argue that only a People's War can sweep away historically entrenched privileges and power of despotic state.

Simultaneously they had argued that Nepal was facing semi-colonial oppression. They maintained following Leninist theory that Nepal is been reduced its semi-colonial fate because of American imperialism. The imperialism enters Nepal through offering foreign aid by firmly based on its neoliberal ideology. While issuing a public appeal on the day of start of their *Janyudha*, they maintained:

> *Where has the present state that has been harping about development and construction for the last fifty years landed Nepal economically?...This state that does not manufacture even a needle in the name of self-reliant and national economy, has handed over the whole economy of the country to a dozen families of the foreign comprador and bureaucratic capitalists. Whereas these handfuls of plunderer have become billionaires, the real masters of this country...the toiling masses of Nepal, are forced to eke out a meagre existence of deprivation and poverty. The sons and daughters of Nepalese peasants and workers reeling under unemployment and poverty are compelled to lead a miserable life of dishonour and neglect in India and different parts of world to earn their daily bread. After piling a massive foreign debt burden even on the future generations of the Nepalese people, the feudal and comprador and bureaucratic capitalists rulers are making merry on it. In the name of privatization and*

> *liberalization under the guidance and for the benefit of the foreign capitalists, the process of mortgaging the whole country to the comprador and bureaucratic capitalists is in full swing now.*[26]

The Forty Point Demands presented by the Maoists to the Deuba government in 1996 also prominently share their concerns of hegemony of India in Nepal. It's very first demand including many others concerned with the removal of unequal treaties and trade agreements with Indian state which they viewed as semi-colonial. The Treaty of 1950 with Independent India or better known as "Delhi Agreement" was built on semi-colonial premise and was a continuation of the 1815's Sugauli Treaty and 1923 Treaty with British India. However, they argued, it was the 1950 Delhi Agreement that promoted unequal relationship of various kinds from politico-economy, to socio- cultural dimensions. They pointed out quite clearly about some specific provisions which made this agreement a recurrent event.

> *At present it is mainly through the 1950 treaty and successive versions of that treaty 'agreed' every 10 years, that Indian expansionism maintains its semi-colonial commercial, industrial, financial and fiscal monopoly over Nepal....the semi-colonial treaty of 195o provides for 'national treatment' with respect to the Indian monopoly capitalists, allowing them to reside in Nepal and to engage in economic activities on an equal footing with Nepali citizens, they are able to monopolize the economy of Nepal completely. At present one dozen India- based billionaire capitalists (mainly Marwaris) exert strong control over Nepal's industry and commerce. According to the estimation of one Indian researcher some time back, about 80 per cent of Nepal's industry and commerce was in hands of Indian capitalists or capitalists of Indian*

26 Op. cit., CPN (M) (2004a [1996]), pp. 25-26.

> *origin. The Indian expansionist state has tended to place restrictions on the international transit facilities that a land-locked country like Nepal is actually entitled to enjoy unhindered. In this way, it has facilitated its hegemony over the Nepali economy..."*[27]

Thus the Maoist proposed, Nepal was as a consequence eventually reduced to total economic dependence. The national industrial bourgeoisie, a class that promotes the development of domestic industry and the production of commodities for domestic consumption, was almost non-existent in Nepal principally because of hegemony of Indian State. Indian capitalist's domination was built in such a deliberate way that self-reliant domestic industries were non-existent and small industries were at brink of collapse. Thus they maintained that imperialism enters Nepal through Indian expansionism:

> *[The]...multinational companies of various imperialist countries like USA, UK, Japan, Germany, etc, sell goods produced in their India-based branches to Nepal, or they open sub-branches of their Indian branches based in Nepal-like Bata (shoes), Hoecht (medicine), Proctor and Gamble (soap, chocolate etc.), Hindustan Lever (soap), Nestle (coffee, milk products etc.), Brook Bond (tea) etc, and products of India joint-ventures with multinational companies such as Maruti-Suzuki (automobiles), Hero-Honda (motorcycle) etc.- are freely sold in Nepal. In this way, world imperialism enters Nepal, riding an Indian expansionist horse.*[28]

Moreover it was also argued by the Maoist that besides making Nepal its captive market for industrial goods, the Indian expansionist exploitation and oppression was manifest over its control of Nepal's natural resources. It was mainly rich water resources which Nepal was considered a greatest water resource

27 Op. cit., Baburam Bhattarai (2003), pp. 124, 126.

28 Ibid., pp. 126-127.

potential in the world. From Nepal's Sharada Dam agreement in 1920 to the Kosi and Gandaki dam project in 1950s to the Mahakali project of 1996, all agreements with Indian state show the unequal and disadvantageous status for the former. This was also echoed in their Forty Point charters of demands submitted to the Nepali state in prior to beginning of their armed struggle.

> *The so-called Integrated Mahakali Treaty concluded on January 25, 1996 should be cancelled immediately as it is designed to conceal the fatal Tanakpur Treaty and it allows the monopoly of Indian Imperialists over all the water resources of Nepal.*[29]

6. PRINCIPLES OF NEPALI PEOPLE'S WAR

It is a widespread belief that the principles of People's War were discovered at a stroke of genius by the Chinese Communist leader Mao Tse-tung. In a war of this kind, it is important that the war is kept subordinate to politics. In this way the concept of People's War has been understood as a higher and distinct form of guerrilla warfare. It has been distinguished from conventional wars between countries in the sense that it demands the active participation of the entire society and does not distinguish between combatants and non-combatants. The novelty of twentieth century guerrilla warfare is not so much military as political in nature. The revolutionary guerrilla wars evolved out of Marxist-Leninist modes of political movements and organisational principles as well as out of the exigencies of anti-imperialist revolt in predominantly agrarian societies.

Mao worked out on ideas of guerrilla warfare while Chinese Communists were fighting a political movement against Kuomintang forces. He modified theory of ancient Chinese theories of guerrilla warfare by developing it over a period of more than twenty years from the time in 1926 when Mao first

29 See, CPN (M)'s 'Forty Points Demand,' in Appendix.

discovered revolutionary potential among the peasantry in Hunan until the spring of 1938-1940s. The result was the formulation of his three essential principles of People's War: the Chinese revolution would be carried out from bases located in remote, rural areas; that it would involve a central role for the Red Army, a role that would be more of a political than a military one; and that the revolution would take the form of a protracted war of long and undetermined length, but one which would proceed through orderly stages. These stages were called as (i) Strategic defensive, (ii) Strategic equilibrium/ stalemate, and (iii) Strategic offensive. Each stage was further divided into several sub-stages consisting of final preparation, initiation, continuation, and advancement. Accordingly, this three staged war would be primarily focussed by stressing role of guerrilla struggle. They had clearly argued that:

> *... people's war is a war of masses, that it can be developed only by relying on the masses and principally on the peasants and the masses are the creators of history; to acknowledge the need and importance of the stages of strategic defence, stalemate and offense of the people's war and to make plans accordingly by accepting the strategic role of guerrilla war as it is the principal form of war in the initial stage of strategic defence; to grasp the importance of developing guerrilla warfare into positional warfare and establishing base areas to capture central power; above all,...to establish leadership of the Party over the army and not to permit at any cost to arise a situation where the gun control the party.*[30]

The guerrilla war was a natural outgrowth of Mao's wider view of revolutionary dialectics, making maximum use of all the ideas within it. These elements, together with the three essential principles, make up the basic concepts of the theory of Maoist

30 Op. cit., CPN (M) (1997), p. 28.

People's War. It is as old as conventional wars. Therefore, the Maoist theory of guerrilla warfare makes an effective weapon for militarily weak masses. However, in the absence of correct political leadership, the Maoists argued, guerrilla war could not achieve much success. The Nepali Maoist emulated Chinese Communist's policy to train its guerrillas through a set of basic rules to wage armed struggle. These were conceptualised as "Ten major Principles" and are following:

1. Attack dispersed isolated enemy forces first; attack concentrated, strong enemy forces later.
2. Take small and medium cities and extensive rural areas first; take big cities later..
3. Make wiping out the enemy's effective strength our main objective; do not make holding or seizing a city or place our main objective.
4. In every battle, concentrate an absolutely superior force, encircle the enemy forces completely, strive to wipe them out thoroughly and do not let any escape from the net.
5. Fight no battle unprepared, fight no battle you are not sure of winning; make every effort to be well prepared for each battle, make every effort to ensure victory in the given set of conditions as between the enemy and ourselves.
6. Give full play to our style of fighting –courage in battle, no fear sacrifice, no feat of fatigue, and continuous fighting (that is, fighting successive battles in a short time without rest).
7. Strive to wipe out the enemy when he is on the move. At the same time, pay attention to the tactics of positional attack and capture enemy fortified points and cities.
8. With regard to attacking cities, resolutely size all enemy fortified points and cities which are weakly defended.

9. Replenish our strength with all the arms and most of the personnel captured from the enemy.
10. Period of rest, training and consolidation should not be in general be very long, and the enemy should so far as possible be permitted no breathing space.[31]

The Maoists laid emphasis on Mao Tse-tung's military strategy from preparation period itself that is –first stage of strategic defence. They had asserted that armed struggle in Nepal *must necessarily* adopt a strategy of surrounding the cities from the countryside. In this way, they grasped People's War as a total war by pitting tactically "ten against one" and strategically "one against ten". Accordingly they set an overall strategy of armed struggle in Nepal and it is following:

> *...give priority to the rural work, but do not leave urban work too; give priority to illegal struggle, but do not leave legal struggle too; give priority to specific strategic areas, but do not leave work related to mass movement too; give priority to class struggle in villages, but do not leave countrywide struggle too; give priority to guerrilla actions, but do not leave political exposure and propaganda too; give priority to propaganda work within the country but do not leave worldwide propaganda too; give priority to build army organisation, but do not leave to build front organisations too; give priority to rely on one's own organisation and force, but do not miss to forge unity in action, to take support and help from international arena.*[32]

Moreover, to win an armed battle there was a constant need to uphold democratic principles between party leadership and

31 Mao Tse-Tung (1966), 'The Present Situation and Our Tasks (excerpts)', in Selected Military Writings of Mao Tse-Tung, Peking: Foreign Language Press, pp. 349-350.

32 Op. cit., CPN (M) (1997), p. 28.

activists. Here come most important principles of People's War that relates with building of guerrilla army. Though, "political power grows out of the barrel of a gun", but it is the communist party who commands the gun and never the gun. Therefore, the guerrilla activists and its military organisation were conceived as a politically motivated activists practising democracy within and working for the communist party. Through this way only, guerrillas would gain strength and support of population.

7. BASE AREA AND MASS LINE AS BASIC CONSTITUENT OF NEW DEMOCRATIC REVOLUTION

The conception of New Democratic Revolution was built by Mao Tse-tung on an application of Marxist theory to semi-colonial situations of China. Based on his experience of industrial societies of Europe, Marx had formulated a theory of bourgeois-democratic revolution. He had argued that with pace of development of society, feudalism is uprooted by a bourgeois-democratic revolution and this subsequently makes way of establishment of capitalism. While capitalist system reaches its over-developed state, a process of decay began with in it in due course and this would be replaced by a socialist system through a proletarian revolution. However, for colonial situation where struggle against imperialism got knotted with a struggle against feudalism too, Marx's theory of revolution was refined by Lenin in 1920. Following Lenin, Mao Tse-tung defined it in Chinese contexts by fusing objectives of anti-colonial movement with anti-feudal struggle together. Mohanty (1978) summarizes Mao's contribution by noting:

> *...that in semi-colonial and semi-feudal conditions like those which obtained in China, the bourgeois-democratic revolution had to take the form of a new or people's democratic revolution which was to be both*

> *anti-colonial and anti-feudal. It was a more advanced form than the bourgeois-democratic revolution because it was led by worker in alliance with the peasants.*[33]

Therefore, the CPN (M) argued that for a society like Nepal in which even the bourgeois democratic revolution has not taken place, only a New Democratic Revolution can usher and institutionalize democracy under proletarian hegemony. Furthermore, what is more important in a struggle of this kind was question relating to political line of the party organization. The Maoist has regarded a correct ideological line of party as the most important aspect in fighting class struggle. They asserted that correctness or otherwise of the ideological and political line decide everything in political movement like this kind. This is theorized as "Mass Line" by Mao Tse-tung during Chinese Communist's battle against Japanese imperialism. The correctness of mass line will set the future of entire course of armed struggle. This is because, Maoist People's War could only fought by relying on peasants, and so agrarian revolution could be carried on. They held that if the ideological line is correct everything is gained, but everything is lost if it is wrong. It is called in the Maoist vocabulary –"from the masses, to the masses".

> *This means: take the ideas of the masses (scattered and unsystematic ideas) and concentrate them (through study turn them into concentrated and systematic ideas), then go to the masses and propagate and explain these ideas until the masses embrace them as their own, hold fast to them and translate them into action, and test the correctness of these ideas in such action. Then once again concentrate ideas from the masses and once again go to the masses so that the ideas are preserved in and carried through. And, so on, over and*

33 Manoranjan Mohanty (2012 [1978]), *The Political Philosophy of Mao Zedong,* Delhi: Aakar Books pp. 37-38.

> *over again in an endless spiral, with the ideas becoming more correct, more vital and richer each time.*[34]

On the other hand, at the heart of the course of New Democratic Revolution is building of base areas which will eventually decide the fate of armed struggle. Mao argued that to defend a New Democratic Revolution, there is a fundamental need of the Communist Party to establish liberated base area. Based on experiences of first civil war period against Chiang Kai-shek and later with anti-Japanese resistance, Mao placed establishment of base areas a strategic importance:

> *...on which the guerrilla forces rely in performing their strategic tasks and achieving the object of preserving and expanding themselves and destroying and driving out the enemy. Without such strategic bases, there will be nothing to depend on in carrying out any of our strategic tasks or achieving the aim of war.*[35]

Mao had categorised a three type of base areas in China based on the communist party mobilizations; in mountains, plains and river-lake regions. It is reported that Chinese Communist Party exercised a parallel political power (i.e. soviets) by forming Kiangsi Provincial Soviet Government in 1927-1934 while fighting against the Kuomintang forces. These Soviets were modelled to carry out democratic reforms (i.e. land reform), to look after peasant livelihood and organise them for struggle. But establishment of such kind of base area was a product of a protracted and painstaking struggle. Many factors such as political mobilization

34 Mao Tse-Tung (1971c), 'Some Questions Concerning Methods of Leadership', in Selected Works of Mao Tse-Tung, Peking: Foreign Language Press, p. 290.

35 Mao Tse-Tung (1965), 'Problems of Strategy in Guerrilla War Against Japan', in *Selected Works of Mao Tse-Tung*, Vol. II, Peking: Foreign Language Press, pp. 93-94.

to military activities contribute towards building it by crossing sub-stages of guerrilla zone, and liberated areas. Mohanty (1978) elucidates by giving a conceptual clarity on this:

> *Base areas must be distinguished from 'guerrilla zones' where guerrilla operations are carried on. There may not be any base in these zones. A further distinction should be made between 'base areas' and 'liberated areas'. The former are meant primarily to support guerrilla war operations whereas the latter are taken to have been permanently liberated from enemy control... It is true that in the base areas political and economic transformation is generally carried out in order to popularise the ideological programme of the party... Revolutionary base areas are central to guerrilla war operations. These are chosen areas not easily vulnerable to attacks by the enemy army. With the support of the people of that area the revolutionary army maintains its supplies, recruits, and trains soldiers; and uses the areas for retreats. They become centres of coordination and planning.*[36]

8. THREE MAGIC WEAPONS OF REVOLUTION: PARTY, ARMY, & UNITED FRONT

The theory of New Democratic Revolution relies on the "three magic weapon" that is the party, army and united front. Of the three magic weapons, the Maoists gave primary importance to the development of a revolutionary communist party over army and united front. They upheld this Maoist principle that it is people who are decisive in People's War but not weapons.

According to the Marxist philosophy, a political party is the product of class struggle. In a class divided society, if an oppressed class wants to mobilize and organise its forces to struggle against the opposing classes and to take over state power, then it must

36 Op. cit., Manoranjan Mohanty (2012 [1978]), pp. 53-54.

build for itself an organisation and a leadership which represents its interests and which concentrate its will. The ideological teachings of Marxism-Leninism-Maoism were taken as a guiding principle to train political activists. The two principles of democracy and centralism were central to develop the party organisation. In this way, a democratic centralism in the communist party means centralism on the basis of democracy and democracy under the centralised leadership. Thus a notion of democratic centralism represents the unity of opposites; though opposites but constitute a unity. In this sense, it is both democratic and centralism. The second aspect of the party organisational principles was based on *Three Do* and *Three Don't Do*. These principles are, "practise Marxism and not revisionism, unite and don't split, be open and aboveboard and don't intrigue and conspire".[37]

Following these basic premises, an overall control of the party remained in hands of its Central Committee. The party General Secretary was called the Party Headquarter and it worked in consultation with Standing Committee, Politburo and Central Committee. The cell committees were the lowest in the party organisational structure and got organised in village development committee. The party organisation coordinates with various mass organisation organised on basis of class politics.[38] These organisations carried out open and partially underground activities. The CPN (M) had also mobilised many non-classes associations based exclusive on caste/ethnicity/region which were facing century's old suppression from the Hindu *Brahmanical* State.[39]

---

37 Patrick Kessel (2008 [1974]), A Basic Understanding of the Communist Party Rahul Foundation: Lucknow, p. 72.

38 These are women, peasantry, labourer, students, youth, teachers, writers, & intellectuals.

39 The organisation mobilized on oppressed caste/ethnicity basis were among following: Dalit, Magar, Tamang, Rai-Danuwar,

The building of a revolutionary army was considered second important magical weapon to wage a revolution. In Marxist perspective, it is the communist party who should control the gun but not vice-a-versa. To wage a guerrilla war effectively, a revolutionary party have had to establish its support base among local population. It is only possible when its guerrilla army grows in power by seizing territories from enemy. Beside, the major role of the army is political rather than military.

In the beginning of armed struggle in Nepal, a three layered combating force came into existence. These were divided into three forms as fighting squad/group, security group and voluntary group. The role of the fighting groups was to carry out guerrilla actions while task of security groups were to execute explosive against state's security forces. The voluntary groups were to conduct propaganda activities in support of the armed struggle.[40] At initial phase of People's War, the fighting groups were inexperienced and armed with domestic weapons. They fought with *khukhri*, and homemade guns. They had only two rifles, the one was called the "Whole Timer Rifle" which was in fact a broken one. Each and every guerrilla unit had a dual leadership structure of political commissar and a military commander. These units were also called fighting squads, which were expanded later into platoons to a full military structure of People's Liberation Army (PLA) at the course of decade-long People's War in Nepal. Moreover, many thousands of semi-trained cadres were organised by them as volunteers called as people's militias. These militias used to be guided by

---

Tamu (Gurung), Thami, Tharu, Majhi, Newar, Kirat, and Sherpa: (oppressed Region) Madhesh, Bheri-Karnali, Seti-Mahakali.

40 Udaybahadur Chalune 'Dipak'(2009 [2066 B.S.]), *Janyudha Ra Janmukti Sena: Saidhantik Aadhar Ra Karyaniti,(People's War and People's Liberation Army: Theoretical Basis and Tactics)*, Sixth Division: People's Liberation Army, Nepal, p. 7.

different party bodies, including the local party committee. They were usually mobilized to help injured members during guerrilla's strike on security forces.

In Maoist view, the united front is the third magic weapon in attaining New Democratic Revolution in a country where "semi-feudal and semi-colonial" social relation prevailed. The idea of united front was not only to be a broad coalition of organisations assisting in the revolutionary struggle but was also to function as an embryonic government. Following Mao, the CPN (M) adopted a premise to unite those set of elements representing "anti-feudal and anti-imperialist, patriotic, democratic and leftist" stand for a development of class struggle and as a seed of the *Jansatta* (people's power) in country.[41] In a multi-cultural society of Nepal, therefore, they argued that the building of united front must gather together the people of oppressed communities and regions representing various ethnic groups (of hill & Tarai), Madhesi, and the Dalits for armed struggle. As the Maoists had expanded its influence in many part of country, they in turn build people's power locally based on its principles of united front:

> *Looking at the historical specificities of Nepal and the experiences of two years of People's War, the broad united front of the oppressed classes and masses, oppressed nationalities and the people of oppressed regions will be concrete manifestation of our Revolutionary United Front... the party regards it as a historical necessity of Nepal to give maximum importance to the question of struggle against national and regional oppression as an integral part of class struggle and democratic revolution. Until political, economic, linguistic, religious, and cultural rights of different nationalities usurped in the*

41 CPN (M) (2004b [1991]), 'Political Line of CPN (Unity Centre)', Nepal: Jandisha Publications, p. 4.

> *course of formation of the centralised state are reinstated democratically and they are guaranteed full participation in the new democratic state and until a great force of national unity based on democracy is created, it will be impossible to smash feudalism and imperialism.*[42]

9. PRACTICE OF PEOPLE'S WAR IN NEPAL: A MAOIST VIEW[43]

First stage of People's War: Strategic Defence

The armed struggle broke out in a carefully planned wave of attacks that swept the country, but it was belittled by the country's ruling class. By the first pamphlet, that was distributed at the beginning of the Peoples' War called upon people to confront three mountains of landlord class, the bureaucratic-capitalist class and imperialism which hindered liberation of Nepali people. According to them, this would only eventually institutionalize a New Democratic State in Nepal –that is "People's Republic of Nepal". To achieve their goal, the CPN (M) formulated many plans to develop its struggle since of first stage of strategic defence. Their objective was:

> *...to make a practical leap into and establish among masses of the people the politics of armed revolution... with a clarion call of "it is right to rebel"... the emphasis was placed on arousing the masses to rebel against the oppressive system and the state, and selection of targets and forms of actions were designed to give correct political message and derive maximum political*

42 Prachanda (2004 [1998]), 'Two Momentous Years of Revolutionary Transformation', in *Problem & Prospects of Revolution in Nepal: A Collection of Articles by Com. Prachanda and Other Leaders of the CPN (Maoist),* Nepal: Jandisha Publications p. 155.

43 For a chronology and organizational structure of People's War, See, Appendix-III and table-IX of Appendix-IV.

> *propaganda rather than to make any material gains in the very beginning.*[44]

By following the 1st Plan, fighting groups carried out five attacks in different parts of country. They had attacked a police post in Holeri of Rolpa district on night of 13 February, 1996. By an armed attack with a few local weapons, both sides exchanged fire for two hours. Before disappearing in the forests, they explained to villagers the aims of armed struggle in country. The second attack was carried out in a security post of Rukum district. With this surprise attack, the police surrendered at once without any resistance. On the same night, they attacked Sindhuligari police post in Sindhuli district of eastern Nepal. Along with these, the two propaganda raids by burning peasant's bonds paper of state owned Agricultural Development Bank in Gorkha and Pepsi Cola plant in capital of Kathmandu.

In the first two weeks, almost 6000 actions were carried out in entire Nepal – including armed assault by the fighting squads on police station, the confiscation of property from landlords and punishment of local tyrants. It was estimated by the Maoists that propaganda and publicity activities constituted 80 per cent of the actions; about 15 per cent were actions of sabotage, while only 5 per cent were guerrilla attacks.

By the end of March 1996, the Maoist evaluated 1st plan by concluding it as successful. They prepared 2nd Plan which began from the end June 1996 with aim of "let us develop guerrilla war in a planned way". Through this plan, the fighting groups were converted into guerrilla squads. The 2nd Plan was designed to attain following goals; (1) mobilize the masses extensively in support of the guerrilla war, (2) capture necessary equipment for the guerrillas

44 CPN (M) (1997b), 'One Years of People's War in Nepal: A Review', *The Worker: Organ of the Communist Party of Nepal (Maoist)*, No.3, (February issue), pp. 8-9.

in a planned manner, and (3) centralize all the activities in order to transform certain strategic areas of the country into guerrilla zones. Many political mobilizations such as the *SAK* campaign[45] was organised in principle zones scattered in different parts of the country. By this campaign, personal weapons were seized from rich peasant and landlords. On 3 January, 1997, they carried a ferocious attack on security post in Bethan of Ramechap district. This attack was evaluated high by the Maoists as "successful" and "one of the most daring acts since the initiation of the people's war"[46]. A large number of sabotage actions were carried out in urban areas including an attack on the house of the then Home Minister Khum Bahadur Khadka by urban guerrilla team in Kathmandu. Simultaneously, the Maoist's mass organisations held countrywide protest demonstrations and meetings including valley shutdown of capital Kathmandu on 21 August 1996 and Nepal shutdown on 12 December 1996. The "anti-national" Mahakali treaty signed between government of India and Nepal was a burning subject which aroused many protest demonstrations but mainly centred in urban region.

The 3rd Plan began with a goal to "develop guerrilla warfare to new heights" from mid August of 1997. During this plan, the Maoists had established temporary guerrilla zones in mid-western districts of Rolpa, and Rukum and successfully boycotted local elections in 1997. It was envisaged as a transitional period to develop guerrilla zone. While the third plan was running, the then Nepal government organised a reign of state terror by organising

45 In Nepali language, its denotation is *Sashatra Kabja Abhiyan* (armed campaign to seize arms). The Maoists has also defined the "*SAK* campaign" in English language, as 'suck blood of enemy of People's War'.

46 CPN (M) (1997), 'The Bethan Raid', *The Worker, organ of the Communist Party of Nepal (Maoist)*, No. 3, (February issue), p. 13.

the Kilo Sierra 2 operation. It was started in May 1998 with a sole objective of "kill all, destroy all, burn all, loot all" and lasted for six months until November 1998. This resulted in hundreds of extra-judicial killing, disappearance and cases of rapes in country. The killing of Maoist supporters as well as general civilian escalated to unprecedented heights and became a regular feature in west, mid-west and eastern region of Nepal. Rape became a central instrument of sexual violence against women. Many were raped in front of their husbands and relatives or after killing their relatives. Even as per government records, more than 2000 people were arrested and only half of them released later. The rest were either killed in fake encounter or declared disappeared.[47] Even prominent leaders of the ruling Nepali Congress party such as Daman Nath Dhungana criticized the state terror by noting that the, "Maoists will go on developing as long as the corrupted people remain in the society."

The Maoists announced their 4th Plan in October 1998 to "go ahead to establish the base areas". Now their policy was to develop guerrilla zones into perspective and relatively stable base areas. They had also built a preliminary structure of the People's Army by transforming guerrilla squads to level of platoon.[48] It was aimed by this plan to adequately respond the brutal security operations of state.[49]

---

47 Bishnu Pathak (2005), *Politics of People's War and Human Rights in Nepal*, Kathmandu: Bimipa Publications, p. 101.

48 Now with formation of platoons, their military power was categorised into a two type of forces; primary and secondary force. The primary force of squads and platoons was responsible for political work (mass political education), organization work (developing mass organisations) while the militia and volunteer groups came under rubric of secondary force and responsible for production and construction (solving people's problem), and propaganda task, (help to carry injured guerrillas, collecting/transporting weapons after raids).

49 Though this plan was initially passed by the fourth extended meeting of the Central Committee of the Maoist held in the mid-August 1998 but was materialized from October onwards.

During this phase, the Maoists formed "first task force" by assembling three platoon level structures located in Rolpa, Rukum and Jajarkot districts. The objective of special force was to carry out boycott election campaign of parliamentary elections in 1999. In some large scale attacks in Dang and Rolpa district, the guerrilla destroyed many police posts completely. The 4th Plan has been considered by the Maoists a successful one as they had set up initial levels of parallel power structures like people's court in many villages. The 5th Plan began in August 1999 in continuation of previous plan with a focus to wage armed struggle systematically. This plan was aimed to establish to "advance in the primary direction of constructing base areas."

By reaching to implement the 6th Plan, the guerrillas greatly strengthened their position by attacking on a large-scale way including in headquarters of district administration. Until now, they had been able to build two full company level army structure first in Rolpa and another one in Bheri-Karnali regional district of far-western Nepal. A major attack in this sequence was on 24 September, 2000 at Dunai, the district headquarter of Dolpa district. With 3 platoons of a permanent and temporary company based in mid-western Nepal, this was one of the first significant military actions which showed a rapidly growing influence of guerrilla war in country. Ogura (2008) reports:

> *After a very hard, long trek on foot through the Himalayas at 4,400 meters above sea level, they arrived in Dunai, government headquarters of the Dolpa district. Once there, the companies carried out attacks on the District Police Office, the District Jail, the District Branch of the Nepal Bank and other government offices. Importantly, they also captured the government District Headquarters. During this military action, 15 police officers were killed, nearly 50 more were injured, all of the local prisoners were freed and Rs. 50,000,000*

> *in cash was stolen. As Ananta, who led the forces as a political commissar, explains, "for the first time we attacked a District Headquarters and captured a Chief District Officer. The Dunai attack was a climax in the armed actions during the Strategic Defence stage in the People's War."*[50]

The Koirala government was stunned by the attack and the then Home Minister Govind Raj Joshi had to resign from his post.

10. STRATEGIC SHIFT OF "*PRACHANDA PATH*"

The Maoists held its Second National Conference in India in February 2001. After initiation of People's War in Nepal, it was their first national level gathering. The purpose was to review the six plans organised in first five year in the stage of strategic defence and to formulate future plan. While, they were still fighting guerrilla struggle by focussing in rural heartland, this meeting reoriented first stage of strategic defence by adopting a new strategy. Now, with a strategic shift, their policy was to combine two military strategies of People's War and insurrection together. Their aim was now simultaneously work to mobilise people in rural region and cities too for a speedy development of People's War in Nepal. This theorisation was known as "*Prachanda Path*" and named after their leader who has been now onwards designated as Chairman of the CPN (M). According to them:

> *Under the leadership of the Party... the synthesis of the experience of five stormy years of People's War has developed into a set of ideas guiding the Nepalese Revolution, which is based on Marxism-Leninism-Maoism. Because of the correct and consistent leadership of General Sectary Comrade Prachanda, a*

50 Kiyoko Ogura (2008), *Seeking State Power: The Communist Party of Nepal (Maoist)*, available at http://edoc.vifapol.de/opus/volltexte/2011/2550/pdf/transitions_cpnm.pdf.

> *strong proletarian headquarters has been developed, as a centre of gravity of the Party, bringing Party unity up to the height of this ideological synthesis. So by "Prachanda Path" the Party means the set of ideas that has developed as a form of centralised expression of the collective struggle...This set of ideas emerging in the form of Prachanda Path will guide the basic line in the forward march of the Nepalese Revolution.*[51]

This conference also decided to transform the guerrilla army to a full military structure that was called as the People's Liberation Army (PLA).[52] While the Maoist was still fighting within first stage of Protracted People's War, they added a new strategic line of "*Prachanda Path*" in strategic defence. They began their 7th plan by organising three military strikes simultaneously in first week of April 2001. The guerrillas attacks were organized against police base camps in Rukumkot of Rukum district, Naumule of Dailekh district and Mainapokhari of Dolkha district. This event created a severe political crisis within ruling class and talks of mobilizing the Royal Nepal Army began against the Maoist's armed struggle. After the Rukumkot attack, government evacuated all of its administrative structure from the VDCs and relocated around 1500 police posts mainly now in district headquarters. It proved to be strategic victory over country's police force and entire state

51 CPN (M) (2004 [2001]), 'The Great Leap Forward: An Inevitable Need of History', in *Some Important Documents of Communist Party of Nepal (Maoist)*, Nepal: Jandisha Publications, pp. 115-116.

52 While the First Peace Talk was undergoing, the Maoist guerrillas met by a national convention at Kureli VDC of Rolpa in first week of September 2001. Through this meeting, a military structure of Maoist's army known as PLA was formed but yet not been declared publicly. Prachanda, the party Chairman was designated supreme commander of the Maoist armed forces.

machinery.[53] These developments in the countryside helped the Maoists to expand party organisations in rural heartland. These events also paved the way for them to declare their first district level people's government in Rukum in December 2000. This soon followed by beginning of 7th plan through a declaration of formation of Rolpa district people's government in March 2001.

11. THE EVENTS OF PALACE MASSACRE AND MAOIST'S FIRST PEACE TALK WITH STATE

It was in this setting that the palace massacre took place in Nepal. In this incident, incumbent king Birendra was murdered with his whole family in June 2001 while at a palace dinner party in Narayanhiti palace in Kathmandu. Though, the government of Nepal claimed that Crown Prince Dipendra was behind this fatal incident because his 'love affair' story. However, he himself had died too, so it was widely believed that he was not behind this massacre. The new king Gyanendra, younger brother of deceased king Birendra was seen as conspirator since he was immediate successor of throne. Soon after this incident, Maoist leader Baburam Bhattarai claimed through his article published in a popular Nepali newspaper that new king had a hand in the palace massacre with active supervision of external forces (i.e., Indian and American intelligence agencies) to suppress Maoist movement. By this article, he acknowledged that his party and king Birendra were maintaining an informal relationship through backdoor channels because of his nationalist credentials by not allowing royal army to be mobilized against People's War.[54] Soon after the appearance of

53 Pasang (2008), *Red Strides of History: (Significant Military Raids of the People's War),* Agnipariksha Janprakashan Griha: Kathmandu, p. 91.

54 This is a public fact and is been acknowledged publicly by the CPN (M) that they were having many round of dialogue with late king Birendra through his younger brother Dhirendra before the Palace Massacre.

Bhattarai's piece in Kantipur Daily prompted Nepal's government to arrest its editor and publisher. He had argued:

> *Why was King Birendra and his family murdered at this particular moment? What was his crime in the eyes of the expansionist and imperialist powers? Whatever your political ideology might be, one thing every honest Nepali nationalists has to agree with is this: King Birendra's relatively liberal political character and patriotic sentiments were seen as his weakness and had become a crime in the eyes of the expansionist and imperialist powers. ...his unwillingness to mobilize the army...to curb the People's Revolution taking place under the leadership of Communist Party of Nepal (Maoist) became his biggest crime in the eyes of the imperialist and expansionist powers...we –CPN (Maoist) and King Birendra –had similar views on many national issues and this has created in fact an informal alliance between us. Obviously, this scared the imperialist powers and their cronies.*[55]

The palace massacre was a turning point which intensified the Maoists to carry massive guerrillas attack in country. Moreover, its mass organisations carried many nationwide protest demonstrations in capital Kathmandu to other urban places. By a successful attack on a police post in Holeri in Rolpa district in July 2001 made Prime Minister Koirala to ask the new king to deploy the RNA against the Maoists. By this attack, they abducted 71 police officers by destroying the police fortification. Though country's national army RNA was mobilized against the Maoists for the first time but police officers were rescued without any armed confrontation between two. It led to the then Prime

55 Baburam Bhattarai (2005 [2001]), 'Lets' Not Legitimize New Kot Massacre', in *Monarchy vs. Democracy: The Epic Fight in Nepal,* Noida: Samkaleen Teesari Duniya, p. 19.

Minister Girija Prasad Koirala to resign due to the RNA's defiance of his order to confront the Maoists aggressively.

While Sher Bahadur Deuba became new Prime Minister of country on 22 July 2001, the same day, the Maoists guerrillas raided an area police post in Bichaur VDC of the far western Nepal district of Bajura and killed 17 police officials. The new Prime Minister was stunned by this incident. The next day, he announced government's willingness to sit in table and resolve armed struggle with peace talk. The CPN (M) eagerly accepted the government proposal. It was their First Peace Talk with Nepali state after five years of their armed struggle and begun from 30 August 2001.

When the First Peace Talks begin, the Maoists started to hold open rallies in Kathmandu and all over Nepal. There were three rounds of talks on 30 August, 13-15 September and 13 November. The Maoist were seeking, "...to find a political solution in the form of an interim government, a new constitution, and institutionalization of the republic" and was keenly prepared "to go for the election of a constituent assembly to settle the question of a republic".[56] Just before the second round of talks was scheduled to begin, the CPN (M) was declared as a "terrorist organisation" by the United State of America following the attack on the World Trade Centre. India followed America by banning Maoist's mass organisations working in Indian cities. The irony was that the government of Nepal was having talks with a political party which was now declared to be 'terrorists' by India and America. The Peace Talks lasted till third round of November 2001. However, the Deuba government rejected to debate on key Maoist's demands following of the September 11 attacks despite the Maoists were "... still open to the proposals of talks if a concrete political solution

56 CPN (M) (2002), *Maoist Information Bulletin-1, Occasional Information Bulletin of Communist Party of Nepal (Maoist), (January Issue)*.

to the country's problem (i.e. abolition of the hated monarchy and institutionalisation of the republic) offered."[57]

12. SECOND STAGE OF PEOPLE'S WAR: STRATEGIC STALEMATE

While the First Peace Talks collapsed on 21 November, 2001, the Maoists argued that their People's War entered into second phase of strategic stalemate. Two days after the declaration of the peace talks as a failure, they carried out two fierce attacks on 23 November. The Maoist guerrillas overrun simultaneously on two district headquarters of Ghorahi in Dang district and another in Syangja. Barshman Pun 'Ananta', a commander of Maoist army, stated the rationale behind these attacks to an interview to a Japanese journalist Ogura (2008):

> *By the time of the Holeri attack [in July 2001] our battle with the police had already ended. We had defeated them. But after the Palace massacre, both the king and the army became active. We eventually discovered that even during the ceasefire period, the RNA had been increasing its forces and weapons capacity in various places. In Ghorahi, for example, the RNA had raised its troop levels from a company to a battalion force in a preparation for attacking us in our base area. We therefore were obliged to attack the army barracks there... Before [Ghorahi attack], we used mobile warfare tactics against the police, that is, 'hit and run' tactics with relatively small forces. But after the Ghorahi attack, we entered into a stage of highly mobile warfare and began to develop a positional warfare strategy, using larger PLA forces against our government targets.*[58]

For the Ghorahi raid an entire battalion with two companies with around a force of 2000 combatants were mobilised. The

57 Ibid.

58 Op. cit., Kiyoko Ogura (2008), p. 17.

Maoist guerrillas had shot dead 21 officers including a Major & Assistant Commander of army barrack. For the first time, they also captured hundreds of sophisticated weapons and ammunitions including mortars, and rocket launchers and a cash of 50 million Nepali Rupees. Prachanda made a press statement on next day by announcing declaration of armed wing of "People's Liberation Army (PLA)"[59] and a united front of "United Revolutionary People's Council (UPRC)" to operate people's power in Base Areas. Two days after these attacks, they made another military attack on Salleri, the district headquarters of Solukhumbu in eastern Nepal. Immediately after this attack, the government declared a state of emergency in November 2001 for six months. Through, emergency, the Nepali state for first time mobilised three forces (i.e., Armed Police Force, Nepal Police, and RNA) in a joint counter insurgency operation against the People's War. In the meantime, calling for establishment of Base Area, the Maoist's united front of URPC organised a countrywide shutdown on December 7, 2001 to protest against imposition of a state of emergency. After the successful attack on the Royal Army at Ghorahi, the Maoist by their Central Committee Plenary Meeting of June 2002 decided to expand the PLA by brigade level under three commands: the western central command, valley central command and eastern central command.

On 16 February 2002, the Maoists carried out a successful attack on Mangalsen, the district headquarters of Aacham in far western Nepal. This resulted in the biggest causality for the government since a total of 147 security personnel including 52 RNA and 95 police officers died. The Maoists also lost 24 PLA including some high ranking commanders.[60] During this attack in Mangelsen, they set free all the prisoners including various Maoist activists from the district jail, seized millions of rupees from banks

59 For organizational structure of PLA, see Appendix.

60 Op. cit., Pasang (2008), p. 142.

and set on fire the centuries old Mangelsen Palace. The Maoists commemorated sixth anniversary of the People's War by organising a nationwide call of Nepal shutdown on 22 February. Besides, various armed actions were carried by destroying communication towers and security camps in districts of Rolpa, Kavre, Syanga, Solukhumbu and Sarlahi particularly.

Soon after these attacks, the RNA launched a joint air and land counter-insurgency operation against their Base Area in mid-western heartland of Rapti region. This made situation grave and many ruthless battles were fought by both side especially in Gam of Rolpa district on 7 May 2002. In Gam battle, the government of Nepal lost its 104 RNA soldiers. Similarly, the PLA failed to defeat the RNA fortification in Sandhikharka and Khalanga. Here they lost more than 100 PLA combatants and over 200 got injured seriously during battle. In same month of May 2002, the Maoists lost first Khara battle to the RNA with over 150 PLA guerrillas were killed. The PLA got a partial victory in November 2002's Jumla raid where they lost more than 50 guerrillas while government also lost 37 security personnel including the Chief District Officer.

In January 2003, the government of Nepal and the Maoists declared a truce and a Second Peace Talks began. The Maoists formed a five member negotiation team led by the UPRC convenor Baburam Bhattarai. They put exactly similar demand as like of previous peace talks. At the midst of negotiations, the Doramba massacre took place on 16 July 2003. Here the RNA killed 20 Maoist supporters and the second Peace Talk broke down.

Now a further course which the CPN (M) took was a decentralised policy by conducting fewer attacks on state security forces but focussed on building its armed wing of People's Liberation Army. By September 2003, their PLA has been expanded by two divisions of (Western & Eastern), 7 brigades, and 19 battalions. According to them, this manoeuvring was intended for more heightened attack against Nepali state. Prachanda argued by a press statement that:

> *All the military strategies and tactics are based on the goals of preparing for going into strategic offensive from the present stage of strategic equilibrium. From a tactical point of view, at present the people's army is going ahead with primary and decentralised resistance so as to feel the pulse of the enemy, tire them out and to prepare ground for the centralised offensive.*[61]

13. THIRD STAGE OF PEOPLE'S WAR: STRATEGIC OFFENSIVE

The PLA once again carried out fierce attacks on two district headquarters on month of March 2004. The first one of this series was where district headquarter of Bhojpur was attacked on March 2 by newly established Eastern Division of the PLA. The guerrillas with a number of over 1500 consisting six companies raided District Police Office by killing 20 police and 12 RNA personnel.

However, second attack of Beni, the district headquarter of Myagdi district, was biggest and strategic one. Here 150 government security personnel died, while the PLA lost its two dozen combatants including high ranking brigade and battalion commanders. According to Ogura (2008):

> *In terms of personnel and weaponry, the Beni attack was the largest-ever PLA military action. A variety of weapons were used and total of some 4,500 people, including 2,600 armed combatants, drawn from all four of the PLA's Western Division brigades, participated in the attack. As Division Commander, Pasang (aka Nand Kishor Pun) explains, "we needed to develop our war*

---

61 CPN (M) (2003), *Maoist Information Bulletin-4,* Occasional Information Bulletin of Communist Party of Nepal (Maoist), (September Issue).

> *from mobile warfare tactics to positional warfare and had to show that we could carry out large-scale military actions." In the attack, the PLA captured the District Police Office and the District Jail. They also destroyed nearly all of Beni's government buildings. Although, they did not capture RNA barracks, nonetheless this action was a success: PLA forces occupied the District Headquarters for nearly 12 hours.*[62]

Following the Beni attack, the Maoist argued they made way into third strategic offensive stage. For a further course of People's War, they held a Central Committee meeting in August 2004 at Phuntibang village of Thabang VDC in Rolpa district. The Maoists were of the view that it would be possible that Indian state would intervene militarily in Nepal to counter the PLA advance to seize capital Kathmandu. They had continually carried out several armed actions including assassinations and ambushes against securities force by using land mines. Many attacks from November 2004 to April 2005 especially in Pandone (Kalali), Khara (Rukum), Ganeshpur (Bardiya) and Pili (Kalikot) were examples of positional warfare which led heavy loss for the PLA in the history of the People's War.[63] The Khara battle of 7 April 2005 between the RNA & PLA was a second one after first unsuccessful attack in 2002. The PLA had mobilized over 4000 combatants from its two Divisions and six brigades for this battle. However, they lost to the RNA very miserably and over hundreds of Maoist combatants dead including many hundred seriously injured.[64]

---

62 Op. cit., Kiyoko Ogura (2008), p. 19.

63 For a research based accounts of these attacks, see, Sam Cowen, (2010), 'Inside the People's Liberation Army', *European Bulletin of Himalayan Research*, Vol. 37, pp. 82-116.

64 For this period, the exact numbers of the Maoist's PLA loss is yet to be known.

14. FEBRUARY 1 ROYAL COUP AND "TWELVE POINT AGREEMENT" LEAD AN END TO PEOPLE'S WAR IN NEPAL

After King Gyanendra's military coup of 1 February 2005, the Maoists suspended all of PLA's armed battles with state security forces. By October 2005, the Maoist decided to build the anti-monarchy joint forum with seven parties. To attain this objective, the Maoist discarded armed strikes without completing strategic offence –the third and final stage of Protracted People's War. In contrast, through Chunbang Plenum, they adopted a different political course by citing adverse international circumstances against People's War:

> *Today, after about four years [i.e. First Peace Talk in 2001] mainly after the royal coup of Feb 1, 2005, with the pressure of situation, the environment and possibility of building such an alliance has immensely increased and the Party is taking initiative to its capacity towards that direction... Now the slogan of interim government, election of constituent assembly and democratic republic that our party, taking into account the international and domestic balance of power, has formulated is a tactical slogan put forward for the forward-looking political way out.*[65]

Following, a "Twelve Point Agreement" was signed between and CPN (M) in November 2005 at New Delhi. This agreement was intended to build a joint forum to wage a peaceful struggle against "autocratic monarchy". Moreover, to oppose king's decision to hold election of local bodies, a few armed actions were carried out by them in different part of country. The PLA conducted a raid against RNA base camp on 9 February 2006 at Sunwal,

65 CPN (M), (2006), 'Document: Resolution of Central Committee', in *The Worker: Organ of the CPN (Maoist)*, No. 10, (May Issue), p. 8.

Rambhapur. The armed strike in Chautara, in Sindhupalchowk district on April 23, 2006 was last one in this series. According to the Maoist, these offensive raids against security forces were aimed to mobilize people to join people's movement against King Gyanendra's regime. Eventually, a peaceful uprising started from last week of April 2006 from Kathmandu and lasted for 19 days continuously. The success of the April mass movement resulted in reinstatement of Parliamentary rule in Nepal and suspension of king's direct rule. Eventually, by the "Comprehensive Peace Agreement" of June 2006 between government of Nepal and the CPN (M), they formally ended their decade-long People's War to establish Democratic Republic in Nepal.

When the peace process started in 2006 after the April people's movement in April that year, the Maoists had seven Divisions and 29 Brigades. After the Comprehensive Peace Agreement of 21 November 2006, the both parties of Maoist & Nepal government asked United Nations Mission in Nepal (UNMIN) to supervise the management of the PLA and state's armed forces. While at times of UNMIN's verification process, the PLA's strength was 19,602 as opposed to their claims of 32,250 combatants. Until recently, the PLA was stationed in seven division headquarters and 21 cantonments in different districts of Nepal.

Thus by concluding Chapter-3 here, I have tried to present various components of the ideology of the CPN (M) by setting its practice in different stages. Besides, it is also been shown of distinct character of People's War in Nepal which went through by a set of distinct practice called as –"*Prachanda Path*". On a one side where with expansion of Maoist movement created a political crisis within Nepal ruling class. While on other side, the Maoists were busy doing manoeuvring of rounds of informal or formal with king Birendra before 2001 and later peace negotiations with government of Nepal. The infamous Palace Massacre of 1 June, 2001 was a result of this amalgam after which royal army was mobilized against Maoist movement. This way, I have argued that the CPN (M) made a strategic shift in first stage of strategic defence itself. Thus without completing first stage of Protracted People's War, the Maoist entered into two other stages of People's War. This eventually led to the Maoist's PLA to suffer heavy loss from state security forces and end their armed struggle in 2006.

CHAPTER 4 People's War in Nepal: A Field View

At the foot of Jaljala, the army is on parade
Like Ching Kyang [Base Area of the Chinese Revolution], the settlements will remain intact

The soldiers patrol everywhere carrying their guns,
(But) our iron fort will remain.
Whatever be the threat over Thabang village
A thousand villages will stand up.[1]

This chapter is based on my ethnographic study of Thabang VDC. Here, I attempt to present socio-political trajectories of a Nepali agrarian scene which gave birth of the Maoist movement in country. This chapter is divided into two parts; first section is deal with times before the People's War and while second part would focus on times after People's war.

The first sections present a concise history of development of communist ideas in Thabang village since birth of first peasant organisation half a century ago in village. By presenting the village setting through its geographical terrain adjoined with social, cultural, economic and history, Thabang came known in nation imaginary as a rebellious village. The peasant's outcry against tyrannical rule of village headman proved to be a polarizing factor which helped them to voice against despotic character of the ruling class. With awakening of its people culminated in voting en mass

---

1 Excerpts of a song titled "*Tyo Kakh Jaljalako*" penned by Lekhraj Regmi, transliterated and cited in Anne De Sales (2003), 'Remarks on Revolutionary Songs and Iconography', *European Bulletin of Himalayan Research*, Vol. 24, p. 16.

for communist candidate in first general election in 1959 to voting against despotic *Panchayat* regime in 1980s referendum. These set of activities make Thabang village a national symbol of resistance. This led Nepali State to organise ruthless security suppression in Thabang by sending the hundreds of Royal Army soldiers in early 1980s. Moreover, peasant resistance did not stop also after introduction of multi-party democracy in Nepal from 1990s. In this way, I argue that the political consciousness of Thabangi peasants broke later in form of armed struggle.

The kind of model of state and society, the masses of Thabang had in mind was essentially a culmination in People's War that kicked off in 1996. The second part of this chapter deals this aspect which made villagers to stand for altering existing social reality. Further, it deals development of guerrilla movement in different phases in the Rapti zone. While the Maoist guerrilla defeated state's security forces mainly Nepal Police, local state machinery in Thabang VDC left and relocated itself in district headquarter. It made the Maoist to fill power vacuum by declaring a base area in Rolpa. The development of Thabang as a Special District was intended to locate Thabang and its surrounding Kham Magar territory as place of shelter, lodging of PLA combatants and preparation of armed offensive further against Nepali state. The various organ of the Maoist governance as popularly called as *Jansatta* is been dealt further. The Maoist's intervention in traditional practices and old customs of village is also inquired. Finally, this chapter gets ended with a brief note on the aftermath events since the CPN (M) suspended their People's War in 2006.

1. THABANG AS A VILLAGE OF RESISTANCE

The village setting

Thabang is situated in a land full of ridges, dense forest and rugged terrain where roads are measured by the time. The Jaljala

Himal Mountain shapes Thabang VDC as a gently sloping valley formed around Thabang stream. The Jaljala Mountain is also a religious spot for Magars and a temple of Barah God is situated here. It is at a height of 3193 meter from the sea level. Thabang is more than a day's walk from the district headquarters of Libang, though the total distance is only 26 km. However, approached from the side of Sulichaur bazaar, it is less than a day's walk.

Thabang VDC lies in a remote part of Rolpa district bordering Mahat VDC of Rukum district in mid-western Nepal. Rolpa is a hill district some 280 km west of Kathmandu in Rapti Zone and its district headquarter is located in Libang and it is a seat of power and authority. Adjoining to Rolpa district are Dang to the south, Pyuthan to the east, Salyan to the west and Rukum to the north. Before the conquest of Nepal by Prithvi Narayan Shah in 1769, Rolpa was a buffer between the *Chaubisi* small kingdoms to the east and the *Baise* states of the west. This region has been known as the original birthplace of the Magar community called the *"Athara Magarat"*. Thabang was earlier a part of Pyuthan district before Rolpa was carved out a new district in 1965.

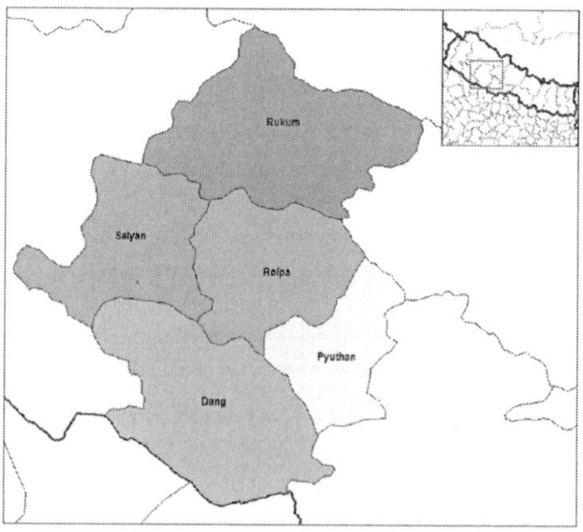

Map-I: *Rapti Zone in mid-western Nepal.*

The Thabang VDC is consists of 12 villages named Phuntibang, Ranchibang, Chalbang, Maghikhark, Gobang, Thabang, Jurbang, Jhakkeybang, Maranthan, Kochibang, Cherlobang, Dhahbang. Out of this Thabang village has been a centre of everything since it has been a village development committee and local seat of government authority. It is also called as *Thula Gaon* (big village) and is centre of many offices. Like all VDCs in Nepal, Thabang is also made of 9 wards. Wards are generally named after a hamlet and many smaller homestead stretches within wards.

Socio-cultural setting

The people of this region speak a distinct language called Kham. In *Kham* language, Thabang means a field of slope (Tha=slope, Bang=field). Since, Thabang VDC lies deep in the *Kham* Magar heartland, therefore the demographic distribution is distinct here with a majority of a Tibeto-Burman community of *Kham* Magars. A significant number of Dalit families do also live in the village. A few household of Gurung and a single household of Hindu upper caste Thakuri are stretch in different hamlets of the VDC. The Magars consist around 90 percent of population. The local population of this region speak Kham language though Nepali is been widely spoken except by older generation.

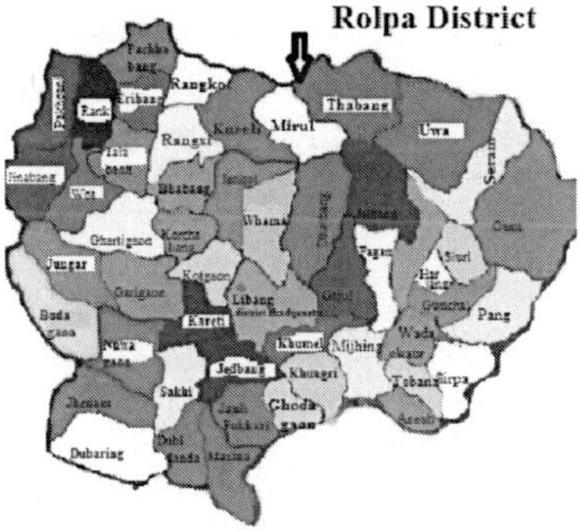

Map-II: Thabang VDC

The 2001 national census survey recorded 4231 people in Thabang VDC. The government records have categorised villagers as Buddhists while the Dalits as Hindu. The Kham Magar population of Thabang has a strong Shamanistic faith with a relatively less influence of Hindu religion. Christianity has also entered the lives of the people after mid the 1970-1980s but conversion form their Shamanistic beliefs have been very few in the past.

The region inhabited by the Kham Magar is surrounded by high caste Hindus Tagadhari populations of Bahuns, Chettris and Thakuri. The exposure to the Hindu belief system is quite prevalent since historically the Magars were ruled by the Thakuri kings. As a result, the Magar settlements in this region are also greatly influenced by the Hindu caste system. However, largely the kinship is defining character of social interaction in Kham Magar society. Here families and individuals are interconnected by ties of kinship. This greatly influences their social identity and future course of life.

According to Nepal's national code of *Muluki Ain* of 1854, the Magar are categorised as *Matwali* and traditionally given ranked below the Tagadhari Hindu upper castes. Due to the centuries old process of *Hinduisation*, the Magars have also adopted caste ideology in their relation to the Dalit communities which has been lowest in the Hindu caste hierarchy.[2] What unites the low caste groups is their ritual impurity relative to those above them. Locally the Dalits are labelled as *nachunay jat* (not touchable caste), *sano jat* (low caste) and *tallo jat* (inferior caste). In addition to their untouchable status in relation to the high castes, there is stratification among the Dalits themselves. Their hierarchy and rank can be seen as which caste would constitute the intermarrying group. The Kamis (Bishkarma or BK, Sunar) are considered highest ranked among the Dalits castes and they work as blacksmith, ironsmith, potters and goldsmith. The Sarki, the second tier provides services as leatherworkers and shoemakers. The Damai (i.e., Pariyar/ Nepali) has been considered to be in the lowest tier in the caste hierarchy which consists of tailors and musicians. The Kami caste constitutes the majority of the Dalits in Thabang.

The Dalit castes settled in area as service castes many generations ago and provide obligatory services to the Magars,

2 Augusta Molnar (1981), *The Kham Magar Women of Thabang*, Kathmandu: CEDA, p.16.

and other communities. For instance the Kami make agricultural tools and household utensils such as sickles, knife, hoes, shovels, plough, nails and axes etc. The Damai are tailors who are also referred to as masters. The Damai men also perform music during life cycle rituals of birth, marriage, death and festivals. The Sarki make leather products from cow and buffalo skin. These include leather sandals and shoes, plough harnesses, saddles and flour sifters. The service provided by the Dalits is similar to the Jajmani payment system of India. It is a traditional practice of labour and grain exchange with rights of patronage called as *Bist Kamaune.*[3] In exchange of their services, the high castes (i.e., Magar) provide grains during harvest seasons. This harvest payment is called *Khalo (i.e., Bist)*. This system binds the low castes to the high castes through economic interdependence following the Hindu caste ideology. In Thabang the harvest seasons are known as *Hiunde bali* (winter harvest) and *Barkhe bali* (harvest of rainy session).

Economic setting

The landholding pattern in Thabang VDC is a mirror of unequal land distribution in a country like Nepal. Besides, it gives an insight of the relative deprivation of peasant population where agriculture is the main source of livelihood. Majority of villagers own land ranging from ¼ to 6 acres plots scattered in various places. The Dalits are the most vulnerable community of Thabang and practice traditional occupation and wage labour regularly. Based on a study by Molnar (1981) suggests subsistence living condition of majority of villagers. Only one fourth household produced more than enough food for whole year. The bulk of population worked as migratory labour on the potato farms in Kalo Pahar (located in outskirts of Shimla, India). In recent times, migration patterns

3 It is also known as *Khalo Kamaune.*

have seen a change and now, to support their families, people of younger generation are migrating to Malaysia, and the Gulf countries instead of India. Like the rest of Nepali hill villages, many young people get recruited by the Indian Army and British Army.[4] Landholdings in the village are fragmented and are on the rugged mountain terrain, with the effect that a bulk of the population cannot grow enough food to feed their families for the entire year. Part of the economic hardship of the peasants is also caused by adverse climate conditions. This makes peasants to borrow money which could be obtained only in high interest rates. The livelihood pattern largely fit for entire region of Rapti zone.

Table-I: Employment pattern in Thabang VDC[5]

S.N.	Employment	Population
1.	Agriculture	1390
2.	Entrepreneur / Shop keeping	103
3.	Government service	15
4.	Labouring (in India)	52
5.	Indian army (Indian Gurkha regiment)	2
6.	Labouring (Gulf region, Malaysia etc)	170
7.	Foreign army (British/ Singapore)	5

By taking insight from above data with inputs of ethnographic study, it is argued that land holding pattern in Thabang should take in view with fertility of land and its location and production of food availability. The peasant population of Thabang VDC can

4 Op. cit., Augusta Molnar (1981), pp. 28-29.

5 Data based on sample survey of Thula Gaon of Thabang VDC only. See, GON, (2008 [2065 B.S.]), '*Antim Prativaden*', Babarmahal, Kathmandu: Ministry of Physical Planning & Building, p. gha-3.

be divided into five classes of semi-Proletariat, poor peasants, lower middle peasants, middle and rich peasants. A recent survey of *Thula Gaon* reveals the level of food availability.

Table-II: Showing self produced food availability in Thabang VDC[6]

Availability of food	Household	Percentage
Below three months	14	6.1%
From 3-6 months	87	38.0%
From 6-9 months	93	40.6%
From 9-12 months	35	15.3%
Whole year & surplus	5	2.2%
Total	229	100%

The first two classes consist of the Dalit and Magar communities makes almost half of households of Thabang. They include landless labourer and marginal peasants who barely grow food for 2-4 months by working on their unfertile and small portion of lands. Many of them under the category go in seasonal migration to India and Gulf countries. Some others works as daily wages labourers in surrounding Nepali cities of Pokhra/ Butwal/ Dang and work in agricultural lands of rich/ middle peasant households on cash payments.

The middle peasants grow food for 9 months to whole year. Majority of this section are from Magar community and half a dozen household are from Dalit community who are also employed in foreign Indian/ British armies. Some are also employed in government jobs in country. Whereas, the rich peasants consist a tiny minority of nearly 5 per cent of village. They produce sufficient food for entire year and partly employ lower section of peasants. At the same time, they give loan on heavy interest and considered as moneylenders.

6 Ibid.

They all are Magar from this class except one of Hindu upper caste Thakuri family. The rich peasants with middle layered peasantry (though partly) own the most fertile land of village.

2. HISTORICAL CONJUNCTION OF A REBELLIOUS VILLAGE

According to the oral history narratives, Thabang has a history of 1700 year and it was organized in four forts. In circa 15th century, a Thakuri king of Rukumkot first came here to stay by making Chapkot as its capital. The king used to involve in suppressing villagers by snatching their grains and exploiting Magar women. The villagers apprehended, if Raja Chapkot would be allowed to get stay, their lives would be a grave danger. The people decided that if they were able to spoil his plan to become rich by accumulating rice harvest, he would certainly have no option but to leave Thabang village. For this they collaborated with a peasant who had become a confidant to the king. They asked him to fry rice before cultivating it in fields. This resulted that there was no crop that year and in frustration the king left. From there he went to build a fort in Jhlubang in Rukum district.

In the 16th century representatives of the king of Rukumkot, Kalu Shahi and Lalu Shahi came to Thabang to extract taxes. They looted grains, cash, vegetables, and poultry and raped Magar women. The people then decided to resist them. The people formed militias and fought them by stoning and beating them in guerrilla attack. Since then no one has dared to come to forcibly collect tax from Thabang.[7] These acts of resistance made people realise the value of armed resistance and inculcated the spirit of rebellion in them.

---

7 Purn Bahadur Roka Magar (2011 [2068 B.S.]), *Krantikari Itihas Bokeko Thabang (Thabang that carries a Revolutionary History)*, Nayabazar: Ganga Jamuna Press, p. 3.

With the Gorkha conquest of Nepal, the area under Thabang was been part of an administrative unit called Thum[8] and was in a jurisdiction of Pyuthan district. In 1961, the administrative unit of Thabang Khuwa Thum was attached with a new district of Rolpa.[9] During the era of the Rana rule, the village was part of a *Birta* land grant given to military officials. Thabang was a part of a grant of *Birta* land that was a dowry present to Princess Shanta Devi Shree who was married to Indra Bahadur Shahi, a grandson of king of Rukumkot. Before the dawn of *Panchayat* regime in Nepal, a *Mukhiya* (village headman) used to collect annual tax of rupees 349 and paid in silver coins to the Gajulkot king Upendra Bahadur Shah.

An examination of the local village administration of Thabang before 1950s reveals that the rule of the *Mukhiya* was oppressive and absolute. The *Mukhiya* was usually responsible for arbitrating local land disputes and other administrative work of the entire village. It was in early 1950s that a despotic order by village headman Krishna Jhankri[10] became a big dispute and divided entire village in two factions. The bone of contention was a new rule introduced by Krishna Mukhiya by ordering villagers to debar pig within household on sanitary grounds. Since, villagers did not adhere with rule as pig was considered a useful animal from producing meat to pesticide for crops. This made village headman to punish peasants which took a violent turn in 1954-1955 after Barman Budha Magar who led people to resist him. Since the *Mukhiya* was well connected with local administration of Pyuthan

8 In pre 1950s, the hill region was divided into many administrative units of Thum. These comprised many dozens of villages which was demarcated with natural terrain of forests and valley.

9 Op. cit., Purn Bahadur Roka Magar (2011 [2068 B.S.]), p. 6.

10 He was appointed as a Mukhiya of Thabang in 1952 by the royal family of Gajulkot. Krishna Jhankri was a retired pensioner of Indian Gurkha Regiment.

district headquarter, Barman Budha and his friends were charged by them as 'communist'.[11] Those days, a label like Communist was considered a seditious crime and this type of accusation was very common in the 1950s. In fact, everybody who dared to attack the authorities was labeled as 'Communist', no matter whether the accused knew who Marx and Lenin were. Consequently, in June 1955, Barman Budha and seven other peasants were jailed in Pyuthan district prison for a couple of month. Here, Barman Budha met some activists of Communist Party of Nepal who were imprisoned on mobilizing peasant movement in region.

In 1956, general secretary of Communist Party of Nepal (CPN), Man Mohan Adhikari agreed Hindu monarchy to work in accordance with legal and peaceful way. Consequently, king Mahendra lifted ban from CPN and its political activities. Therefore, in accord of Nepali government, communist activists like Mohan Bikram Singh and friends were also released from Salyan jail. While returning to their home, planned to stay some days in Thabang since they were knew about conflict between two groups of Thabang. They stayed couple of days in Thabang. Mohan Bikram Singh was succeeded in persuading both factions of Barman Budha and Krishna Mukhiya to end their enmity. He also convinced them instead a form a peasant organisation where they can deal with villager's day today problems. Thus a village committee of All Nepal Peasant Association was founded in Thabang on July 3, 1956 in leadership of Burman Budha Magar. Krishna Mukhiya passed way from a long illness of Tuberculosis in 1958 and then Burman Budha was appointed a new Mukhiya of Thabang village. After returning to his hometown Pyuthan,

11 Kiyoko Ogura (2007), 'Maoist, People and the State as Seen from Rolpa and Rukum', in H. Ishi, D. Gellner and K. Nawa (ed.), *Political and Social Transformation in North India and Nepal*, p. 456.

Mohan Bikram Singh dispatched Khagulal Gurung to look after Communist party activities in Thabang. The countrywide first general election held in 1959. The whole Thabang village voted for CPN's candidate Khagulal Gurung who was standing from Pyuthan constituency. Though Khagulal lost election but Thabang came into radar of district administration.

3. VILLAGE AWAKENING WITH FOUNDING OF PRIMARY SCHOOL IN THABANG

However, around same time, it was with the founding of first primary school that made early roots of communist politics in Thabang village. The school got official recognition from the *Panchayat* government in 1965. At the behest of Mohan Bikram Singh, Pyuthan committee of Communist Party sent Khiman Singh Gurung to work as teacher in primary school. Gurung opened a night school and taught for two years. Deepak K.C., a prominent communist teacher of Pyuthan was later send to Thabang as a school principal. It was Deepak K.C. who was responsible for inspiring a young generation of villagers to get mobilised in communist politics. The seed of a primary school was gradually grown into a Thabang High School. Till early years of 1970s, that it was Thabang High School that became a centre of political activities in region.

This was a time; the *Panchayat* government issued a order to ban *Raksi* (homemade liquor). Since, production & brewing of liquor had been an essential component of every household of region and Kham Magar culture, so soon this became a peasant outcry. The peasants accused Nepal government that it wanted to promote factory made liquor duly licensed and permitted as per state rule. This was resulted in a political campaign against government order and manifested in a conflict between two groups who supported and opposed this move. Ram Kumar

Budha Magar was a staunch supporter of this government order. He was also been served as *Pradhan Panch* (elected village mayor), therefore had influential connection in state administration. However, Barman Budha Magar, who was then mayor of village with his communist associates had opposed against administrative order. In view of continuous anti-brewery campaign in village, government arrested Kaman Jhankri Magar and other peasant leaders in 1973. However, these arrests could not deter villagers in their defiance of brewing and producing liquor.

In such a view with the arrival of Comrade Jaljala in 1974, which brought anti-brewery campaign as a full blown political movement in entire region.[12] Her efforts were successful immensely by culminating in mass mobilisation in which hundreds of women opposed government efforts and its stooges like Ram Kumar Budha Magar to build a liquor factory in village. This women's group organised many meetings and rallies in High School ground of village. This had in effect made district administration to slap false criminal cases against many villagers. More especially, who were considered close to the women's movement faced false cases. The tussle turned violent and resulted in many incidents of firing by both sides.[13] The anti-brewery movement also witnessed incident concerning poisoning of Lalmani Budha who was a deputy head of village. When the matter was taken to district administration nothing was done to the culprits. This was because Ramkumar had become important for the administration for suppressing the communists.

---

12 Comrade Jaljala is a *nom de guerre* of women activist of CPN (Fourth Convention). His original name was Vidya Dhakal and she hailed from Chitwan district. See, Op. cit., Purn Bahadur Roka Magar (2011 [2068 B.S.]), p. 8.

13 Purn Bahadur Roka Magar (2008), Documentation of Purn Bahadur Roka Magar, Thabang.

Besides, there was another event which angered local peasants. Following a road of developing rural Nepal, the *Panchayat* government had banned production and sale of hashish and marijuana in 1976. In western Nepal, as a commercial crop Hashish has many utilities from generating cash income to making ropes, bags, clothes and used in consuming by making pickles. The hashish production has been a key source of family income in the Kham Magar dominated region because of majority of peasantry barely produced enough food for their subsistence. Before enacting ban, government has many shops in capital Kathmandu to regional centres like Nepalgunj, where people used to sell hashish balls. But now under the Drug Trafficking and Abuse Acts 1976, many who defied order were arrested.

These set of government decision made people go against state administration. To voice people's protest, student's activists of Thabang High School in tacit support of communist party had formed a cultural association in 1978. But soon, on behest of Ram Kumar Budha, local policeman had a crackdown and arrested many on false charges of disrupting law and order in village.

This was a time when country was witnessing a nationwide students and teachers mobilization to protest against Julfikar Ali Bhutto's hanging by government of Pakistan in 1979. Since, Nepal was ruled by a party less government, so these protest demonstrations were also intended to oppose *Panchayat* government for establishment of multi-party democracy. Since, Thabang was the second SLC centre in entire region after Rolpa district headquarters of Libang. So students of adjoining villages and Rukum district too used to stay in village to study in school which was till then famously known as 'communist school'. There was a massive student movement took place in Thabang in early 1980. The district administrative took events in Thabang as surprise. The student activists with a wide support of villagers had taken charge of administrating the village. Ram Kumar Budha and his supporters who were known as 'anti-social and anti-people element' of the village were punished and were forced to either leave the village or correct their ways.

4. FIRST MILITARY CRACKDOWN IN THABANG

The student movement was largely influenced from nationwide protests in Kathmandu. The *Panchayat* government believed that it was dangerous to run the administration in village and a movement in a village such as Thabang was least expected. In the wake of countrywide demonstrations, King Birendra announced for a national referendum in Nepal. Thus, to decide whether to continue rule of the partyless *Panchayat* system or to introduce *Bahudal* (multi-party democracy), a referendum was held in 1980. The entire village voted in favour of multi-party democracy. The district administration largely made *Pradhan Panch* (village mayor) Barman Budha mainly responsible for inciting villager's unanimous vote for siding with democracy. Immediately after this referendum, he was arrested and spent more than two years in different jails of Ghorahi and Libang.

After winning the referendum, government organised general elections in 1981. Since the Fourth convention had given a boycott call of election, the peasants of Thabang also followed party's call. Thabang became an only village Rolpa and also of country where not a single vote was casted in this election. The ballot officials forced to return with empty ballot boxes. The referendum and election boycott by peasants frightened the state machinery in Kathmandu, resulting in a massive crackdown by a joint security operation of Royal Nepal Army and police forces in October 1981. In vocabulary of government, now Thabang became Communist. Thabang High School became a central location of state brutality and security forces stayed her for many weeks. Balaram Gharti Magar, the then defence minister of country was main architect of military crackdown.[14] Eight local activists of the communist party were arrested on October 19 and false cases of sedition were charged on 24 people. They were detained in Tulsipur jail in Dang district for the next two and half years.[15]

After 1981's security operation, a police station was established in Thabang. This resistance established Thabang on the national scene of Nepal. The military operation was conducted to terrorize the people who till then were only using their basic rights to vote and protest against the government. The administration had thought that after the operation people's confidence on the communists can be shattered. However, the operation worked exactly the opposite that anti-state sentiments grew stronger.

5. FIGHTING A RURAL CLASS STRUGGLE IN EARLY 1990S

Thus in 1990, the long standing demands and struggles by peasantry finally resulted in culmination of movement for democracy popularly called as *Jana Andolan-1*. And it was just impossible that Thabang could be untouched from country political churning. A pro-democracy rally was organised in grounds of Thabang High School in March 9, 1990. This was a time after split in Mohan Bikram Singh's led Fourth Convention in 1983, the communists of Thabang had sided with Mohan Baidya's led CPN (Mashal)[16] and its political mass organisation of *Samkuta Janmorcha, Nepal* (SJM, Nepal). With restoration of multi-party democracy, the SJM had organised a cultural and

14 Balaram Gharti Magar hails from Khungri VDC of Rolpa. He was known *Panchyat* architect in Rolpa district and he had persuaded villagers of Thabang through his supporters like Ram Kumar Budha which was largely unsuccessful.

15 Op. cit., Purn Bahadur Roka Magar (2011 [2068 B.S.]), p. 10.

16 Also known as *Moto Mashal*.

political campaign in district continued for a whole year until the announcement of general elections in country. Starting from Thabang, these campaigns lasted from March-April and in July 1990 in eastern part of Rolpa to rest of district.

The first general elections were held in June 1991 and both constituencies of Rolpa district won by the SJM candidates including Barman Budha Magar.[17] This victory of Barman Budha was celebrated in Thabang village by organising a big rally in the district headquarters of Libang.

After Nepali Congress led Girija Prasad Koirala led government came into power in 1991, in district like Rolpa and Rukum where the SJM had strength, began to take account of development projects. Their victory in Rolpa made a further ground for the SJM to expose inefficacy of parliamentary democracy, and raising class consciousness of people were sought to be developed through by cultural campaigns. The performance of revolutionary songs exposed acts of state brutality, propagated the ideology of Maoism, and implored the people to build resistance against the state for achieving radical social change. These campaigns also sought to garner support for the People's War in Peru and to impart an internationalist perspective to build a new kind of future. The rural class struggle took several forms, including public humiliation of government officials, and moneylenders by blackening their faces, burning of loan papers. At impromptu public hearings organised by the SJM in rural region, many of the VDC officials found guilty of taking advantage of their offices. Many political activists of ruling party were also accused of pilfering state resources were also targeted by the SJM activists. Most of government officials were associated with ruling Nepali Congress party or former *Panchayat* regime.

At the time of *Tihar* festival in Thabnag village on November 2, 1992, police arrested four SJM activists on the charge that they

17 The other winning candidate was Krishna Bahadur Mahra.

were indulging in illegal activities. These arrests largely were outcome of peasant's opposition to the Jumleni' sisters[18] attempt to cut down the tress by capturing forest land at Portekhani which was a community land and grazing sight for animals. With help of Ram Kumar Budha, they had met district police administration in Libang and reported about underground activities of the SJM in village and bribed the police officer.

6. CHALLENGING STATE TERROR BY *SIJA* CAMPAIGN

The beginning of October 1994 brought in village (and region adjoining to it) an occurrence of similar to what Thabang suffered in 1981. This was a time when a security operation called Operation Romeo was organized by then state. Many contingents of armed police were mobilised for this search operation in the whole region described in the state's phraseology as 'deeply affected from communist guerrilla activities'. These regions were initially identified as Thabang and 13 other adjacent VDCs of Rolpa district. Later, this police operation was extended to almost all the VDCs of Rolpa and Rukum and other districts. By the end of the year, the ruthlessness of security operation became a heated subject of discussion in national politics. Dr. Baburam Bhattarai, the convenor of the SJM, told a national Nepali daily in December 1995:

> *Around 1,500 policemen, including a specially trained commando force sent from Kathmandu, have been deployed to let loose a reign of terror against poor*

---

18 The *Jumleni* a nick name of a rich peasant family which patriarch was Ram Kumar Budha Magar. Ram Kumar had two sisters living in Thabang village at the time of these happenings while he himself now lived in Libang after his alleged hand in 1981 security operation. The family had a big business of hashish by collecting from villagers and sell it in Kathmandu and Indian cities.

> *peasants... there has been indiscriminate ransacking and looting of properties of common people, molestation/rapes by the ruling party hoodlums under the protection of the police force. More than 10, 000 rural youth, out of a population of 200,000 for the whole district, have been forced to flee their homes and take shelter in the remote jungles.*[19]

Though state repression continued, the SJM held a series of cultural campaigns in Rolpa and Rukum districts.[20] Known as *char tayarri* (four preparations), these events aimed at strengthening the party organisation and preparing a ground of giving armed resistance to government. While began in September 1995, these preparations had four elements of ideological, organisational, logistic and technological. First of its kind was called *Sija Abhiyan* (*sija* campaign) began in Thabang from May 1995. A senior Maoist leader, Comrade Badal led these campaigns in Rolpa and Rukum. The *Sija* campaign was named after the two mountains, the Sisne Mountain in Rukum and the Jaljala Mountain in Rolpa. Besides, the Maoist also defined as it is pronounced as similar to a spelling in English language that is "siege". Thus *Sija* campaign as part of preparing a ground for seizure of power from landlords ruling class (including seizure of weapons form the hands of the police and seizure of property and bonds of the landlords and moneylenders).

A pamphlet published by the SJM describes this campaign in following manner:

> *... the Sija name comes from the two high mountains called Sisne in Rukum and Jaljala in Rolpa. ... These two districts could be said to be under developed. The mode*

19 Arjun Karki and David Seddon (2003) (eds.), p. 21.

20 These kinds of cultural campaigns were conducted in places which was directly affected from state's violence in rural heartlands of Jajarkot, Gorkha, Kavre, Sindhupalchowk, Sindhuli, Dhanusha and Ramechap districts.

> *of production of these areas is rudimentary and there is a lack of education among the masses. Majority of the people of these areas belong to ethnic community. These people were not only exploited by the state but also by the newly sprouting NGOs and INGOs which exploit in the term 'Bikas' (development). …Sisne was popularly known as Sija among the city dwellers. The Sija was basically the process of educating masses through cultural programs, debates and meetings about the exploitive character of the 'Bahudal' State which was as anti-people as the 'old' Panchayat regime. …The origin of Sija can be traced in the social-economic and cultural dynamics of this society. However since communists worked here for a long time the idea was based on the guiding philosophy of Marxism-Leninism-Maoism. This campaign was actually a development of Maoism in the context of Nepal. This campaign was not at all based on ethnic identity as was hyped by the media and Kathmandu-centric intellectuals at that time. They termed this campaign as an act of terrorism. The Sija is neither an act of terrorism not was a totally ethnicity-based movement. It was rather a preparation for the class struggle led by the proletariat. The only way for the emancipation of the masses of the semi-feudal and semi-colonial countries is path of Protracted People's War.*[21]

The other campaign was the *Miteri Abhiyan* (friendship campaign) which also simultaneously organised along with the *Sija* campaign. By this, it was aimed an exchange of views and experiences among political activists, helping them to get to know each other. The mode of exchange included through performances of revolutionary songs, dances, and theatre. After these campaigns, the party organized a special campaign focusing the youths in

21 Op. cit., Purn Bahadur Roka Magar (2008).

Thabang VDC. It was known as *Jangiti Abhiyan* (progressive song campaign) and was run for around two months in entire Rolpa district by mobilizing the youth from Thabang. The *Jansewa Abhiyan* (serving people campaign) focussed on construction of schools, footpaths and resting places in the region. During these campaigns, the peasants of Thabang with adjoining VDCs erected a three-dimensional martyrs' column on top of the Jaljala Mountain. It was believed by Maoist activists that the Jaljala Mountain would bless their revolutionary struggle to become successful and goal of revolution in Nepal to be realized.

7. PEOPLE'S WAR BROKE IN THABANG

These set of political campaign resulted in the SJM charter of "Forty Points Demand" in first week of February 1996. By this, it was demanded to then government to stop state's atrocities in countryside. The state instead intensified armed operations in a ruthless manner. The firing by security forces took place in dozens of village in Rolpa including Bhabang, Badachaur, Uwa-Juttar, Charka, Pachabang-Sallakhot and Kureli.[22] The district of Rolpa became a police camp where except leaving two VDCs, armed police commando camps were established in 49 VDC. There were only seven armed commando camps in Rolpa before these incidents. Thus state terror operation eventually became the immediate reason for launching the Maoist's People's War.

Amidst of police repression in region, the party organization of Thabang organised a training class for its activists. Many top leaders like Comrade Badal were guiding these training sessions on ideological and political questions. Likhi Bahadur Budha

22 Nirmal Pun (1995 [2051 B.S.]), 'Gramin Varg Sangarsh: Kehi Anubhuti Ra Shiksha', *Sisne, Akhil Jilla Sanagathan Samiti*, No. 3, Rolpa. (December issue), pp. 11-18.

recalls such a training class in the forest located near Rachibang hamlet of Thabang:

> *Just some month before the setting off of armed struggle, Comrade Badal came to take party classes. The village comrades had asked, "The government has a big army, lots of weapons and money, so how can we fight such a strong force?" Then he told us, "let we should initiate the war. The government itself will bring the weapons for us and we will be able to build an army for ourselves. Moreover we will get the money too." I didn't believe all these. I thought, "How could it be possible?" Later he was proved right. We initiated the war and we got the arms and even money from the enemy.*[23]

Bar Prasad Gharti Magar was a member of village fighting squad at that time and was a member of the youth front. He remembers scenario in Thabang just the night before commencing People's War on 13 February, 1996.

> *That was a harsh winter night in and snowfall was so much that it was very difficult to walk. The party committee had organized a food celebration in house of Lali Roka Magar. We ate dal-bhat with pork meat. So everyone drank a little amount of liquor to keep warm. We had planned to start the wall painting in respective areas starting from midnight and finish before 3 am in early morning.*

The implementation of early phase of strategic defensive stage went as smoothly prior as planned by party activists. The fighting squad carried its first sabotage action on 15 February by destroying Jumleni family's apple nursery plants in Patikhore hamlet. Next day the police arrested 17 people allegedly for attacking the Jumleni's apple graden and beaten up mercilessly.

---

23 Interview, Likhi Bahadur Budha Magar, 17 Novemebr, 2010, Rachibang, Thabang.

8. POLICE TERROR LED EXPANSION OF GUERRILLA MOVEMENT IN REGION

While armed struggle went ahead, the Maoists had divided country into four commands eastern, central, western, and Kathmandu valley. In first early years, western command was centre of guerrilla activities and Thabang was its nerve centre. But since, the western command was stretched in a vast territory; therefore the Maoist had later divided it into four sub-regional commands namely Gandak, Rapti special, Bheri-Karnali and Seti-Mahakali. The district of Rolpa and Thabang VDC was geographically located in Rapti special regional bureau. To carry out guerrilla activities, the CPN (M) carved out three types of guerrilla zones (i.e., main, secondary and propaganda). Thabang was located in main guerrilla zone where conducting guerrilla war was first priority while activities such as sabotage and annihilation of enemy were done to complementary basis.

With expansion of guerrillas movement in Rapti region gave a momentum to the people's resistance in Thabang too. On 17 January 1997, the police arrested four villagers from Phuntibang village including Lali Roka Magar, a senior activist of All Nepal Women Organization-Revolutionary. Next day on 18 January in police custody, Lali Roka was brutally gang-raped and shot dead with another party activist Dilman Roka Magar. The police hanged their bodies from tree nearby Thabang river stream. By the end of the CPN (M)'s first early plans, more than 150 people were reportedly killed in Rolpa alone.

After these gruesome killings, the reign of police terror was established in region. To counter police terror, the Maoist guerrilla carried out a sabotage attack on store of Mulya Roka Magar on midnight of 26 February, 1997 but he was escaped. It was maintained by local party committee that he with his Nepali Congress supporter had acted as police informer in killing of

Lali and Dilman. Mulya was associated with Ram Kumar Budha's group and was considered a notorious moneylender of region. The fighting squad killed Mulya Roka Magar and Manjit Gharti Magar on 8 March, 1997.

Soon after this incident, police made a flag march in Thabang VDC. A company level of police force was deployed from district headquarter of Libang to reinforce the VDC's police post. A jungle combing operation started from 13 March, 1997 and continued till 28 March, 1997. Property worth lakhs of rupees was destroyed. Criminal cases were registered against 40 people on various charges. All the people from young to seventy year olds were forced to hide in the jungle. Nimu Roka Magar and Miljita Roka Magar were brutally murdered in their own house by Nepali Congress members in collaboration with the police on 29 June, 1997. The blame was put on the Maoists and sixteen villagers were also arrested by the police and sent to jail.[24]

While Nepali state largely failing to contain guerrilla activities made a crisis in national politics. The Nepali Congress government declared a mid-term general election which was held in June 1997. The CPN (M) had boycotted these elections and it was successful in the most of VDCs in Rapti region. With a new coalition government of Nepali Congress and CPN (UML) planned a new counter insurgency operation from mid year of 1998.

In infancy years of People's War, the government claimed many times that the Maoist guerrillas are a small gang of dacoits and would be easily defeated. But they were also planning to figure out how to stop the Maoist movement which was now spreading and gaining support in rural heartland of country. Then after a lull for some months, security forces carried out a big security operation called Kilo Sierra-2. This was a 'search and kill' operation and run in 'Maoist affected areas' from 26 May to 7 November,

24 Op.cit., Purn Bahadur Roka Magar (2008).

1998. Thabang also became a witness of state's brutality. The police had destroyed tons of grains and razed many households in main village of Thabang VDC. Most of the villagers were forced to leave and to live in far away jungles on the Jaljala Mountain for many days.

The police brutality provided a reason for the CPN (M) to escalate guerrilla strikes in throughout country. The fighting squads have till now taken initial shape of temporary platoon level of the Maoist military wing. With this strength, they carried a series of attack in Rolpa and Rukum districts. Two large settlements of armed police in Thabang-Uwa border and Jelbang VDC were attacked and destroyed completely on April, 1999 and May, 1999 respectively. The September 1999's Mahat attack in Rukum district considered a fierce one. With 3 platoons of the Maoist combatants organised as special task force raided a well fortified police riot base camp. This attack was totally successful in destroying the police camp which was responsible to run operation Kilo Sierra-2 in region. Thule Rai, a commanding officer with dozens of policemen was abducted by the guerrillas as a prisoner of war. They were kept in Thabang for many days and were released after a mediation of International Red Cross in exchange of a Maoist leader Dev Gurung.[25]

These offensives were assisted by two more simultaneous attacks on police posts in Roolbang and Narabang by assassinating many policemen. These offensive followed by a successful attack in November, 1999 by which police post in Thabang VDC was completely destroyed. This made security forces demoralised and government of Nepal was forced to re-locate dozens of police posts including Thabang's in district headquarters of Libang. The large scale and successful Maoist's armed strikes on security forces

25 Pasang (2008), *Red Strides of History: (Significant Military Raids of the People's War),* Agnipariksha Janprakashan Griha: Kathmandu, p. 40.

made guerrilla zones to expand quite considerably. Two successful strikes at Namule and Rukumkot in April 2001 made it clear to the then state that the Maoists have defeated Nepal police completely. These two raids forced all elements of the state machinery to evacuate from the rural region.

9. MAOIST GOVERNANCE IN THABANG SPECIAL DISTRICT

It was this context, which prompted the CPN (M) to orientation of establishing *Jansatta* (people's power) once presence of the then state became nil and void in rural region. Soon after since 2001 victory over police, the Maoist declared their first *Adhar Ilaka* (base area) to be centred in Thabang.[26]

It was during 7th plan; Thabang *Bishes Jilla* (special district) was formed in April 2002 in a central committee meeting of CPN (M). The purpose of forming this district was to establish a people's power in a distinct region of Kham Magar population. It was carved out from 13 VDCs of Rukum and Rolpa districts. This included north Rolpa's six VDCs namely Thabang, Uwa, Mirul, Jelbang, Rangkot and Kureli. The remaining seven VDCs from Rukum's eastern region were Chunbang, Mahat, Kankri, Kol, Taksera, Hukum, and Maikot. Thabang VDC became capital of this special district. The *Bishes Jilla Jansarkar* was declared public in Thabang High School ground on 25 February 2003 in the presence of thousands of people. With formation of Thabang as a special district, it became country's

26 It is observed in a report of united people's committee that a 'temporary level' of people's power in village begun taking shape in between from 3rd plan in October, 1997 to 5th plan in 1999. However, until this time, these committee were organized on ad hoc basis and did not functioning openly as police post existed in village. See, CPN (M) (1999 [2055 B.S.]), '*Prativaden, Samkuta Gaon Jan Samiti*,' Thabang: Rolpa.

"76th" district of Nepal comprising 75 districts. Its first chief was a veteran communist leader Tejman Gharti Magar alias Dirgh.

According to a handwritten document of *Samukta Gaon Jan Samiti* (united village people's committee), the development of people's power in Thabang had developed in various phases. Initially, these united people's committees later to be called as *Jansatta/ Ga-Ja-Sa* (village people's committee) came into existence months after the Maoist's destructed area police post of Thabang. Initially, this committee was formed taking representation from all nine wards from different frontal organisations from peasantry, women, worker, ethnic group, Dalits, intellectual, cultural committee and shopkeepers. Three representatives from the village guerrilla squads were also nominated. By a pool of a general people's council would responsible to elect 13-15 member committee with its chief and deputy chief. The constitution of village people's government also ensured through right to recall its chief or deputy chief if they proved to be inefficient or corrupt.[27] The basic thrust of village *Jansatta* was to educate the people about Maoist politics and in continuing the struggle.

Pratap Roka Magar was a member of Thabang village people's committee in 2002. He explains about rationale of establishing *Jansatta* in the Thabang VDC.

> *In any society either in times of war or peace, the people must have to feel about state power. Before the beginning of people's war, the people had experienced the nature of old state so it was natural that they wanted to revolt to this idea of state. In the very beginning of people's war the local administrative village unit flee to district headquarter and national capital in Kathmandu*

27 CPN (M) (2001[2057 B.S.]), '*Niti Tatha Krayakram, Gaon Jan Samiti,' 2057* (Policy and Program, United Village People's Committee, 2001), p. 1.

> *because of Maoist 'terror'. This resulted in a power vacuum in the village of the space of old monarchical state. Then the higher committee of the party made instruction to local committee to initiate discussion with villagers and in this process the higher committee helped us to organise people's power in Thabang. If there is no presence of authority then it becomes very difficult to solve contradiction among people and to provide justice in land quarrel or give punishment on violence against women or take care of theft matter. In absence of this power, the people feel themselves Tuhuro (orphan). So, this way people's power begins to take initial shape.*[28]

The most important issue of Thabang special district was to give security of population living under its purview. Therefore, department of public administration was established. The security department under every village government created people's militias to provide security in region. According to its policy every area and VDC was given the right to form their own militia.[29] These militias had to identify the police informers and also gave elementary arms training to villagers. Besides, they were also potential recruits for the Maoist army. In cases of battle with state armed forces these militia used to participate as volunteer force to the PLA. Shram Roka Magar recalls a chaotic situation in village after state's security operation in May, 2002.

> *Fearing the royal army, the entire village had followed militia instructions and went to the jungles. The royal army had burnt down fifteen houses on the second day of their arrival in Thabang. On a later day they had a heavy battle with the PLA which made seven militia comrades*

28 Interview, Pratap Roka Magar, June 27, 2010, Libang, Rolpa.

29 CPN (M) (2005 [2062 B.S.])), '*Niti Ra Karyakram', Magarant Syayattya Gantantra Jan Pratinidhi Sabha*, p. 2.

> *dead. The security forces retreated only after a counter attack made by the PLA in Gam base camp of the RNA.*[30]

The other important aspect of the Maoist governance was their effective intervention in country's judicial system. The judicial system of Nepal is very exclusive, expensive, discriminatory and corrupt. To get justice depends on conditions of paying larger amounts of fees to lawyer and thus it make villagers in heavy debts. Moreover, the courts are based in cities and district headquarters. Solving a case is so slow and it keep pending for years. In contrast to an expensive and discriminatory judicial system, the Maoist people's court charged a meagre fee. When the village people's committee received any complaints, the first priority was to solve the issue at the local level and if by any chance this failed the complaint was forwarded to the people's court. The people's courts were mobile in nature and were governed by a set of directives.

In serious criminal cases like spying, the judgment was delivered by consulting the PLA. In cases of rape and murder, the accused had also to pay financial penalty while also undergoing labour punishment. The labour punishment was usual mode of punishment though an open jail was maintained in Jhakkibang village. By process of punishment, the convicts had to stay in the village where he/she would help villagers in various labouring activities as per the *ga-ja-sa* need. The time period of punishment used to depend on the nature or severity of the crime committed by him/her. If the accuse try to elope without completing punishment then people's court had a right to extend time period of his/her punishment.

10. THE LAND QUESTION: COMMUNE AND COOPERATIVES

As the landholdings in the hilly areas were scattered and relatively small, a cooperative farming system was promoted in Thabang

30 Interview, Shram Roka Magar, 16 June 2010, *Thula Gaon*, Thabang.

special district. Accordingly, fertile land seized from moneylenders and mischievous elements was converted into model farmlands. Here, new varieties of vegetables and grains were produced.

The village people's government took over to the work of land registration in Thabang. The peasant had to pay Rs. 10 affidavit for every land transaction. However, there was no policy of redistribution of land for poor peasants. The revolutionary land reform was absent from the Maoist policy and practice in the base area. Prakash Adhikari worked as a secretary of agricultural department of Thabang special district and Magarant autonomous council from mid 2002 to February 2006. He explains about CPN (M)'s policy on the land question.

> *Primarily we took the issue of the chaklabandi (collectivization) of land. For instance, if one peasant had many portion of land scattered in five or more places, by collecting in one place was promoted to increase agricultural production. But our policy was not successful, although some 5-6 families came together and worked together for some time. The campaign of collectivization succeeded only in the context of building communes in Rachibang village. Though, we had seized land from oppressive and anti-social elements like informers but re-distribution of this land among peasants was not in the party's central policy and it did not take place in Thabang. So from those rich people who supported our struggle, we used to take seasonal taxes from them while those who were against People's War, we used to seize their property. Yet there were many suggestions for this to our committee from activists belonging to the poor peasantry.*[31]

31 Interview, Prakash Adhikari, 19 April, 2012, Jhumri, Pyuthan.

In direction of collectivization of farm land, a commune was established in Rachibang village on 1 June, 2003.[32] It was named after memory of commemorating village Maoist activists who laid down their lives for course of the People's War. Known as the Ajambari commune (immortal commune), it was established by a group of 34 families of deceased Maoist activists. A People's war time document depicted founding of commune in Thabang as:

> *"...the best achievement of a decade-long People's War. They are ideal model of defence, experiment and advancing ideology of Marxism-Leninism-Maoism and Prachanda Path. These communes are the embryo of Socialism and Communism."*[33]

Now only 9 families with 39 persons live in this commune and it was on the verge of breaking.[34] Tejman Gharti Magar alias 'Dirgh', the chief of Thabang Special District had opposed founding of commune by arguing that until we seized Kathmandu and established Socialist state power in Nepal, establishing a commune would be an idealist and immature move. That is why his family did not join it.[35] To support everyday necessities of the PLA and villagers, a co-operative industry was set up in commune after Jaljala Mountain. In these factories a wide variety of dry fruits related products to shawl, garment, soap, candle, paper and shoe was manufactured. These industries had initially set up with a capital of 1.5 lakh rupees which turnover was 10 lakh when it was closed down with end of armed struggle in 2005.

32 Other than Thabang, 3 more communes were established districts of Rolpa, Rukum, and Jajarkot.

33 CPN (M) (2004 [2061]), 'Prativaden, Ajambari Jan Commune Thabang', Thabang, p. 2.

34 This observation was based on my first visit of Thabang in June, 2010.

35 Interview, Ajay Gharti Magar, eldest son of Tejaman Gharti Magar alias 'Dirgh', 14 November, 2010, Gobang village, Thabang VDC.

A rudimentary form of mobile banking was organised by pooling shares from peasant families in September, 2002. It was known as Jaljala Financial Cooperative Fund later to be called by *Janbadi Bank* in August, 2004. Ruz Bahadur Roka Magar alias Regan was responsible for co-operative bank. He gives the rationale behind its set up,

> *Though, moneylenders had all left the village, but peasants still needed to borrow money. To solve this problem we established this co-operative fund. It was handled jointly by cooperative department and its resources were many from tax from hashish traders to fines received from people's court and land registry.*[36]

The bank, however, failed to win confidence of peasants since it functioned in an irregular manner and closed down in 2005.

11. MAOIST MODEL OF DEVELOPMENT

Many construction projects were carried out in Thabang by the village *Jansatta* with consultation of special district administration. This could be included to construction of hydroelectric power stations, to pedestrian road tracks, rest houses, village gates and school. Out of this, establishment of hydropower stations were significant to mention. Though, on a small scale, one of its first kinds was established at the end of 2004 in Phuntibang village with a capacity of 4.5 kilowatts. This power house brought electricity in Rachibang and Phuntibang villages though its supply was only for lighting at night. Until commencement of end of Maoist war, 4 hydro plants were providing electricity for entire Thabang VDC. One of such plants was destroyed in a security operation by the RNA in 2005.

Besides this, construction of a 93 kilometre road network was commenced on November, 2004 by newly declared Magarant autonomous government in grounds of Thabang High School.

36 Interview, Ruz Bahadur Roka Magar, 2 November, 2010, Bibang, Thabang.

It was named after memory of martyrs and called the Dahban-Thabang *Sahid Marg* (martyr's road). This road was to connect Thabang by networking key locations of special district's Kham Magar heartland of two districts of southern Rolpa and Rukum. Building such a road in a mountain region where a journey is measured by time other than distance was conceived by the Maoists that people are real makers of history. Based on a premise of *Aafno paurakh aafnai gaurav, hamrai prayas hamrai bikas* (our prowess our glory, our effort our development), thousands of villagers from 13 districts of Magarant autonomous state were involved to build it. By 2005, a 17 kilometre by connecting Nuwagaon and Tila VDCs had been completed and 10 million rupees was spent in construction of first year itself.[37] In 2008, the Nepal government took responsibility to complete remaining project.

A Maoist education policy was one more aspect of development projects taken in Thabang special district. It was believed that it is the education policies which ultimately decide nature of society and state. Comprehending this notion, a primary school was established. The building of school in Thabang was an outcome of a necessity as due to security concerns; children of the Maoist families were unable to attend government run school. Thus the *Sahid Smriti Namuna Bidyalaya* (martyr memorial model school) was opened on 12 February 2005 in Gobang village. Initially, it was run up to the class III standard which was later upgraded by the 4th standard. The L shaped residential campus had a one story building with seven rooms which was built from community labour of villagers. The school provided uniform and stationary free of cost to children from martyrs families, Maoists activists and poor families. The syllabus of model school encouraged education in the

37 Kiyoko Ogura (2008), 'Maoist People's Governments, 2001-05: The Power in Wartime', in D.N. Gellner and K. Hachhethu (ed.), *Local Democracy in South Asia: Micro Process of Democratization in Nepal and its Neighbours,* New Delhi: Sage Publications, p. 206.

mother tongue and its curriculum for class I to V had a necessary element of social sciences.[38] There was a large plot of land where the teachers and students together cultivated potatoes, cauliflowers and various other vegetables which were used for the school mess. Here, national anthem in praise of monarchy was replaced by the Communist International. The students and teachers ate together and were responsible for washing their own utensils.

At a tender age of 6 year, Jivan Roka Magar lost his father in a war incident in 2004. He belongs to Mirul VDC and studied in model school till 4th standards. He recalls his experiences while studying in Thabang:

> *We were 80 students when i came to attend the school in 2004. Fifty were hostellers and rest came from outside. Our school began at 10 o'clock in the morning and our prayers begun with the Communist International song. When we entered the class we used to say Lal Salam (red salute) to the teacher and sing the class song. One song as I remember now was, 'aaj hami kokila chau, bholi thula hun chaun' (today we are little kids, tomorrow we'll be strong). At two occasions in 2005 and 2006, I remember entering of royal army in our school. We used to run away and hide. A helicopter of army fired on us while being in school in 2006. According to me, People's War was started in a reaction of police terror. So, people took arms to defend them from police and oppressors from Nepali Congress and CPN (UML) who used to set fire in villages. Those who kill other people and loot them are feudal and so why People's Liberation Army was born.*[39]

38 CPN (M) (2005 [2062 B.S.]), '*Pathyakram, Naya Janbadi Shiksha-Kaksha 1 Dekhi Kaksha 5 Samm*', Kshtriya Janshiksha Bibhag, Kendriya Aadhar Ilaka.

39 Interview, Jeevan Roka Magar, 21 October, 2010, *Thula Gaon*, Thabang.

The model school was closed down in June 2008, soon after the elections to the Constituent Assembly. At that time, school accommodated 287 students with a teaching staff of eleven.

12. REDEFINING CULTURE

With establishment of Thabang special district, the CPN (M) also promoted a cultural movement which was termed as progressive culture. It was believed that as long as the class society exists, literary community would also be divided into two camps of oppressor and oppressed. By adhering, this premise that all cultures have a class character, through various genre (i.e., literature, songs, and theatre) depicting people's struggle were propagated in place of hero-worship and *Brahmanical* symbols of power relations. The traditional Hindu festivals of *Dasain* and *Tihar* were replaced by festivals commemorating People's War, martyrs, cleaning drive, and literacy campaigns in village.

Moreover, the *Jansatta* also redefined popular folk festivals of the *Bhume Mela*. The festival begins every year on the first of *Asar* month (June 12) and continues for five days before the arrival of monsoon. By this celebration the people offers prayer to earth goddess for a good harvest every session. The *Mela* began traditionally by keeping two older persons at village outskirts traditionally two days before. They would leave this place only after entering of young Magar boys and girls with traditional Damai musicians in Jaljala Mountain. Afterward the villagers sacrificed buffalo and perform prayers. The special district administration stopped prayers but sacrifice remained the same. The custom of shitting of two old persons was replaced respecting the two oldest people of the village on first day of festival. These new changes were successfully brought in the celebration of the *Bhume Mela*. Santosh Budha Magar gives reasons behind this set of new changes introduced during his tenure of being chief of Magarant autonomous people's government in 2004:

> *These changes were brought by the Jansatta in accordance with the idea of Cultural Revolution, which we conceptualized as Parimarjan ra Bikas (modification with development). A culture of prostitution, gambling and consuming liquor was a common tradition during the Bhume Mela. The basic form of dances and celebrations were kept as they were but the centuries-old orthodox elements of shaman's healing prayers of spirits/ghosts were modified. While our Jansatta banned these practices amid opposition from people but supporting outnumbered them. We did not use force on the question of prayer and belief but we were successful by convincing them.*[40]

It is important to note that the Maoist intervention in the Bhume festival was not a one day business but it was an outcome of political mobilization of priest and shaman community also. Many campaigns in form of cultural movement were propagated in the region. One of such *Jansatta's* initiatives was to mobilize shaman community of Kham Magar heartland. It was known as the *Dhami-Jhankri Bhela* (shaman-sorcerer convention) was organized in Thabang. The main aim of this convention was to mobilize shaman to make conscious about the *Jansatta's* policies & political programs. Many persons of this profession were terrorized after believing rumors that the Maoists might torture or kill them. This convention was held in Thabang on 25 March, 2004 and 76 shamans attended this. Prakash Adhikari, an organizer of this event observed about shaman convention:

> *Through this campaign, the shamans were told that they were respected by the Jansatta for their knowledge and healing skills. They were asked not to exploit the masses in treatment and help to raise the*

40 Interview, Santosh Budha Magar, 23 June, 2010, Thula Gaon, Thabang.

> *consciousness of villagers. They agreed on the Maoist position that meaning of religion was to pray and serve the poor, distressed, and exploited masses.*[41]

In addition to propagate policies to transform everyday lives of people, the CPN (M) developed a set of media communication practice in Thabang. They begun publishing a weekly newspaper and established a Maoist radio station. Printed in lithographic machine in special district, the Ladi Janprasarit (later renamed as Naulo Janjwala) newspaper was based on contents of Maoist organ Janadesh. Moreover, in a country where more than two-thirds of the people are illiterate or semi-literate, radio journalism became an important propaganda tool. The Radio People's Republic was established in October, 2004 and located in Jaljala Mountain. The Magarant autonomous state government financed the radio with a logistic support from village *Jansatta*. Most of its programs broadcasted related to news related with Maoist's battle with security forces and disseminated news of probable security operation in region. The radio station broadcasted socialist literature through progressive songs, radio play and news features. A substantial amount of radio broadcasting time was allotted on programs on peasantry, Dalits and gender inequality. The radio was closed down just before the beginning of the Peace Process in 2006.

13. IN LIEU OF CONCLUSION

Following the Peace agreement with Nepal government, the CPN (M) leadership suspended its *Jansatta* in Thabang village from June, 2006. A series of talks between the Maoist and political parties resulted in holding elections to the first Constituent Assembly in 2008. Meanwhile, government of Nepal re-established area police office in Thabang VDC amid a wide opposition in village. Nevertheless, the entire village supported Maoist leader

41 Interview, Prakash Adhikari, 22 April, 2012, Jumri, Pyuthan.

Prachanda in constituent assembly elections who won the Rolpa seat with an overwhelming majority.

It can be concluded from above discussion that it was state atrocities that led to People's War in Thabang and thus in entire Nepal. With expansion of guerrilla movement in region, the CPN (M) was able to build people's power as expressed in village people's government. The establishment of Thabang special district was channelized thus both as a necessity of Maoist party organisation and an embryonic model of alternative state as opposed to Nepali state. The village of Thabang was capital of first of special district which was later organised in federal level as Magarant autonomous state. The Maoist administration was thus a by-product of People's War and with its calling off, it also was got an end.

CHAPTER 5

Voices of Thabang

Do not cry, do not laugh, but understand.

— Rosa Luxemburg

This chapter tells story of peoples of a Nepali village. Thabang is just one symbol out of thousands of villages of Nepal. I have made an attempt to tell voices of people as accurately as possible. These individual stories of their life was observed and sometimes recorded in informal setting in different times. Here, six selected life histories is been presented which are intrinsically connected to previous chapters. My objective of writing life histories is essentially to portray the historical setting of Thabang which accompanied five decades of history of class struggle.

Throughout human history, the telling of stories has been widely regarded as a tradition of oral narratives which are passed down across generations through which we could know their social realities.[1] The people provide an essential element to ethnographic research. When it comes to a work which is based on political sociology and social history then it becomes even more important.

The selections of life histories are based on an interwoven thread with each other. These representative stories deal with their childhood, education and adulthood to political believes which was a reproduction of a larger reality of collective conscience of

1 Ken Plummer (2001), 'The Call of Life Stories in Ethnographic Research', in Paul Atkinson et al (eds.), Handbook of Ethnography, Sage Publications: London, pp. 395-406.

Nepali society. In the following histories, everybody talks about the People's War that erupted in Nepal by recollecting historical memories of continued state repression from the *Panchayat* days to multi-party democracy. They narrate how they were influenced by the Communist ideas and their appreciation of ideology of Maoism which politicized them for to put a resistance by taking respective roles over the years. These stories are specifically critical of the existing society and show a deep hatred against state formation. It shows how confronting the questions of subjective and objective world, people negotiated in the development of different phases of their lives. The life histories presented in the following pages are interconnected in the setting of Thabang in the specific and Nepal in general.

1. PATRIARCHY AND THE PROMISE OF WOMEN'S LIBERATION

Name: Raj Kumari Roka Magar

Age: 52 year

Education: Illiterate

Profession: Peasant

Born in a middle peasant family on October 1960, my father Purna Bahadur Roka had three wives. He was a famous communist activist of village and was also called *Molo Mukhiya*.[2] After separation from his first wife Sarjita Roka, he married my mother Jamansari Roka. From his first wife, he has a son named Satya Roka alias Bhatt who is a prominent Maoist leader of village. From third wife, he had two sons and a daughter. I was not allowed to attend school because it was believed that sending girls to school could be dangerous. My father was very feudal and

2 Her father had served as a *Mukhiya* for few months in absence of Barman Budha Magar tenure of village headman, in 1963.

conservative in the matter of sending girls to school. Though some of my childhood friends attended school but could study till 2nd or 3rd Standard. They were forced to leave their studies to assist in family's household chores. I am illiterate but my elder brother studied till class 6th Standard in Thabang High School.

(Raj Kumari Roka Magar ploughing her fields)

At an age of 17 years, I got married with Chandra Jyoti Budha of Phuntibang village. Ours was a love marriage and my husband who a year older than me was studying in class 10th. My father gave him gold and money as dowry at the time of our marriage. By selling this gold, my husband had opened up a chemist store in *Thula Gaon* and worked for many years.

I had a newborn baby when military operation took place in village. My husband was not around as he had gone to Butwal town three days ago. It was a fresh winter early morning, when I saw hundreds of royal army soldiers surrounding main village. My neighbours had told me not to open the door and to be inside home. They were interrogating people randomly. A young soldier had knocked on my door too and asked a few questions. I did not answer since I did not understand his language. I only knew Kham language and never spoke Nepali before in my life. As he saw my newborn baby, he left without further interrogation. The army stayed here for many weeks, camping in the High school. They had also interrogated my mothers to get to know my father's whereabouts since he was deputy chief of village *Panchayat* council. Hundreds of villagers had fled from village and went to safer places including my father. I got to know in between that they had arrested many persons for allegedly supporting the communist party's call to boycott national elections. Those days it was very unsafe to go out even in the daytime. So I did not go out anywhere till my husband arrived from the town.

Later I came to know that security forces had looted gold & cash and had beaten up even old people. Dozens of women were molested and raped. Those days, there was not a single household in the whole of Thabang VDC where they had not gone to search and interrogate. Ram Kumar Budha Magar and his supporters were responsible for particularly naming communist families where security forces made out loot and make their house just like debris.

My father was also named in sedition case including many who had defied king's despotic rule. It was only after that incident did I got to know about the political situation of country. I had not seen the king and didn't know who he was. This memories of state brutality had a long lasting impact on me and over the years, what I realise is this: *Junai jogi aaye pani kannai chireko* [all rulers (governments) are alike]. Even nothing has changed after the multi-party democracy replaced the *Panchayat* regime in 1990s.

Kishore Budha Magar, my only son was five years old when my husband married another woman from a nearby village of Uwa. My parents had objected about his second marriage therefore he just eloped with her one day without closing down even chemist shop. Those days, it was common for men to marry twice or thrice and it was a socially accepted practice. Later I came to know that he had left for the Kalo Pahar with his second wife.

After a period of many months after finding no chance of his arrival, I went to India in search of him. Those days, hundreds of villagers used to go in search of jobs. When I located my husband with the help of my kinsman, he was very reluctant either to accept or give divorce. So after a month, I returned home. My father was very shocked and angry at my husband He fell ill and soon passed away in 1984. He was only 51 years old.

At that point in my life, my mother and relatives had asked me to remarry but I was reluctant to do so. I had a son and it looked difficult to find a man who would have accepted me with my son. Our Society was very conservative those days but my mother stood by my decision. All the family land was in my mother's name and I was given a plot of land and settled in brother's house, which remained my only source of livelihood. My mother also believed that everyone should get land irrespective of their gender.

Time passed by nurturing my only son and taking care of brother's family. When the *Bahudal* system was established in 1990, a procession was organised in our village. Thousands of villagers including people from adjoining villages were chanting slogans in praise of multi-party democracy and revolution. The procession went around in the all wards of village which was led by students and teachers of the High School. My brother Bhatt too was seen raising slogans. The procession concluded in the evening in a big gathering near my house and speeches continued until late in night. A group of women led by Samjhana Gharti Magar, and Lali Roka Magar sung many progressive songs.

It was the end of 1991 and election was supposed to held in few weeks. My brother had told me that we have to support

Barman Budha Magar in the election. Those days many cultural programs were organised in High School. I had also attended cultural programs in the High school where students performed songs and plays. My brother too was very active in supporting cultural events. Many young girls and boys who were studying in the school were part of the cultural team. The cultural team used to start the program by a welcome song and entertained us by singing revolutionary songs. I do not remember those songs exactly but these songs give us a message that we should get ready to fight against the exploitative tyrannical forces and the police/army who constituted the *Rajyasatta* (state power). The *Shosak/ shamant* (exploiter/ feudal landlord) in our context was the Jumleni family and their chief Ramkumar Budha. They were very rich and known as big oppressor of region.

The whole village had supported Barman Budha Magar and only few casted votes in his opposition. The opposition was constituted naturally by the gang of the Jumleni family and their supporters. Barman won the parliamentary elections and a victory torchlight procession was organised. To celebrate this occasion, Lali Roka had asked me to join the food festival where buffalo meat was cooked.

The victory of Barman Budha was just a beginning and from then on a series of political meetings and cultural programmes followed. Almost everyone in the whole of Rolpa and Rukum knew about the revolutionary enthusiasm of Thabang. This resulted in police repression and from then on we used to hear stories of police atrocities in neighbouring villages like in Uwa, Mirul, Mahat, Jelbang and Seram. My elder brother was quite active in peasant organization. He would often tell us that about difficult task pertaining party's responsibilities. Those days, many senior Maoist leaders like Ram Bahadur Thapa alias Comrade Badal and Dr. Baburam Bhattarai visited village without letting us know who they were.

People used to tell us that the Maoist party had started People's War. The apple nursery of the Jumleni family was attacked by the one night. Thereafter, police repression was organised in a manner similar to the 1980s army operation. In the name of interrogation, they stole our belongings. We were not allowed to go out of our homes after five in the evening. In between, my brother's wife started to quarrel with me and my brother was also reluctant to let me live with them. Then I decided to live separately from them. My mother rescued me and we came to live in our [present] house. Since land was in my mother's name, my brother's wife could not suppress me anymore.

It was one afternoon of January, 1997 when I was having some discussion with a relative near health post. My friend Lali Roka was arrested by police when she was giving polio drops to children. It happened in my presence and we were helpless. At that time, she was working as a health assistant in the VDC health post. We could hear her voice on the day of her martyrdom. She was beaten up severely and raped by many for two days continually in police post. She was shot dead and hung along with Dilman Roka Magar upside down near Thabang River. Two years ago, western lady had asked me what Lali's fault was. I told her categorically;

> *Look, she was not at any fault at all. She was working in a women's organisation and mobilising them to unite and oppose the society's ill-treatment of women, opposing polygamy,* ***jari***[3] *and wife-beating. The police informers gave information about her activities and involvement in the party work. She was not very educated but a very good human being.*

She and Dilman were the first martyrs of our village. In retaliation, the Maoist guerrillas annihilated Muley Roka Magar and

3 A practice in Nepali hills by which a man takes away another's wife by paying him compensation for the loss of his 'property'.

some of his associates after three months of their murder. Before that, the party had not killed any police informer of the village. Muley was one who had behind these killing and was given also police security in the village. The police atrocities rose in unprecedented ways thereafter and hundreds of villagers (mostly men) became underground including brother. In the meantime, I sent my son to a relative's home in Dang district so that he did not get into trouble.

I faced one of the biggest troubles of my life in the month of *Sawan*[4] in 1997. Since my brother was not in village and was absconding from many months, I was worried as to who will plough the land. I knew one woman, Rammaya Budha Magar of Khairbang village, who herself ploughed her land for some years. It was difficult to find any men except very old men. So many women were forced to do this work by themselves. Then we held a small meeting of women and shared stories from other villages where many peasant women were forced to plough the land a few years ago during years of police repression. It was customary that women would take care of household jobs besides working in the fields, while ploughing and putting seeds were considered a sin if performed by women. At this meeting, Rammaya told that if women could take up guns, why then can't we plough our land. It was absolutely true because many young girls of our village had joined Maoist guerrilla squads.

Then, that year, I along with my brother's wife ploughed our land. It was very difficult as we had never done it. It is a very tough job but over the years it turned out to be fruitful. Not only ploughing but also that year, though a few did other "manly" jobs such as carpentry, and woodcutting. Now for last ten years, I am not dependent on any man but plough land myself.

---

4 According to English calendar the Sawan include month of July and August.

I think it was the end of 1999. The Maoist guerrillas used to come at night some times and we used give them shelter in my home. They used to tell us that they were fighting for the revolution. I don't know what a revolution is if you ask me. But it has something to do with the advancement of the country and the village. This is what the guerrillas said in their conversations with us. After some time, the guerrillas used to come in large numbers. One day, I had gone into the jungle to look after sheep and collect woods. There I met Sahansila[5], Roopsari Pariyar[6] and other from our village as well as my brother. They asked me about the condition of the village and police activities. The same night the guerrillas had attacked village police post. We heard firing at midnight for a few hours. In the morning, somebody informed that the police post had been destroyed by the Maoists and police had fled. It was true and in the afternoon hundreds guerrillas converged in village. We were happy that at least the police will be no more to oppress us now. Some days later, many of the absconding men of village returned home.

The royal army arrived in February of 2002 and made a camp in Taligha and stayed there for nearly a month. At that time, I along with my mother went to the jungle with hundreds of people. During this period, army arrested many young girls of village. Katkari Roka Magar and Jyoti Ghari Magar, two of cultural activists

5 She was a member of guerrilla squad (and later in PLA) died in 2004 in Siraha district.

6 One of first Dalit girl of Thabang VDC who had joined the PLA on 13 February, 2002. She was platoon commander in the PLA. She lost her left leg in second Khara battle in April, 2005. She married a fellow PLA combatant from Tharu community and till recently she was living at a camp of *Salim Mandal* Memorial Brigade of Fourth Division of People's Liberation Army located in Jhyaltungdanda. Interview, Roopsari Pariyar, 3 February, 2012, Jhyaltungdanda camp.

of village were tortured for weeks by security forces and were later killed. A village squad gave security to us. Many pregnant women had given birth to their children in that period. When the army left village, they had looted houses, destroyed VDC building and burnt many houses including mine too.

After this incident, the village was calm for some years. After this, hundreds of PLA combatants used to stay in the village. At the founding of the Thabang Special District in February 2003, my mother was felicitated and honoured for giving me an equal share in family property. Many dozens of parents of region were honoured that day who had given their daughters equal share in paternal property. Women cannot claim a share in the paternal property once they get married. I too had received a *lalpurja* (*Jansatta* order) recognizing my share of land but, I lost it same year during a security attack in village.

When Thabang special district government was functioning here, our village people's government too was running smoothly. At times, I used to join the people's court proceedings. Most cases usually pertained to quarrel between husband and wife. One of my neighbour's daughters was married at age of sixteen year. When the *Jansatta* came to know of it, both the boy and the girl were summoned. We all were present there. My brother, a member of people's court proceeding told a large gathering in VDC office ground that the marriageable age for boys was 22 and for girls it was 20 years. Both were assigned to serve two months of community service to work in mess run for PLA combatants by giving them a labour punishment.

My brother was also active in the *Jansatta* and in 2005; he was nominated as a chief of Thabang *ga-ja-sa*. They ran industry, registered land, built school and also had built a commune in Rachibang village. I along with our group of villagers had gone to build martyr road. Drinking liquor was restricted at that time. If anybody was found drunk, he would face strong action from the people's government. In my view, it is wrong that men have the right to marry two wives. The village people's government made a ban on polyandry practice. This was the most important change the *Jansatta* had introduced [but this practice is reappearing in the last few years since 2008 after the party stopped running its government]. They had also prohibited *jari* and punished those who practised it.

I don't know much about women's liberation since I don't know how to read and write. But one thing I knew was that it was far better to be in PLA and to be a part of the advancement of the people and the country than to be trapped in prostitution rackets in the brothels of India because of poverty. Many girls of Thabang became part of the militia and married within the party sometimes inter-caste marriage with Tharus, Gurungs, Tamangs and with Chettri which one could hardly imagine before Maoist movement.

My mother passed away in 2009. After her demise, my elder brother Satya Roka, a known Maoist leader and ex-chief of *Jansatta* started saying around that;

> *I would not get any paternal property and land for being a woman and a daughter in the family. Though he is my brother, how cheap could he be? He hadn't changed after being active with the party for so long.*

Just some days ago, I fought with him one whole night. He says that he won't recognise the Thabang Special District government order which had recognised mother's land share in my name. He told me that even the government will not listen to me since the decision of the *Jansatta* is not considered legal according to present law. I have asked party activists to solve my case. Some have objected to his wrongdoing, but he is not ready to give me in writing that I own the land. We stopped speaking to each other since then. It remains unsettled.

2. JOURNEY OF A WOMEN MILITIA COMMANDER

Name: Deumaya Budha Magar

Age: 39 years

Education: Literate

Profession: Ex-militia commander & Housewife

Born in *Thula Gaon* in 1973, my family could grow food for 9 to 10 months with all our efforts. My father was a retired Indian Army pensioner and had two wives. After failing to get children from first wife, he married my mother through which I and my brother were born.

My parents did not send me to school. At the age of 18 years, I joined an adult school in 1991 which was run by a NGO. Many girls of my age group had joined that school but it was run for a brief period. Soon it was closed off since its organisers were involved in spying for the district administration about the political activities in our village. It was at that time when Barman Budha Magar had won election. Those days, many cultural programs were held in village and we also joined those programs. In mid 1992, the *Akhil Nepal Mahila Sangh* (All Nepal Women's Association) had opened night classes exclusively for women in village and I joined it. Lali Didi [Lali Roka Magar] had initiated this campaign and we were taught sometimes by people of our age and sometimes elderly party activists. It was fun those days. In every class, we would perform some folk songs which typically narrated a peasant's worry about harvest and oppression face from landlords, police and anti-social elements. Initially I did not understand those things. It was later only by learning about 1981's military operation in Thabang, I could understand.[7]

7 During this incident, I lived in Dehradoon, where my father was posted in the Gurkha Regiment battalion. It was only 1984, that I returned to village.

(Deumaya Budha Magar with daughter of building of new house)

Our village was the centre of all political activities in Rolpa district. I was only twenty years old when I got attracted to cultural activities in village. In early 1993, a cultural campaign were organised by the SJM. Samjhana Gharti Magar, my friend of night classes had asked me to come with her. Although, I was reluctant to join but she convinced me. My father permitted me to go since many girls of my age were also going. We were a cultural group 38 members led by Santosh *dai* [Santosh Budha Magar] and Manohar *dai* [Manohar Budha Magar] led us in this travelling mission to dozens of villages. At that time, we had visited entire northern and eastern parts of Rolpa. We used to walk in the daytime to reach the village and organised cultural programs during the night. This was the time when the Koirala government was suppressing and killing people on everyday basis in region. So we were also blocked from holding programs in many villages by the Nepali Congress supporters. Our last program at the end of the campaign was in Libang district headquarters. By this time, our group grew to a large collective of two hundred. However, our way was blocked by the police and vigilante from Nepali Congress party. The police had charged batons on us but soon they stopped when hundreds of villagers gathered and rescued us. Only then did the police allow us to enter district headquarter and a cultural program was held attended by five thousand villagers from the surrounding areas of Libang. We had sung a song on Peruvian revolution which depicts anti-imperialist resistance movement waged by the Peruvian Communists against America.

> ***O Yankee go home, dirty Yankee go home*** *[O Yankee go home, dirty Yankee go home]*
>
> ***Hamro rato jhanda Peru ma phar pharaunde cha*** *[Our red flag is fluttering in Peru]*

Through this cultural campaign, I could understand that Nepali Congress and police is our enemy and they want to suppress the poor. And I began to relate many incidents in our village where local police misbehaved to peasantry on an everyday basis. It was towards end of 1993 that I associated with party's women's organisation with a view that it would be good for me and my family. Women in Thabang were culturally oppressed and victims of orthodox traditions. Women were only confined to household. She would not decide for her own but men took every decision. The practice like polyandry was prevalent and men were allowed to have more than one wife at same time whereas women would never dare to think about this. By being in the women's organisation, we stood against all this.

Gradually, I got to know that my father was also a party supporter which enabled me to get more freedom in organising women's movement. This was in early 1995 when the party had organised a series of cultural campaigns from *Sija* to *Jansewa*. Our organisational leader was Lali Didi. I and Samjhana Gharti from our ward worked together in the *Jansewa* campaign by visiting different hamlets and build women's organisations, do wall-paintings and distribute leaflets. We would give classes to women and tell them to stand together to fight against patriarchal values which are rooted in our society. We have also formed the *Aama Sangathan* (mother's organisation). The mothers association played vital role in collecting money and grain for campaign. It was during this time, Lali Didi gave me party membership and soon after I was nominated as president of women organization of ward-4 Jurbang village committee.

As our campaigns advanced, the police repression on our activities also increased. On an everyday basis, we used to listen to stories of police atrocities in nearby villages. Hundreds of false cases were registered against many people. Our party evaluated this situation and concluded that armed struggle was the need of that time to counter state repression.

On 12 February, 1996 the night before People's War broke, we did a wall-painting in Barman Roka's house. Barman Roka Magar was a supporter of the Jumleni family and a police informer too. He was also known to be a ringleader of gang led by Ram Kumar Budha Magar. On the next day, nobody knew that we had done the wall-painting in Barman's house. The next evening, the women & youth organisation had organised a torchlight procession and I along with nearly three dozen women joined this demonstration from our ward. After some days, I too was part of the group that destroyed the apple nursery of the Jumleni family.

Soon the police started to register criminal cases against many people. On 18 January, 1997, Lali was murdered by the police along with another comrade Dilman. This was the beginning of my underground life including my father. We left our house of *Thula Gaon* and shifted in a far away forest of Dullidanda village. The murder of Lali was major event since she was the district-level woman leader, known and respected in Rolpa. For many of my generation's political activists, she was a torchbearer.

Till 1999, our women's organisation was expanded in the entire VDC. One day, we seven women activists were called by party area committee to attend a political training programme in the Jaljala Mountain. The party committee of village had formed a women militia group of seven of us and I was nominated its commander. Pawan Roka Magar, a member of village squad gave us initial level of military training. Initially, we had no modern weapon except two homemade guns but had sticks, hammers, cycle chains and dozens of *Khukhri*. The women militia's task was to provide security to meetings and programs and work as couriers. Our work was quite different from squad who were involved in guerrilla attack on police and sabotage actions. Sometimes, while attacking anti-social elements (i.e., rapists, moneylenders and thieves) our militia also took part with fighting squad.

Some in our group were nominal literate; however, a recurrent problem was the dependence on a few literate members every time a party circular or secret letter arrived. To solve this issue, the party began adult education classes for us. Samjhana and Chiring Roka Magar were initially assigned as our teachers and later many more taught us. This adult education programme helped many of women guerrillas who could read and write because of the party's adult education program intertwined with political-military training during these years.

Soon after our squad's action against police informers, a heavy police crackdown ensued by mobilizing a 'Search and Destroy Operation' in Rolpa. During this operation, many of our supporters were killed and many more were detained for many months in police custody. At this point, the party asked us to go underground, so we more than 86 comrades went underground including my father. The police had selectively made search warrant against underground political activists and vandalized my house as well. My 62 year old mother was severely beaten up by dragging her out of house and taken to the police station. My younger brother who was just twelve years old was also beaten up. She was released from police custody after nine days through intervention by a Nepali Congress supporter and my neighbouring uncle. I could not step inside the village for nearly two years after that incident took place. At this time between 1998 and 1999, the village guerrilla squad carried out two ambushes and one mini raid on the police search campaigns in Dishari forest and Bibang village. At this time, our women militia also participated along with guerrilla squad to collect weapons in region by a campaign known as *Sak Abhiyan*.

Until now, a large gathering of police force was stationed in region with its locus at Jelbang Police Base Camp from where they were conducting regular counter insurgency campaigns. We attacked Jelbang post in one moon light of 2 May, 1999 which was located along with other two police posts of Rulbang and Narbang. We with a total force of 116 including 29 women assembled in a Jaljala Mountain cave and our commander was Pasang. They were more than 56 armed policemen led by an Inspector with sophisticated weapons whereas we had some rifles, homemade twelve bore guns and many types of explosives. The hunting police dogs had smelt our activities from a distance and began barking. But we managed to destroy Jelbang police camp completely by killing three policemen and injuring 16 in this attack. This was my first and only experience in frontal battle with the police.

Our successful attack made a made local police fearful and for a time being stopped search operations. This was a period when our Rolpa district committee decided to build base areas following the central plan of the party. At this time, our guerrilla squads had also expanded in quite a considerable manner and formation platoon level force was in progress. This was also a time when a woman journalist from America had visited Thabang.[8] We were told that she is a member of the Revolutionary Communist Party of America and she has come to meet us. Our militia provided security cover to her visit in region. This made us proud that Nepali revolution had attracted worldwide attention.

Then in July 1999, Rolpa district committee of women's organisation deputed me to Pyuthan district along with Samjhana. The area of Puja VDC, we were assigned was a propaganda zones dominantly with the Magar population. This region was not a guerrilla zone like Thabang but we had many supporters there. The peasantry of the VDC were heavily oppressed by Chhetri landlords who supported ruling Nepali Congress party. We had to start building the party organisation amid insecurity but this village was relatively free from police repression. After eight months of political work, we were successful in building village & ward committees of peasant and women's organisations.

It was early months of 2000 year when our party concluded that the task of building base areas was gaining new heights. Our party had declared formation of first district level people's government in Rukum and people's army had also developed greatly. At that time, we planned a mass action against a landlord of Chettri community. He was also a district level leader of Nepali Congress in Pyuthan. He was not only known among villagers as a moneylender but also responsible for suicide of a Chettri woman who he exploited sexually and made pregnant. A month before this attack, we had formed a fighting squad in Puja VDC. The squad along with hundreds of villagers attacked his house and burnt down hundreds of bond paper. All of his cash and gold were seized by guerrilla squad. We detained him under our custody and

8 Referring to a left wing American journalist Li Onesto whose was given excess freely by CPN (M) leadership. She has reported widely about Nepal's Maoist movement by numerous reports and a book.

was made public next day in the presence of hundreds of people. His crimes were put before the public. People hated him and they wanted to kill him. His face was blackened and he was paraded on a donkey with a placard saying, "I am a moneylender and a notorious rapist. Any punishment by people would be accepted by me." This was first guerrilla action in region and it made us popular in village. We stayed in Puja VDC till July 2001 and by this time all of mass organisations were formed in entire VDC.

This was time in middle of year in 2001 when base area was established in Rolpa and Rukum in and a new king was crowned in country after a palace massacre. It was early July 2001, I came back to Thabang to visit sick mother. She was very ill since the police torture which put her into a state of paralysis. She died after three days of my arrival. This made my father too fell ill. The crisis in family made a first ever practical helpless situation to what to do. I asked the party organisation, what should be my duty? How was I to continue to do party work? Who will take care of my sick father? The area party leadership could not answer satisfactorily, and none could convince me. They told me that I have to leave everything to accomplish the party mission. I was very uneasy with their attitude, especially on the question of caring my sick father who had given many years to the party. I decided to stay at home.

At that point, *Jansatta* was just taking shape in Thabang. I thought that I could be active in Thabang itself, at least until my father recovered. It was time when the first peace talk ended unsuccessfully and the RNA was mobilized to fight us. At this juncture, district women's organisation had convened a meeting in Thabang on September 2002. I met Samjhana there and shared my thoughts that why the party organisation did not take my questions seriously. Her answer could not convince me that I should return again as fulltime activist since nobody was there to keep an eye on my father.

My political activism ended with father's death in March, 2003. It made me totally helpless since nobody was around me with whom

I could share my thoughts and feelings. I ploughed land this year with by help of my younger brother. Until this time, I was unmarried since I believed that marriage led to limit women freedom by containing herself in household work. Lali *Didi* used to tell us "don't marry early, first work for revolution". I followed what Lali *Didi* had taught me. I had realised it that why women in Thabang are oppressed because they marry really early, even before turning 18 years. During our night classes, we were made to understand that woman's life ends when she marries. Once she gets married, she will have kids that become an obstacle to achieve our goal. Even Lali *Didi* was unmarried when she was killed at the age of 33 years.

Finally at the age of 33, I got married in 2004. My husband is a labourer and worked in India for twelve years. We have a one & half year old daughter and a 3 year old son. We are the toiling masses and to fulfil our goals, we worked for the party. However, the Maoist movement was ruined at the later stage. This whole notion of the republic was confusing since we have not fought for a constituent assembly but for goal of revolution.

3. A DALIT PERSPECTIVE OF PEOPLE'S WAR

Name: Dhan Bahadur Nepali

Age: 52 years

Education: class 8th (incomplete)

Profession: wage labour & tailoring

I was born in 1960 in a tailoring family. Our house was in situated in Dalit ward (ward-5) of Thabang VDC. I was eldest one in a family of five sibling brothers and sisters. As per Hindu social order, I was born in a Dalit family and country's social order as per law of *Muluki Ain* described that, I am from Damai caste. My father performed traditional occupation of Damai caste that is becoming *Bist* through a patron-client Jajmani relationship to Magar families. He was fine tailor master who would also perform music at ceremonies on birth, marriage and death. We were not landless but the land he owned barely produced food for even three months. This situation remains the same even now. From very childhood, I began working as a farm labour of various kinds to rich Magar household. I was seventeen year old only when poor economic condition forced me to leave school in 1986 without even completing 8th class.

(Dhan Bahadur Nepali (right) with younger brother at their house, Thula Gaon)

Soon after, I went to Kalo Pahar and worked in Kannur district under a shopkeeper who had a business of collecting herbs. One night, the contractor and his men came to collect the herbs. They abused supervisor of our group who were responsible for arranging food and lodging for us. They blindfolded us and threw mercilessly into snow-covered jungle. They put all our utensils, pots and stoves in a bag and threatened us with dire consequences unless we left immediately. Then we somehow managed to get back home after doing some petty jobs in Shimla city. Unable to get another job, I returned to village after six months. I began to render help to my parents in tailoring work and started looking after family.

It was beginning year of after arrival of multi-party democracy in country. While as a child I was attracted to communist politics especially of their standing for truth and their take against exploitation. Gradually I became an activist of the peasant association and activist of the SJM. As my political participation grew after this period, I was interested to work for empowerment of Dalit community. As a child, I had observed that caste hierarchies in Thabang were very rigid and the practice of untouchability was very widespread. It was reason that while studying in class 6th, I was attracted to the communist politics. I have many of childhood memories of Magar people discriminating the Dalits on an everyday basis. For instance, if a Magar sees a Dalit person on his way towards public tap, he would start verbally abusing him and would ask to go away. The Dalits had to step outside small footpath while any Magar passed by.

I was elected the president of the district committee of the *Dalit Mukti Morcha* (Dalit Liberation Front) of Rolpa district in 1992. I worked with organization for two years and had to move from village to village in the whole district. With commencement of Dasain festival that year, we decided to hold *Bhailo* programs by propagating villagers against caste discrimination. A cultural team of 25 Dalit youth (including seven women activists) was formed in my leadership. This team used to perform progressive songs and dance from one village to the other. I remember some lines of a popular song team had performed;

> ***Manche manche auta ho.....sheep chal cha*** *[all human are equal... our skills is utilized]*
>
> ***Tar pani kin hamro paani chaldaina*** *[Why our water is not accepted]*

We had decided that we will forcefully enter Magar households during the Bhailo performance. However, if Magar abuse and try to beat us up, then we would resist it. During these five days of cultural campaign, we entered in Magar households located in Thula Gaon, Jurbang, Jhakkebang and Maranthan.[9] There was some resistance from the older generation but not of a violent kind. A majority of the Magar youth had supported our effort but they did not have courage to come out publicly by fearing family backlash.

This entire event had made a big impact region and adjoining VDCs. This made others to follow and anti-caste campaigns were held in other parts of Rolpa. The anxiety among the older Magar generation was later reflected in local party committee meeting of village. I was called as "an anarchist" Dalit leader but as many leading Magar activists of district committee stand with me. Tejman Gharti Magar alias 'Dirgh'[10] sent me words of appreciation from Libang through a villager. Eventually, I was awarded the Party[11] membership in mid 1993. From then on, I was called "Comrade Ranko". In Kham language, *Ranko* stand for fire. The rural class struggle in 1994 made another occasion for us to convene anti-caste agitation along program taken by the SJM.

Just before beginning of People's War, a village party committee meeting was organized in Phuntibang village's Chelbhatebang forest and fifteen of Dalit activists had participated. In 1997, I reorganized district committee of dalit front in a view to recruiting Dalit youths for guerrilla movement. With course of movement I was assigned responsibilities in area level of the party committees from 1999. This was a time when the party had initiated forming a committee of activists whose name was not warranted in police list.

9 These four villages cover three fourth territory of Thabang VDC.

10 Dirgh was the highest ranking leaders from Thabang who died during People's War. He was a member of advisory board to CPN (M)'s central committee and also elected first chief of Thabang Special District People's Government.

11 Then the party was called CPN (Unity Centre).

With the establishing of village *Jansatta* and subsequently developed as Thabang special district, we held a Dalit conference in 2003. After Dalit conference, we organized a program of forcefully entering Magar households in Chittibang village. Comparing to entire village, village of Chittibang had been known as a centre of hostility against Dalits in whole region. It was because this village was established by Roka Magar priests who have been hereditary priests of the Barah Gods Temple situated on Jaljala Mountain. With a hundred Dalit activists holding flags in our hands, we left for Chittibang in a procession raising slogans against Brahmanical system and untouchability. After reaching there, we were surprised to see that all the houses were empty as everybody ran away to nearby mountain after locking their houses.

Few months later, we again planned such program in Chittibang. Taking a lesson from earlier embarrassed situation, party's special district committee, and village *Jansatta* supervised this program. We had organized a convention in playground of martyr's school which was a five minute walk from Chittibang village. A majority of 31 Magar families[12] attended this convention where Dalit activists performed progressive songs opposing caste discrimination followed by Magar and Dalit activists to share their life experiences by relating politics of People's War. A food party was held in the middle of convention in which Magars ate food served by us. It was the first such event in my life when the Magars shared tea, lunch and water. It was also a breakthrough from

12 This village comprised of 34 Magar families only. At present, [while conducting fieldwork of last phase in 2012], remnants of untouchability do exist in this village. Though, I can enter any Magar household and their kitchen and they do offer me food and a place to rest. They respect me for being a Maoist leader but not as a Dalit. Still, they would not treat other Dalits as same way as me.

their earlier attitude of boycotting such programs. Eventually, it prompted special district's people's government to declare Thabang as an untouchability free village.

The decade year old armed struggle made a situation for villagers to fight enemy collectively. When security army operations conducted in village, the entire village would relocates themselves to jungles. This made a gradual weakening of untouchability, as people were forced by situation. Very few houses had food, so whichever household had food would have to share it with others, whether it was a Dalit, or Magar or any other caste. Thus survival became more important than caste boundaries during war and strengthened feeling of unity and solidarity amongst us.

I had participated in the Maoist movement as a full time activist but saw many problems while visiting home. My family was living a miserable life as they neither had enough food nor even proper clothes and sleepers. The conditions at home become worse in March, 2001 when security forces burnt down and destroyed my only house along with more than two dozen other households. For a whole year, my family was begging for shelter and food from one place to another but comrades did not take our issue seriously. The harsh material condition of family made me utter helplessness. I have time and again put forth family's miserable condition to concerned party committees but it was not dealt seriously. This was not only my case, but of many activists coming from the poor peasant background from upper to lower castes. The leaders urged that this wasn't the time to raise such issues and told that once we capture state power, these issues could be solved accordingly.

My inner struggle on this issue was growing day by day which finally resulted in my resignation from the party organization in July 2005. It was last phase of People's War and I went to abroad for employment within a year by arranging a loan of 1.5 lakh rupees. A local party leader named Ruz Bahadur Roka alias 'Regan' gave me three-fourth amount of loan on "an interest of 5 rupees per hundred". The interest rate was very exorbitant and quite contrary to *Jansatta* policy which had set a maximum of two rupees per hundred for loan on interest. I borrowed remaining amount from a relative living in Kankri VDC without any interest.

I went to Malaysia and stayed for nearly five years. However, I could not overcome my problems even there. The medical test conducted by the overseas company declared me as medically unfit and the company manager snatched away my three months salary. After realizing that I won't be able to pay back my heavy debt back home, I ran away one day from company's residential settlement. I was thereafter living in Malaysia as an illegal resident for around four years. I was employed by a local poultry farm but my earnings were not adequate to get me even enough food. This forced me to take up a security watchman's job. I was able to return Nepal by the end of 2011.The major portion of the debt still remains due. Though I have paid back the money I owed to my relative, I could not paid back debt of Maoist leader. With the yearly interest of 5 rupees my debt amount now comes around 4 lakh rupees. I have frequently pleaded to him that I will soon pay back his debt. But Regan and his loyalists have threatened me time and again by publicly announcing that if I would not pay back my debt, then they would forcibly capture my land and household property. They are threatening me on a daily basis and I can only plead to them to show some mercy after my hardship in Malaysia. The entire Thabang village has been ruled over by rich Magar families. Earlier, Barman Budha Magar ruled over putting a Communist mask and now Regan or likes are ruling by making Thabang as their fiefdom.

However, I was not only person who deserted movement in middle but there were a large chunk that had left movement for other reasons. The number of these youth rose very high by

2001 during First Peace Talks between the government and the Maoist. Though people went in foreign but there numbers were approximately five to eight people per year. But in the According to my records, a minimum of 100 youth from Thabang VDC went for foreign employment. Most of these youths were either active in village squads, militia or local party committees. The reason for this sudden rise of youth fleeing village was based on a fear that "to save one's life is more important than being end up being a Maoist guerrilla".

We were taught by our leaders that Marxism is a science and according to the laws of this science we have to see the essence behind the thought. Without the laws of the science of Marxism, it is impossible to understand Thabang. The village has a semi-feudal social base and this is a problem from our past. For instance, the leaders and activists made speeches about revolution. They were supposed to establish the politico-ideological line of People's War among people by becoming role model. At the same time, the same leaders had accumulated wealth and doing money lending business on heavy interest rate. In the early days of Maoist movement, we had never observed it. Thabang saw a practice of fully developed money lending activities from a period between 2001 and 2003. It is ironical that our party had punished many such moneylenders in the past and it was against policies of People's War. But many moneylenders were taking birth within our own rank and file.

Most of this leadership came from a rich background comparing activists like us from lower committees. In context of Thabang, rich means who can get sufficient food for a year and have some surplus as a bank balance. They constitute around on fourth of the families in Thabang and belong to the Magar communities. Some other Magar activist families produced food for six to eight months. However, around ninety percent of the Dalit activists did not produce food for even three months.

Even though I may be targeted to put this bitter truth but their hypocrisies should be exposed. This is why the co-operatives and bank could not be run properly during the *Jansatta* period. We live in *jhupdi* (hut made of wood), but they live in houses made of *dhunge ghar* (stone and cemented houses) and now they are making buildings. Tomorrow, when vehicles start plying here in Thabang, they would buy buses, jeeps, cars and will make money out of this. The situation today is that most of the leading Maoist activists have pilfered lakhs of rupees from the budget passed by the government and projects run by many NGOs. By making money out of this, some have bought tractors and one of them bought a truck as well. For instance, a former village *Jansatta* chief Bar Prasad Gharti Magar alias Inkar bought a tractor and a truck soon after first Constituent Assembly elections in 2008.

There was a large participation of Dalits in Maoist government on both level of Thabang special district government and village level. But the Dalits generally did not get leadership positions in the *Jansatta* committees but always led by the Magars. It was because, we have a practice of the *Bist kamaune* which make us to follow traditional jobs as assigned by *Muluki Ain*. Due to this, the Magars have generally treat us in lower order and like '*das sarah bujhne*' (literally seen as slaves).

This was the primary contradiction between us. For instance, we (Dalits) do not have enough food to eat and have no other economic resources except of caste occupation. At the same time, the party leaders' households are wealthy and have enough food for a year apart from grain collection. During any natural calamity, they sell us grains at high prices and lend us money on high interest rate. There are only five dalit household in Thabang who hold sound financial condition since their family member have jobs in the foreign army. The remaining 95 percent of the Dalits depended on their traditional jobs.

Land distribution was a central issue which often led to various debates in the *Jansatta* period in Thabang village. In those days, we debated in the party classes the question of carrying out revolutionary land reforms once after Thabang Special District was established. I argued many times in the party meetings that those whose (rich and middle peasants) lands were not used for growing any crop and remained unused for many years should be distributed to the poor peasants who hardly produce sufficient food. By distributing this unused land through the policy of land ceiling, we could provide land to poor peasants who usually own small unfertile plots. In this manner, our party could serve the masses well and it would have been easy to mobilize them in support of struggle for a longer period.

However, it was never done since our party had a vague understanding on this question from the very beginning of People's War. The first *Jansatta* document published by the party in 1999 does mention that a revolutionary land reform would be implemented in hill region. However, later this policy was amended by maintaining in other documents that it was only in Tarai region where revolutionary land distribution would be carried out. In the hilly regions, focus was to be on a co-operative system of agriculture. The village *Jansatta* job was only to carry out registration of land and moveable property. The rich and the upper middle peasants who owned large plots of land were not "disturbed". The reason was also that these same rich-upper middle peasant classes constituted the party leadership (i.e. regional and central level) and hence any discussion on radical land reform was kept aside.

There is only one case when this question was dealt but with a "public interest". For example, we can take the case of building martyrs School in 2003. The land for school was seized forcefully by the village *Jansatta and* it belonged to most notable communist leader Barman Budha Magar's family. Initially Ganesh Budha, an eldest son Barman Budha Magar's who was in the *Jansatta* committee had resisted this plan. This plot was part of community land located in Bibang village which was illegally acquired by Barman Budha during his tenure as *Mukhiya* in 1974.

Moreover, the concept of collectivization, co-operative industry and commune was promoted without redistribution of land which failed miserably. The main reason behind its failure was related to vague policy of the party. Added to this was the opportunistic line of rank and file of leadership as they owned a major portion of land and household property of Thabang. These failed experiments were directly linked to petty bourgeois class nature of central leadership of People's War.

Other than this issue some problems existed in cultural matters, such as question related to religion, and prohibition of child marriage. During tenure of Barprasad Gharti Magar as a chief of village *Jansatta,* an explosion took place outside his home in November 2005, which also happened to be a militia post. At that time he was heading a committee to investigate many cases of underage love marriages held recently in village. According to the Maoist policy, we had prohibited underage marriages and it was mandatory for bridegrooms to write to the *Jansatta* committee for getting married. After this explosion, many youths summoned and some were detained by militia for a week. It was found out during investigations that bomb explosion was outcome of handling of marriages with a bureaucratic way by party leadership.

The celebration of Bhume festival in 2002 made another issue on this relation. The village *Jansatta* committee had formed a committee to look into modification of age old orthodox practices of animal sacrifice with prayer to the Barah god. The animal sacrifice was so widespread that festival used to become a site of 'slaughter house'. We modified this sacrifice by putting a limit per person without replacing the prayers practice. The villagers objected on our modification efforts by abusing us and fierce reaction. Gradually, we were able to calm down their anger and they accepted our efforts of reforming festival.

The village *Jansatta* committee was qualitatively different and progressive compared to village administration committee of *Panchayat* and multi-party democracy period. When the *Jansatta* was running the village, nobody dared to beat anybody or used to steal things from others. At that time, women used to travel at night and felt safe and nobody would dare to abuse them. The practice of gambling and drinking was put in controlled and villagers felt empowered. This could be said the achievement of the *Jansatta* in my view.

4. A TEACHER IN THE PEOPLE'S WAR

Name: Man Prasad Budha Magar
Age: 44 years
Education: SLC
Profession: former teacher

I was born in main village of Thabang VDC in 1968. We have a family of five members with my two brothers and the parents. Since there no other female member other than our mother in the house, we used to do all the household tasks on our own. We were a self reliant peasant family, with food for the whole year produced and we also did animal husbandry, keeping dozens of cow and sheep. After managing food requirements for a whole year, my parents used to sell one or two *muri*[13] of maize crop. My father was a *Jaysi* (astrologer) and had received elementary education in night school run in village during 1959-60. He also knew the old Magar script dialect known as *Mangre*. During those days, those who knew *Jaysi* used to be much respected as a knowledgeable person in the village and worked as an assistant of shaman.

13 A measurement of grain in Nepal.

(Man Prasad Pun with his family, Dullidanda village)

As a child, I remained shepherd for many years and feel sad as many of my childhood friends like Pratap, Chiring, Santosh[14] went to school. My father used to tell that instead of attending school like my sibling brothers did, I should learn *Mangre* language and become a *Jaysi* like him. One day I ran away from home to attend school in 1979. Though, father was unhappy since he thought who will take care of animals. This was how my studies finally began and I was registered directly in Thabang High School at age of 13 year in 3rd class.

It was in 1981 when before the examination of 6th class, the RNA carried out a military operation in village. Many villagers were arrested in this operation. The security forces had destroyed many houses, stole valuable property, scattered the grains and mixed urine in it. Those who were arrested were taken and imprisoned in Tulsipur jail and were freed only after two and a half years. After this operation, Santosh Budha Magar whom I admired as an elder brother and friend went absconding. He was active in student union in Thabang High School and was studying in 9th class. He had run away to India and returned only after one and a half years when government had quashed warrant against him.

14 Some became Maoist activists later and some are in foreign countries and some dead.

He joined High school in 1985 and began secretly organizing the student's organization.

In 1982, while studying in 9th class, I got attracted to student politics. I used to deliver letters of the party to local comrades in secret way. It was a dangerous thing because if something of this kind was known to police, they used to beat and keep whoever in prison for a long time. At that time, Mohan Bikram Singh and Nirmal Lama were in the same party known as CPN (Fourth Congress) and were called 'Chao' and 'Mao' of Nepal respectively.

A team of senior party leaders comprising Prachanda, Badal and Bishnu Pokhrel came to Rolpa and Rukum to give political classes in March 1986. When they arrived in Thabang, Chiring Roka Magar[15] and I were part of volunteer team for managing this event. It was organized in the deep forests of Ghare jungle in Phuntibang village and continued for three days. On the last day, we both were awarded party membership in presence of them. It was a happiest moment of life that I was give membership of party which was known as CPN (Mashal)[16] after splitting Mohan Bikram Singh faction. What I had thought those times that feudal *Panchayat* system is enemy of Nepali people and source of poverty and exploitation of our country. We had to end the monarchy's rule by waging a communist revolution and a communist party would never achieve its goal without a people's army.

At this period, I was mainly associated in the student organization. While my SLC exam results were awaited, I was assigned the task of coordinating the regional bureau of the student's organization. We had a convention in Dang in an underground and student activists from Rolpa, Rukum, Salyan, Dang and Pyuthan districts participated. A student conference was also organized in leadership of Krishna Bahadur Mahra in

15 Later became important Maoist leader of Rolpa district.

16 It was also called as Moto Mashal.

Libang which was attended by student activists of Libang, Rangsi, Ghoragaon, Gajul and Thabang villages. By this conference, I was elected as secretary of All Nepal Student Union of Rolpa district committee.

After passing out SLC successfully in 1986 and failing to get admission in Dang campus for 11th class, I took up a teaching job for primary level classes on a temporary basis Thabang High school for nearly a year from 1987. I shifted to Phuntibang Primary school after a year and continued party work. In 1989, I got selected at Nepalgunj campus for 11th class. It was a period when a massive student movement was on the horizon in capital Kathmandu. The rallies and demonstration were organized in daily basis by various students' organizations in Nepalgunj. To escape from administrative crackdown many students went to India and many were arrested. At this time, I returned home from Nepalgunj. While at home, I got to know one day that police is searching for me. I went underground same day. Since I was working as a teaching job in Phunibang village, veteran party comrades Dirgh and Dharam Bahadur Roka advised me to present myself before district administration and get dates to appear when summon. We[17] five went to Libang and presented us before Chief Development Officer of Rolpa. Here, we got to know that our names were in police search list but issuing warrants against us only a rumor. Thus we were allowed to return home with a warning if we participated against Panchayat government, we will be punished severely.

Eventually, after a prolonged nationwide people's movement, the *Panchayat* system fell in country in 1990. The advent of multi-party democracy in Nepal attracted teachers and government

17 Other includes were activists like Pratap Roka Magar, Jhamendra Roka Magar, Chiring Roka Magar and Greesh Pun Magar.

employees of towards our politics. Since I was a teacher in Phuntibang, I was assigned a task of building teachers' organization in Rolpa district. I had become a whole timer party activist until now and working for party in veil of teacher. The general election took place in 1991 and our party's organization SJM put two candidates from two constituencies of western & eastern of Rolpa district. Though, our party won both seat of Rolpa district by big margin but stiff resistance faced for eastern constituency is worth mentioning. Here, Barman Budha Magar was standing against a *Panchayat* politician and ex-minister Balaram Gharti Magar of Rashtriya Prajatantra Party. At this hour, I was a polling agent of Krishna Bahadur Mahra for western constituency at Pakhapani VDC where Surendra Hamal from Nepali Congress party was our opposing candidate. After polling I returned to Libang with government officials carrying vote containers. Balaram was our main enemy and was adamant to win this election at any cost. The counting had already begun. Then he suddenly entered Tundikhel ground with his daughter led vigilante group to capture polling containers. While his goons tried to create anarchy, our supporters and people armed with sticks seized all their weapons and beat them up. Balaram might not have escaped that day if police did not have escorted him. As our both candidate Krishna Bahadur Mahra & Barman Budha Magar won elections, we organized a victory demonstration. With this event, a phase of rural class struggle took preliminary shape hereafter in Rolpa district.

I passed Intermediate in Commerce stream in 1993 from Mahendra Multiple Campus and joined a diploma course at Dang campus. But my expenses were becoming high, therefore I decided not to stay in city but managing studies from village. I had already got married in 1991 and it was difficult to manage family with a teaching salary of 5000 rupees. My father and elder brother were very supportive for my studies and at the same time stood by my politics. I was registered in the Dang Campus as a regular student in 1994 but in reality I was a part-time student fulfilling all responsibilities of party activist, a teacher and a student. I asked sometimes my friends to teach in my place at Phuntibang School while in my absence so this way my name remained in school register. I used to pay nearly fifty per cent of salary in this way as an exchange of friend's help. It was nearly 1800 Rs. In between, our party had boycotted 1995 general elections amid severe state repression.

This was a period when the party was holding *Sija* and *Miteri* campaign in region. I was Area Committee Secretary for a region consisting of Thabang, Jelbang, Uwa, Mirul and Kureli VDCs. While holding party's meetings in Gam VDC, we were attacked by Nepali Congress and CPN (UML). Moreover, police fired on our supporters and killed two brothers Man Bahadur and Lok Bahadur in Iribang VDC. These two incidents forced our supporters to hold the view that we should also give armed resistance to government. As a rehearsal to actual armed struggle, our party carried out some people's actions by beating the exploiters, vigilante and landlord elements by managing a team of fighting group.

It was a largely a phase as we termed a preparation phase called *Char Tayarri* (four preparation) when we had organized a meeting of area committee in a deep jungle in Thabang just a month before the initiation of People's War. Since I was a teacher at the school and was keen on completing campus education, the party decided that I was not fit to hold responsibilities as area committee secretary. Sharad[18] was elected as new secretary while I was assigned to work as a member of area committee.

18 Sharad hails from Jelbang VDC. Till recently he was Division Commander of the 3rd division of the disbanded PLA and was also CC member of the UCPN (Maoist).

Though, the party initiated People's War from 13 February 1996, I did not go underground and still was a teacher in Phuntibang. I was not identified in village as a Maoist activist until brutal murder of Lali Roka Magar in police custody made me to go underground with many other people in January, 1997.[19] Just after fifteen days of murder of Lali and Dilman Roka, the party annihilated Mulbahadur Roka and Manjeet Gharti because they were the main police informer responsible.

At this hour, our party policy was to make elephant blind. The elephant connoted security forces and government while vigilante groups of police informers was its eyes. When the elephant suspects, it kills and suppresses. As we exterminated some of police informers, elephant became blind and hence mad and carried out large scale repression. However, since it does not see anything was incapable of doing any serious harm to contain expansion of guerrilla movement.

The beginning of underground life had a effect on family too. So just after a few months of going underground and our joint family was broken. This phase of our life was very hard and my wife had faced many intense hardships and distress. Looking back those years, I feel like cry and grieving. While this continued, I stayed in Gam and Seram VDCs for an entire year in organizational activities. After a year in 1999, the party again sent me to Pyuthan district to work there for more than a year. I could return to Thabang in 2001 and was assigned to work as party secretary of Thabang area

19 At this hour in Thabang, only five party activists were underground. They were Tejman Gharti Magar alais Dirgh, Santosh Budha Magar, Tara Prasad Roka alias Shang, Chiring Roka Magar, and Manohar Budha Magar. Dirgh and Shang were killed later in course of decade long People's War.

committee. I was elected for District Committee of Rolpa in October 2001. By this time, we had completely defeated police forces.

I got seriously injured in a PLA's attack on Solukhumbu district headquarters in November, 2001. This incident made an end of my further active political life. Though, I was elected as President of the *Magar Rashtriya Mukti Morcha, Nepal* (Magar National Liberation Front, Nepal) of Thabang Special District Committee. But my health did not allow me to continue in organizational activities.

In 2005, some foreign doctors from international fraternal Maoist parties visited Thabang village in February, 2005. They had come to train health assistants of our party's newly built People's Model Hospital at Oat-Ghorneti village situated in Rukum district. Considering my health paralysis conditions, these doctors advised me to live with them in hospital. I was treated by them for an entire year at Ghorneti hospital.

I am relatively fit and look after management committee of model hospital which I visit occasionally. I now live in Dullidanda village with family where we plough our land and rear cows and pigs. We shifted here in the middle of People's War when our house of Thula Gaon was destroyed by the RNA in one of its security operation in 2002.

5. REMINISCENCES OF A PLA COMMANDER

(Bin Prasad Pun Magar at Tila Cantonment, Dahban, 5 June, 2012)

Name: Bin Prasad Pun Magar

Age: 34 years

Education: Intermediate (incomplete)

Profession: Ex-Brigade Commander, Jawar Memorial Brigade, Fifth Division, PLA

I was born in family of retired Indian army soldier on 28 January 1978 Tipla village of Thabang VDC. Our grandfathers had migrated from Dolpa district to Thabang some hundred years ago and had married daughter of the *Mukhia*. They also got a huge plot of land in dowry. My grandfather had one brother and my father had three. So when land was redistributed, my father could acquire only a small plot of land. However, my mother had no brothers in her family, so he also owned her family property. Due to posting of my father in India, he came to see us in duration of two to three years. While his arrival, we felt him like a guest. It is because of this reason that I hardly ever had an attachment with father in contrast to mother.

In my childhood days, it was a general opinion in village that it is essential to know at least elementary education in order not to get deceived by educated people. A minimum qualification for the British and Indian Army jobs was class 4th. There was no other pressure up on me and I did not face any hardship in childhood. I still remember 1981's army attack in village. There were two young men who were forcefully taken while beating on footpath by security forces. While asking to mother about this incident, she told me that she did not know. This incident always haunted me in my teenage life.

Our village was very crowded and packed and everybody had many pigs kept within houses. As a child, I used to go toilet in the pig house. Everyone used to the same because it was a custom passed down from generation to generation. The human waste also used as a fertilizer for agricultural production and pigs eat all human waste. I heard about modern toilets in 1986 first time and this practice was normal till 1998 in region. It was only after awareness campaigns later post People's War that villagers started using closed toilet.

I was ten years boy when King Birendra visited village in 1989. We had a prepared a welcome ceremony at Thabang High School ground but he did not turn up that day. He visited Thabang after three days later. We rushed from school to see him. Queen Aisharya was clicking photographs and distributing pictures to us. Dressed in army dress, he was guarded by royal guards. The village mayor welcomed him and while we chanted slogans.

> ***Hamro raja hamro desh pran bhanda pyaro cha,***
> *(Our king, our country, more lovable than our life),*
> ***Panchyati raj amar rahos,***
> *(Long live **Panchayati** system),*
> ***Hamro bhasa hamro bhesh pran bhanda pyaro cha,***
> *(Our language, our culture, more lovable than our life).*

We did not know meaning of these slogans at that time and used to recite in a song form much later while been grown up boys. After a few months of the king's visit, we heard in 1990, the *Panchayat* government fall down and *Bahudal* rule has established in country. Many villagers got free from jail. This included my relatives Jhamendra Roka and Dhaplal Pun who were arrested in 1981. I had heard that my aunt took membership in some party organisation and my mother also supported it. Santosh Budha and Renu didi was frequent visitor. They used to come at night in garb of playing cards but they discussed politics in these meetings which held till late night.

I was 13 years old when got attracted to cultural activities held on banner of people's committee. These committees were organised by student organisation and met weekly on every Saturday holiday at High School. We used to listen to many revolutionary songs like '*folkland ko tapu bata*' which was penned by revolutionary singer Mani Thapa. It was about a Nepali soldier in the British Gurkha Army. While during battle, he sees some people who were torn apart due to war and become poor. Seeing this he would write a letter to his family. This song was banned by government. I remember a little one song by Khushi Ram Pakhrin;

kalo ban ko bichaima	[in the middle of a dark jungle
Khetalako gaon	there is a peasant village
sana sana jhopari	with tiny huts
chainan aama baw	no parents in there
bhoka nanga nani haru *duli rahane thaw*	only hungry and naked children
hamro desh ko bewestha	to see the system of our country
herna teha jaw.	You go there!!]

I went for a month-long cultural campaign led by *Jaljala Sanskritik Sangam* in 1991. It was part of an election campaign of Krishna Bahadur Mahara who was the SJM candidate from Western constituency of Rolpa district. In some villages, we were attacked on performance stage by vigilante groups. The cultural front was led by Santosh Budha Magar with a team of fourteen volunteers armed with Khukri. The leaders used to tell us that being students it is our responsibility to guide the society. During this trip, our leaders taught us to question hereditary rule of monarchy. They strongly believed that King is against the people and development of country. Only a good man with capacity should run a country and not through birth rights. And that good man can only be a communist. The *Panchas* (*Panchayat* supporters) cannot be a good man. We were a group of 40 to 45 young people and ate together sometime in nights eating biscuits and noodles only. The poor peasants influenced by our songs and felt that our songs as their own which talked their life surrounded with suffering.

I had performed role of a husband during a play in which Samjhana Gharti Magar played role wife. The wife fall sick and medicine did not cure her. The husband has not enough income to take her to hospital. To treat her illness, a shaman is called who informs that reason of her illness is *Mukhia* (village mayor). He is a devil and a ghost soul. To make everything well, his family must rise against him. Though, our party did not believe in ghosts and spirits. But the situation in village was like that and this particular play was liked by people. It carried message of exploitation and suffering and talked of a struggle against ruling class.

While returning home from trip, my uncle and aunt discouraged me from getting involved in politics. They told me since we had no political history in our family. They told me that until I pass out SLC, I should focus on studies. I heeded to family wishes. Therefore, I was not part of the *Sija* campaign but I was definitely aware of it.

While People's War broke out in 1996, I had taken up a teaching job at the primary school in Phunibang village. While being a teacher I organised a convention of Young Communist League in forest of Dullidanda village in 1998 where I was given membership of the CPN (M). In August 1999, the police arrested me in Uwa VDC while going to Dang district for appearing in Intermediate final year examination. I was tortured and interrogated for two days continuously in police custody. But they had to release me since they were not able to extract any information about guerrilla activities. This incident made a turn in life and I decided to part of the Maoist guerrilla army. I told my parents and wife and they stand with my decision. Our twin sons were just born when with beginning of year 2000 commenced my underground political life.

For nearly a year, I was asked to work in the district headquarters of Rolpa. My task was to courier top secret letters. In September 2000, a political-military camp was organised in jungles bordering Uwa and Thabang. It was organised by three commands comprising western, mid-western and eastern region and a selected 400 Maoist guerrillas took part. Here, I was promoted as the Area Committee Member of the party and Political Commissar of a guerrilla squad named Narendra guerrilla squad. I was in management team during Rukumkot attack in April, 2001. Twenty Policemen were detained as a war prisoner in Rukumkot attack and kept at Thabang. My squad was responsible to take care of these policemen. They turned out friendly and supportive to our cause when we release them after a month.

The PLA attack on Holeri[20] was my first combat experience. It was a successful attack where we had arrested 72 policemen as a war prisoner on 12 July, 2001. While we were returning our way to Thabang, many peasants offered us water, bananas, curd

20 Holleri police post was also attacked on beginning of People's War on 13 February, 1996.

and bread in road. They were very happy to see policemen in our custody because it region was full stories of police atrocities. Our attack made far reaching impact when then Prime Minister Girja Prasad Koirala government crumbled and eventually he resigned. With Sher Bahadur Deuba took over as new Prime Minister, First Peace Talk begun between our party and government from 30 August, 2001. It was during this period that the party held a national conference of Maoist guerrillas held in Kureli VDC of Rolpa district. All senior leaders including Prachanda, Baburam, Kiran, Badal participated along with two hundred representatives of Maoist guerrilla army.[21].

There were separate messes for leaders and guerrilla cadres like us and this was first time I felt discrimination. The senior party leaders were provided with mutton meat with rice and pulses whereas we were provided with *dhido*[22] and cow meat. Our leaders should have eaten same food as we lower activists did. But then I thought this favouritism was done not by leaders themselves but by those who were involved in the preparations. I thought that we should not find fault in it because the leaders were our guests. But only now I think that it was a reflection of petty bourgeoisie tendency which was prevalent in higher rank leadership. Otherwise, such a culture of separate mess system was not promoted during People's War.

The Kureli conference passed a resolution to make a nationwide structure of *Jansatta* and party's armed wing. Thus United Revolutionary People's Council (URPC) and People's Liberation Army (PLA) was formed. The conference debated ideological and political line of People's War that was called Marxism-Leninism-Maoism with input from *Prachanda Path* as guiding principle. While applying ideology in the concrete situation of Nepal we have

21 That time we had 2500 to 3000 guerrillas in entire country.

22 A dish made of maize floor.

to ask what we have been able to add or develop in the arena of ideology. According to this understanding based on the *Prachanda Path*, now PLA task was to fight a struggle based on principles of:

> ***Dhakka krambhanga mahabipatti ra chalang***
>
> *[Revolutionaries must give a conscious push to make forward armed struggle].*

This principle was based on It is true that the Nepali revolution will gradually develop by taking its own route. The task of revolutionaries was to work as its catalyst. Once they break its usual motion by giving it a push it will create huge crisis within ruling classes. Our task was to blow down enemy where it lands. This would create a situation where a revolutionary party utilizes in its favour to attain victory.

We at those times were in process of forming regular companies and battalions of the PLA. We recruited only those youths, who crossed over 18 years of age, otherwise they should be in either the people's militia or Young Communist League. A notable difference marked between militia and PLA was that later were Whole Timer armed combatants.

With the First Peace Talk got inconclusive results, we attacked Ghorahi barrack on 8 November, 2001. This was first PLA attack after its formation on a large camp of a joint security force comprised of 325 RNA soldiers and 235 policemen. We had a force of 1100 combatants that included one full battalion. We 25 comrades including nine women combatants from Thabang participated in this battle which begun at 11 Pm in night and got over after a four hour long duration. The Ghorahi battle was a total success and camp was destroyed completely. Eight of comrades were died while government lost its 21 security personnel including an army Major. We seized 21 army trucks full of ammunitions and many weapons including many mortar & rocket launcher. We also detained SP & CDO of Dang district who were released later in Dahaban.

Afterword, my battalion took part in attacking Sandhikharka, the district headquarters of Arghakanchi on September, 2002. Though, we won this battle but with a huge lose on our side, including 72 PLA comrades and a Company Commander. The government lost 74 personnel but this battle was a difficult one to defeat a small contingent of 284 security force. We attacked thereafter the district headquarters of Jumla on 14 November, 2002 where RNA soldiers were trained by the U.S. Army. In Jumla, our victory was a partial one and we lost 27 comrades.

Afterword the PLA lost many battles except winning occasionally. We lost battles at Khara, Tauliwha, and Bhirpustam. We had attacked Khara twice but lost both with many dozen comrades died. The first attack was carried on 27 May, 2002 and second on 7 April, 2005. The Tauliwha and Bhirpustam battle took place respectively on 24 February, 2004 and 16 November, 2004. The PLA could not destroy security fortifications of security forces. We were unable to defeat government forces militarily. During those days, one week of military training was considered enough to fight battles where RNA required six months to do the same. Till 2002, both political and military training used to go hand in hand in the People's Army. At platoon level, we held political classes on every two days. But later especially since 2003, the party were unable to hold political training regularly and focus was more done for military training. It was period when the PLA was largely fighting positional warfare; therefore political training of combatants was neglected.

The party's assessment that we were in the strategic stalemate stage in 2003 was not correct. The subsequent understanding since 2005 of reaching to strategic offensive stage was a blunder.

At this stage we were asked to fight to win even with heavy loss of exceeding any number of combatants. This was a wrong policy followed by party leadership and it is why many of PLA comrades deserted us during People's War.[23] Prachanda had then in 2005 begun arguing that it is only through political tactics that we can crush enemy. Thus a tactics of constitutional assembly was put in third round of Peace Talks. With a success of people's movement of 2006, our PLA had grown into seven divisions and 29 brigades. The party's plan was that half of armed force will merge with Nepal Army and remaining would join YCL. We had thought that there is no need to defeat enemy if each one of us can convert three army soldiers to our side. We thought that we will go for Constituent Assembly elections and with a huge majority will form our own government. If this situation doesn't arise we will give a call for insurrection. Thus, we thought of capturing power politically and militarily rather peacefully.

A peace agreement was signed in June, 2006 between the party and government of Nepal. With this People's War was suspended and PLA kept under supervision of the United Nation Mission in Nepal (UNMIN) from 2007. According to the party's plan, hundreds of senior comrades and political commissars of PLA were transferred into YCL for organizing insurrection in near future. During the verification process, the UNMIN did not know much about military structure of the PLA. Those who could articulate suitably were considered "fit" and those could not present were declared "unfit". The faulty categorisation made nearly 4000 PLA combatants unfit and disqualified in name of "child soldier". However, the truth is that thousands of activists

23 For instance, we were 184 combatants from Thabang VDC in 2001. But once we started to suffer heavily from mid 2003, our number reduced to 84. During the Peace Process in 2006 we were only 42 comrades. 19 of them got died during battles and many others were injured, while others left.

had joined the PLA before it came under UNMIN supervision. They were not involved in battles at all and left the cantonment after receiving 5 lakh rupees.

This was a time that I was working as Brigade Commander of Jawar Memorial Brigade of Fifth Division stationed as Tila Cantonment in Rolpa district. In early 2012, I took voluntary retirement from the PLA and received a cheque of 2.5 lakh rupees. I refuse to join the so-called Nepal Army merely because its "royal" prefix has been removed after the Maoist joined bourgeois parliamentary system. We never imagined such a day and grieve sometime for comrades who died before my own eyes during battles and we could not save them. We had dreamt that either we would be martyred or be successful in making Nepal a socialist country in twenty first century.

6. A REAL STORY OF COMRADE JUNG

(Hitji Jhankri Magar with son and grandson in his home)

Name: Hitji Jhankri Magar alias Comrade Jung
Age: 55 years
Education: Class Four
Profession: Peasant cum shopkeeper

I was born in Maranthan village of Thabang VDC on 8 April, 1958. When I was eight years old, when my parents left for Kalo Pahar in search of job. My parents worked in potato farms as wage labour in a village nearby Shimla city. I attended primary school here and studied till class 4th in village. I was 17 years old when I returned home with mother in 1975. I was the eldest son in family therefore farming was made my responsibility. We were a lower middle peasant family and able to produce food for 9 to 10 months. The father stayed back in India and married another Nepali woman. He returned in 1990, bought built a house in Ghorahi city in Dang district. He died nine years ago in 2004.

I got married at age of twenty years with Samjhana Jhankri[24] and have two sons & a daughter. Later in 1983, I fell in love with another woman and married her without divorcing Samjhana. Afterword, she did not live with me for ten years. Now, she lives in Koizabang village with her sons. I have four sons and two daughters from second wife. I divide my time between the two wives but mostly I live with second wife in Mangra Khola village.[25]

The practice of polygyny was a common practice those days in entire region. Barman Budha Magar, the founder member of Communist Party in Thabang had married twice. Many senior activists from Kaman Jhankri to Ruz Bahadur Roka alias 'Regan'

24 My first wife was actively participated as a leading activist of All Nepal Revolutionary Women Association and a party member of CPN (M) in 2002. She was also active in the *Jansatta* period as a member of the people's court committee of ward no.7 in 2005.

25 It was during the *Jansatta* period that I realized that my second marriage was a mistake.

married twice and thrice respectively. Suryalal Budha Magar married twice while being a secretary of Communist party's Rolpa district committee in 1988. The party took action against him by suspending his primary membership. He was re-admitted in the party only when he divorced second wife.

Those days my friends had formed a cultural group in mid 1970s in guidance of teachers of Thabang High School. It was called *Dhikure Samuh* and to mobilize villagers to oppose anti-social activities of Ramkumar Budha Magar's gang. Ramkumar operated in whole region with active aid from administration and police. Ramkumar's gang had also hand in killing of some businessmen and stealing in daylight, looting had become everyday stories. His gang's terror spread from Sulichaur bazaar to southern part of Rolpa district.

My friend insisted that I should also take interest in politics but I refused. I did not felt that government is oppressive and exploiting us. Nepal at the time was in turmoil since of student movement all over in country. Thabang was also influenced by these countrywide events. A referendum was organized by the *Panchayat* regime in 1980 which was boycotted in Thabang. Though, military operation of 1981 had fresh memories in mind but I remain largely indifferent.

It was only in 1988 when I attracted to politics. The same years, I had taken a teaching job at newly open primary school in Maranthan village. While I left the job by 1990, multi-party system had been instituted in country. Being part of the teaching circle, we used to have discussions on politics. I also become active in peasant organization and elected as president of ward-7 committee of village unit of All Nepal Peasant Association.

By the end of 1992 and beginning of 1993, the mass mobilization by the SJM expanded to nearby VDCs of Rolpa and Rukum. One of chief target of our struggle was against Jumleni family patriarch Ramkumar Budha Magar. With advent of democracy, now, he had become a Nepali Congress leader. Two of his associates were punished by the SJM activists in district headquarter of Libang in broad daylight by blackening their face and made walk on donkey. It was known in whole region that they had sold many Nepali girls in brothels of Indian cities.

Our peasant front decided that we have to collect seasonal contribution for political campaigns organize by the SJM. We were given responsibility to collect a definite amount of grains [maize] and 4 rupees per month. In the ideological-political classes, we were taught earlier *Panchayat* system had exploited us for 40 years, and now so-called *Bahudal* system want to exploit us in name of multi-party democracy. When the *Sija* and *Miteri* campaigns started in 1995, we used to visit small villages located in different wards of Thabang VDC. By holding small meetings of villagers which convened usually at night, we shared life struggle.

I was given party membership on 9 July, 1995 by giving me *nom de guerre* 'Jung' which meant war in English language. Our Maoist Revolution was intended to abolish monarchy and establish a New Democratic society which would be Socialism opposed to present feudal and capitalist system. A New Democratic society would be a system in favour of the poor and landless peasants and would uproot oppressive social, economic and cultural system which the police, landlord, money lenders and anti-communist parties wanted to maintain. I was convinced by the party's view that without political struggle nothing can be achieved. We united everybody who could be united in Thabang village. For instance, in a family, if men would be a member of peasant front and party, his wife would be in women's organization, his son and daughter would be in student front, militia and YCL.

Soon after initiation of the People's War, I was advised by the party comrades to go underground but I did not go underground immediately. With the pace of expansion of armed struggle, government unleashed massive terror campaigns in region. On 30 March 2002, the RNA burnt down my house located at Mangra khola. I had a small shop which also was burnt and I lost property worth around 2.15 lakhs. The joint operation of police and army made a big camp at Taligha for forty days. Seventeen more houses situated in Thula Gaon were completely burnt down and property of million rupees was lost. We had taken shelter in jungle and stayed in caves of Jaljala Mountain for many weeks. They did not only destroy houses but looted grains & chicken, stole cash and killed pig, buffalo, cow. They left Thabang only on 7 May when the PLA combatants attacked Gam military barrack and destroyed it completely by killing more than 100 soldiers.

By 2003, I was elected as Area Committee Member of party village unit. This was also a time when Thabang Special District was formed by the party in a view to exercise *Jansatta* in Kham Magar region. I was soon made a member of its Thabang Special District Committee due to my long association with movement. After two years of serving for the Special District People's Government), we were told one day that Special District was disbanded in a view to exercise *Jansatta* at bigger level (i.e., Magarant Autonomous State). We were somewhat angry with the party decision since the *ga-ja-sa* committees were beginning to take shape in many VDCs. We thought that our task was to consolidate instead of dissolving Special District.

With dissolution of Special District, our committee was attached with party's Rolpa district committee. I was responsible for managing food and logistics during military attacks conducted by the PLA and party activities. While PLA took military raid, we arranged shelter, food, medicine and sleeping arrangement in village by mobilizing dozens of peasants committee. Our management committee mobilized hundreds of people to bring together 50-35 kilogram packet from Nepalgunj and Dang by walking on foot. We did not pay any money to them instead distributed rice and other grains as per their family need.

We had organized two types of kitchen during those days. The first type mess cooked for the higher leadership of comprising members of Central Committee & above of the party organization. We served them usually *Khasi* (mutton), rice and wheat bread with local dishes. The second type mess was for lower level leadership comprised of Regional Bureaus, District Committee & PLA combatants. We served *Ranga* (buffalo), *Sungur* (pork) and sometimes cow meat with *dhido* and sometimes rice too on its availability. While for a large gathering of the PLA, we served them *dhido* with buffalo & pork since cooking rice or *roti* was not feasible. This was a mess arrangement until end of 2005. Thus, there was a hierarchy between higher committee and lower committee. We believed that the senior leaders are our *Pahuna* (guest) and we should serve them best food available. When the Phuntibang Meeting held in early 2005, we served food for entire party leadership. Even though dozens of Central Committee meetings were held in Thabang, it was the only occasion when party's central leadership including Chairman Prachanda took food with lower cadres like us. We had served buffalo and rice for everybody.[26]

More than 200 cadres and supporters left Thabang village for foreign employment from 2001 to 2005. More especially with battles of Arghakanchi's Sandhikharka in September, 2002, youth began to abandon the rank and file of the PLA. The PLA attack on Myagdi district headquarters on 20 March, 2004 made a boost to mass desertion from the Maoist movement. 125 young cadres had left the PLA and the party organization that year in Thabang

26 We were 350 activists including 65 Central Committee members and a company of the PLA providing security of meeting venue.

Special District itself.

> ***Ragat ko khola bagna thalyo*** *[A river of blood began flowing!]*

These young people were deeply involved from initial phase of guerilla movement. These youth had joined People's War out of necessity since state treated everybody in Thabang as Maoists. Two kinds of people joined the People's War: ones who were forced by state repression and their number was high. The others were those who had joined the movement with a political consciousness and their number was less. The party did not impart proper political-ideological training to first kinds and focus was rather given on military training in contrast to a political one. Therefore, once the PLA started suffering heavily in battles, they began to leave movement and village altogether. Some went for studies and while majority went to the Gulf countries for employment.

The reason behind desertion of youth was located in political line of our party. From the last months of 2001, the line of Protracted People's War and insurrection was combined as per guiding principle of the *Prachanda Path*. The line of organizing the *Janbidroh* (insurrection) was began propagating onwards this period. But, insurrection might get organize for a very short period and cannot go on for a long period for years. According to my view, this was a root cause from where problem started in People's War. During ideological classes, our leaders used to strongly argue that we have to capture central power as soon as possible and only through organizing insurrection, we can attain it. This line of *Shigrha vijay* (quick victory) was a widely accepted position by the higher leadership and soon it became a mainstream discussion in our everyday life. Prachanda used to tell us in those days in 2004:

> *We are now in strategic offensive stage and we have to capture state power as quickly as possible by following*

> *the line of mass insurrection. We have come very near to capturing state power. We have been flying a jahaj (plane), and now we have to hit it on chattan (rock). Otherwise we have to give it a new direction.*

While listening to Prachanda, we, the local activists thought that we are going to capture power of Kathmandu very soon. We were intoxicated by this whole idea. But the plane eventually did not hit against rock comprised of feudalism and capitalist ruling class. Prachanda made us swing in a wrong direction in between and our plane lost its original direction.

I was elected as deputy *ga-ja-sa* chief of Thabang in January, 2006. The villagers followed rules set by our *Jansatta* committees by not indulging in gambling, prostitution and consuming excessive liquor. Our militia had arrested many thieves and we used to punish guilty by awarding labour punishment lasting from a week or months depending on crime. The security personnel arrested as a war prisoner were treated with respect by us. They were kept in open supervision of villagers without any concept of jails. Selling of liquor was not allowed, though brewing homemade liquor is a part of our Magar culture and it was also not produced much those days. The villagers feared that if the *Jansatta* came to know, then they will face strict actions or public humiliation. Many times we seized and destroyed hundreds of liquor bottles. The women of the village were happy because the husband could not drink, family quarrels could be avoided and money could be saved. The *Jansatta* discouraged villagers from holding expensive ceremonies on ritual of birth, marriage and death. The Kham Magar has a grand tradition of spending excessively on death ritual by investing from 60, 000 to 200, 000 rupees. According to our policy, last rites should be completed in three to five days and must not be expensive.

The villagers were living a primitive life before the People's War and only after establishment of Thabang Special District, a qualitative transformation begin. Littering was done in open and footpath. Defecting within household pig huts was an age old tradition. We discouraged people and asked them to avoid defecting openly. At that time, some NGO/INGOs also wanted to carry out such activities in our region, but initially Special District government did not allow them to work. However by 2005, the party began accepted assistance from them. The *ga-ja-sa* committee collected raw materials (cement and toilet seat) from them and passed a definite budget to build toilets in village. Some families built toilets themselves in their houses. The foundation for this consciousness was prepared by the *Jansatta*.

However, with disbanding of Maoist government in village has reversed these new practices. While with signing of Peace Agreement in June, 2006 between government and our party, the *ga-ja-sa* committee was also disbanded. Now in 2012, the state of Thabang is similar to what was before 1996. The moneylenders have born again in large number in the party organization and our party activists such as Ruz Bahadur Roka alias 'Regan', Ganesh Budha Magar, Resham Shah and others are charging 5 to 6 rupees per month as interest from the people going to the Gulf countries and Malaysia. During the initial period of People's War, we had punished moneylenders but now Maoist leaders themselves have got converted one among them.

Practices like polygyny have reappeared again in the village. Recently, Dalman Budha has married a 27 years old Dalit girl at an age of 73 year. Tek Sunar's son married twice this year. During the *Jansatta* period, nobody dared to such acts. We took action against them by awarding labour camps for one month extendable to a year depending upon the case and age difference. Ghangaru Budha Magar was in village peasant committee when he married second time in 2002. He had also fathered a girl child from her. When it was reported to us through his family, he was discharged from party responsibility and was awarded one full year of labour punishment. Her second wife was given three months of labour punishment. He was given stricter punishment because being a party leader he presented a bad role model before people. He divorced her and she re-married another person within a year in Uwa VDC.

We had run *Jansatta* in Thabang VDC from September 2002 to June 2006 successfully. Though, a people's committee was formed October 12, 1999 but it was run in a secret form since police post existed in village. It was after PLA's successful Rukumkot attack of 1 April, 2001 by which we made out a strategic victory over police force. The formation of base area and Thabang Special District was built only on this basis to run the *Jansatta* publicly so we could save people from state repression. The villagers feared to visit district headquarter those days due to terror of government security forces. The police used to detain villagers on the way itself and used to interrogate. Immediately villager would put in police custody.

> ***Kaha ko manche ho?*** *(Where are you from?).*
>
> *[If their answer was Thabang, they would immediately say,]*
>
> ***Aei Thabang! Tyan ta sabai Maobadi chan*** *(Oh! Thabang! Everybody is Maoist in Thabang).*

Therefore, we needed a structure of *Jansatta* to intervene in everyday affairs in village. But the senior leadership at the national level made agreements with the bourgeois parties to disband and overturn decisions made by the *Jansatta.* All cases of land registration and judgments of people's court have been nullified by a single agreement of Comprehensive Peace Agreement, 2006. Our PLA has surrendered their weapons following the Peace Process.

This is the reason why our party is on the verge of a split.[27]

Re-establishment of the police post in Thabang was most painful experience for us. We fiercely opposed it which was constructed by the state on the eve of Constituent Assembly elections in 2007. When the district administration sent a team of policemen for building the area police post, nobody in Thabang VDC gave them shelter. We made a signatures campaign and held mass demonstrations in August, 2007 at district police headquarters in Libang. The entire village said in one voice that they don't want a police post in Thabang.

> ***Luteri/ balatkari/ hatayri police murdabad***
>
> *[down with the robber/ rapist/ murderer police!]*

We, the villagers knew very well difference between a PLA and government security forces. We were successful in blocking district administration's plan through our mass mobilization for three months. Then the chief of party regional bureau and Central Committee Member Com. Srijal came Thabang to convince us. He told in a big gathering:

> *The police will not misbehave from now onwards and since we have already signed the Peace Agreement, we have to do it. All policemen are not bad and rapist and we have to differentiate between a bad and a good policeman. Now onwards we should not differentiate between us and the police. In fact from now on they are our own people since they were no more a police force working under monarchy. Now they know it and have become* ***janta ko police*** *(people's police).*

Finally, the area police post was re-established in Jhakkeybang

27 Some parts of this life history were recorded at a time (May 2012), when the UCPN (Maoist) were verge of split. Eventually it happened in mid-June 2012, as CPN, Maoist led by Kiran split away from Prachanda led UCPN (Maoist).

village towards end of 2007. Many leaders from Libang district headquarter from Nepali Congress to the secretary of CPN (UML) attended opening of police post ceremony. In their speech, leaders of Nepali Congress and UML and said;

> *That the police will neither enter the village from now onwards nor will they drink liquor. Forget about mis-behaviour to women, the police would not even think about it for a moment.*

The Deputy Superintendent of Police said that,

> *We are not the old police. We will show you that we have become new policemen. We are here to serve the people.*

However, the fundamental character of police remains unchanged even in 2012 after 5 years. A six month ago in a social gathering organised by an NGO in Thula Gaon, a local villager told that the police is no good and they are harassing villagers in name of settling cases by bribery. We later came to know that he was detain for a night in police post and was beaten up mercilessly.

Recently our Chairman Prachanda came to Thabang for a special program at Ajambari Commune in Rachibang village and told us:

> *Our fight will not be like the ones in China, Russia or Peru. The setback in Peru was because of the arrest of Chairman Gonzolo and the Peruvian party's inadequacy to forcefully overthrow state. We had fought with the royal army in past but now there is no royal army after the abolishment of monarchy. Now, there is only Nepal Army. We don't have to fight with National Army, therefore we don't need weapons.*[28]

I wanted to ask a question to him that had any change took

28 This visit held on 13 March, 2012.

place in basic character of Nepali state once the party went in government? But the organizers said Chairman had very little time and did not provide any space to debate. He came by helicopter and left within one hour. Three dozen policemen, who had suppressed us during the People's War, were providing him security. Some party activists had planned to show him black flags because of his role of causing split in the party but the commune leaders made them silent by showing fear of police. He, though had also said,

> *Our party will not split, we are unified and the discussion is going on at a higher level. When I was the General Secretary, allegations were made against me that I have become rightist since we participated in parliamentary elections of 1991. But I led the People's War amid these allegations.*

It was a meeting with a small presence of less than a hundred people and villagers boycotted program. We have a feeling of betrayal and hate towards leaders like Prachanda and Baburam Bhattarai. But at the same time, we believe in Maoism and we will fight and resist the state until our New Democratic system is realized. We are prepared for another People's War, but it all depends on senior leadership. It depends on how they make correct policies and implement them by transforming themselves while staying with us and not in the safe places in India.[29]

We stood with Maoism and sacrificed in favour of the proletariat class. At least 15,000 people were martyred and over 10, 000 people are disabled. During state emergency period, it was Thabang who had fought in the PLA and faced ruthless state repression. The peasants managed everything from food to shelter to sentry for the PLA. But the Maoist-led government could not arrange a minimum financial package for us. Our houses were

29 The Maoist senior leadership stayed mostly in Indian cities during decade-old armed struggle in Nepal.

burnt down and more than 50 million rupees property of Thabang VDC was destroyed security forces from 1996 to 2005. We were forced to live in jungles for months for our belief of Maoism. We were just used so they could sit in the *Singh Durbar* by destroying our dream of a new society. Our leaders are living a royal life in Kathmandu in contrast to our hard life in the village.

The party line as argued by Chairman Prachanda, and Baburam Bhattarai on "state restructuring" is nothing new but an illusion. Though, old power structure of monarchy is been abolished but everything has remained same in Nepal. These leaders are creating illusions after the Peace Process to retain their chair at the *Singh Durbar*. In contrast to the party having serious contradictions on "class character of Nepali state", we the villagers of Thabang have no doubt over it and never agree to the view of these leaders. We will support only those who will come with us to realize our goal of a new society and not Kiran, Baburam or Prachanda.

CHAPTER 6

Making of 'Cash Maoism' in Nepal

Correctness or otherwise of the ideological and political line decides everything. If it is correct, everything is gained, but if it wrong, everything is lost.[1]

In the earlier and recent history of Nepal, a series of popular resistance, many of armed revolts, occurred which hardly find any mention in the official history where the oriental idea of 'peaceful Hindu kingdom' was been celebrated. In Nepali psyche, however, struggle has been understood as synonymous to armed struggle because the century's old state formation has been based on exploitation and violence. This fact can be seen from contemporary history of Nepal when political movements by the Nepali Congress and the Jhapali took place in decades of 1950 to 1970s. Looking at nature of various peasant movements which was chiefly against the landowning class and Hindu monarchy, it can be argued that its nature often had elements of guerrilla war and mostly resulted in violent suppression.

Following chapter-2, it can be argued that Nepal's agrarian history witnessed some characteristics features which more or less instigated many of armed revolt and peasant movements. Over a many hundred years of state formation since the Gorkhali conquest to until recently in early decades of 1990s, these became a permanent feature of Nepali society and state. First point was

1 CPN (M) (2004 [2001]), 'The Great Leap Forward: An Inevitable Need of History', in *Some Important Documents of Communist Party of Nepal (Maoist)*, Nepal: Janadisha Publications, p. 46.

large-scale migration from the village Nepal for employment purposes to destinations either in India or the overseas destination of the Gulf, and East Asian countries. Without remittance, the rural population was hardly to survive and it became a pan Nepal phenomenon. Second point relates to successive government's continuous apathy for agriculture sector. On a one side, the advent of development of country was projected by a heavy dependence on foreign aid money but life of peasants remained miserable. Finally, the growth of industry had little meaning and this concentrated only in urban centres. Apart from Kathmandu valley, the process of urbanisation was limited in surrounding administrative centres of district headquarters. In this background, the People's War emerged in an inherently unequal and exploitative political economy and by product of these above features. The ten years of the People's War could be seen only in this background and if any of above mentioned dimensions is not outlined then a true picture can never emerge.

1. MECHANICAL APPLICATION OF PROTRACTED PEOPLE'S WAR IN NEPAL

It has been noted in the chapter-3 that People's War broke up in specific situation of "semi-feudal and semi-colonial" setting of Nepal by every nook and corner of the country. Following the first stage of strategic defense, the Maoist movement went forward by guerrilla attacks on security force, banks and landlords and moneylenders. This was based on Maoist ideology that People's War in Nepal will take a protracted route by encircling the cities from countryside through waging guerrilla warfare and area wise seizure of political power.

Besides this, the Maoists had argued that specific situation of Nepal demand establishing of base areas like the Communist did in China. They had pointed out of four districts of Rolpa, Rukum,

Salyan and Jajarkot would be their strategic zones where base area would be established after its transformation into guerrilla zones.[2] This was a reason that guerrilla actions for initial plans (first three Plans from February, 1996 to August, 1998) were mainly carried out in these districts where thirst was to development of guerrilla war in a systematic way. Until 3rd Plan, the Maoists were following the mass line of Protracted People's War and firmly rooted with guerrilla strategy.

But a qualitative difference emerges during the 4th Plan of October 1998 when a call is given to "Go forward in great direction of building base area". It is a surprising view that once a strategic zone has to be developed into guerrilla zone which would be realized in a long period and by protracted way. Though, they acknowledged their error in their one of party document in 1998 but they seldom give a thought over to correct it.

> *We are entering the fourth sub-stage "base area" and making a plan under it, after passing through "initiation" and simultaneously crossing over the second and third sub-stage of "continuation of initiation" and "guerrilla zone". The reason why we were not able to define this way last time was because* ***we lacked clarity in understanding guerrilla zone and base area*** *[emphasis mine].*[3]

According to this, until early 1998, they had not been fully successful in a situation to transform strategic zones into guerrilla zones. But a call of building base area was issued by 4th Plan to at the end of 1998 but ambiguity about guerrilla zone persisted in Maoist leadership. For instance, while the goal of 4th Plan (October, 1998 to July, 1999) was to "go forward in great direction of building base

2 Two more regions one each located in western and eastern districts of Gorkha and Sindhuli were also marked for this purpose.

3 CPN (M) (2004 [1998]) 'Experiences of the People's War and Some Important Questions', in *Some Important Documents of Communist Party of Nepal (Maoist)*, Nepal: Jandisha Prakashan, pp. 40-41.

area", whereas 5th plan (August, 1999 to March, 2000) call was "go forward 'a bit more' in great direction of building base area". The 6th Plan's (April, 2000 to January, 2001) was similar as earlier one in continuation since October, 1998. It means until early 2001, they were unable to consolidate and establish base area.

While implementing the decision of building base area in the mid-western region, the Maoists had mobilized a military attack on Dunai, the district headquarter of Dolpa on 24 September 2000 which comes in 6th Plan. The district of Dolpa was categorized by the Maoist as a propaganda zone and hence it did not come under their categorization of guerrilla zone. The government security forces knew beforehand possibility of a guerrilla attack in Dunai but the Maoist attacked in mid night. Pasang, a guerrilla's commander of Maoist forces remembers Dunai attack:

> *We did not think it appropriate to return back only on the basis of such baseless news. If we had to return back twice, we had never to attack again. It could result on the wastage of the people's investment, party's labour, financially a great loss, and losing the reliance of the people. So, at last we decided of going to raid, t**aking whatever kinds of risk** [emphasis mine]**... In spite of knowing that it was the white area, we behaved as if it was the base-area, and we tried to make camping in fortification style, as a result the planning was opened among the enemy; and made us retreat from the first plan... we could not arrange the secrecy and security system. We lacked the route and survey, got confusion on the mid way** [emphasis mine].*[4]

The Dunai attack was clearly a departure from mass line. This incident was a reversal of the basic principles of Protracted

---

4 Pasang (2008 [2065 B.S.]), *Red Strides of History: Significant Military Raids of the People's War*, Kathmandu: Agniparishya Janprakashan Grah, pp. 83, 89.

People's War, because this attack was carried out without having a mass base in region. My field insight suggests that the Dunai attack was not only a single incident which went against key ideas of guerrilla warfare. In reality, this tendency of forcing a People's War had began once they could not come clear on difference between a guerrilla zone and base area starting from late 1998 (i.e., 4th Plan).

The very first task was related to building of base area, which means that it will not be consolidated in a wider region until the Maoists defeat government security forces. While implementing of 7th Plan, the Maoist claimed that they got strategic victory over Nepal police by Rukumkot attack in April, 2001. After this attack, most of the police posts in rural region were re-located by the government in district headquarters. Now their main obstacle was to fight with the RNA, which was not mobilized against them until this time.

According to theory of New Democratic Revolution, *Jansatta* or people's power should be build after establishing of base area and in a linear direction starting from village to district level. But it is astonishing that without consolidating village level people's governments, the CPN (M) had already declared formation of district level of Maoist government in many places beginning from late 2000. For instance, the first district level people's government was announced in Rukum on December 20, 2000. It was followed by declaration of Rolpa district people's government in 16 May, 2001 through a mass meeting in Bhabang VDC.

As the above discussions shows that no significant development in the consolidation of base area and hence local village people's power took place till 2001. By these declarations, one can argue that the Maoist leadership was either lacking conceptual clarity of theory of People's War or they were in a great hurry. Moreover, this vagueness and lack of clarity continued for a long period starting from 4th Plan to the 7th Plan until 2001. The goal by the Maoist for nearly four years revolves around expansion of base area and establishment of *Jansatta* locally. Eventually, this hurry was reflected in their new decisions following theoretical tool of "*Prachanda Path*" taken in Second National Conference of February, 2001 which according to them would help them to capture state power successfully. Now, according to them, a fusion between Protracted People's War and insurrection was necessary to attain victory at central level that is- storming national capital Kathmandu. This was in sum an upside down turn from military strategy of Protracted People's War and its necessity in state and society of Nepal. It was an ugly turn from their adherence of 'ideological clarity' set in 1995 party document which reads:

> *The synthesis of all the specificities clearly shows that it is impossible for the armed struggle in Nepal to make a quick leap into an insurrection and defeat the enemy. However, it is fully possible to finally crush the enemy through systematic development of the armed struggle in Nepal. It can be clearly derived from this that the armed struggle in Nepal must necessarily adopt People's War strategy of surrounding the city from the countryside.*[5]

This was a fundamental departure from a mass line propagated through 1st Plan to 7th Plan to itself where the Maoist efforts were centred on building of base area for accomplishment of a New Democratic Revolution in Nepal. But now onwards hereafter, all of the CPN (M) successive efforts from mid-July, 2001 was achievement of an "Interim government, new Constitution and Institutionalization of Republic" in Nepal.

Based on these 'tactical' slogans, the Maoist and government sat for first peace negotiations in August, 2001 amid changing

5 CPN (M) (2004 [1995]), 'Third Expanded Meeting Document of the CC', in *Some Important Documents of Communist Party of Nepal (Maoist)*, Nepal: Jandisha Prakshan, p. 20.

dynamics in national politics after palace massacre and emergence of a new king. But this process of peaceful settlement of the People's War had already begun from September, 2000. Prachanda, in his press statement on the same evening of the Dunai attack made willingness to hold dialogue with the government in an "institutional way". Therefore, the Maoist participation in the successive official and informal peace talks with the "old state" was not a surprise move. However, this is another matter, that these negotiations were unsuccessful in attaining the Maoist 'new' goal of a "Republic Nepal".

Moreover, with the falling of first peace negotiation, the CPN (M) declared entering into second stage of Protracted People's War that is strategic stalemate. It was a quite contrary move without even achieving goal of first stage of strategic defence. The first stage had been realized only by defeating royal army effectively, but the Maoist deliberately entered second stage and later in third stage of strategic offensive in 2004. With this, what came into effect was large scale violence between the Maoist's PLA and government's mobilization of the royal army against Maoist's armed struggle. This period also set a tone of declarations of base area, and formation of *Jansatta* at village, district and central-level people's governments. But the aim of these declarations was to build pressure on Nepali state for further peace negotiation. Since the Maoists had not only abandoned the strategy of People's War but in essence they cut short its *protracted* nature which affected on everything. Now their goal was to attain what their leadership outlined in 2002 that "... only an interim government, constituent assembly and institutionalization of the republic can guarantee the liberation, peace and progress of Nepal and the Nepalese people...[6]

---

6 Chairman Prachanda (2002), 'Press statement, dated March 27' in *Maoist Information Bulletin-3 [Occasional Information Bulletin of Communist Party of Nepal (Maoist)]*.

2. THE THESIS OF 'CASH MAOISM'

This had a direct influence on Thabang too.

Thabang village of Rolpa district was one of the main revolutionary centres of the People's War in Nepal. My work showed how the peasants of this village had rebelled against the monarchy. The arrival of multi-party democracy in the 1990s did not make any difference in their life. Though, it was they who had favoured for multi-party system in Nepal by defying party less *Panchayat* rule way back in 1980s referendum and faced state suppression. However, the multi-party government treated them identically as the *Panchayat* government while they began questioning corruption of Nepali Congress government and efficacy of its development projects. Then, they realised that the post 1990s government was nothing more than a mere replica of the previous one. How could this happen that the peasants of Thabang demarcated so sharply that there existed no difference between two forms of government before and after the 1990s? Here comes the role of communist ideology which began taking roots with opening of school in village half a century ago. A significant role was played by primary teachers in their journey to internalize Maoist ideology. A bird eye view of Nepal's Maoist movement shows that a majority of Maoist leadership were teachers at some points of their life before entering into communist politics. This can be seen from top leadership including Prachanda to village level leadership of Thabang as depicted by three life histories (4, 5, and 6). Their narration makes it clear that majority of then leaders who were active in building communist movement in Thabang were primary teachers. They were also backbone to mobilize cultural movement in region which disseminated the radical ideology of Maoism in region by plays and songs by exposing the anti-people character of government.

Thabang was an ideal rural setting where the radical left political consciousness could grow in region albeit development rhetorical discourse propagated through Rapti Development Project. The political consciousness provided by Maoism as an ideology was idolized by peasantry as a belief in a new society which would able to transform a crisis ridden agrarian society where rooted multiple form of exploitation based on class, caste and ethnicity based discrimination to patriarchal violence. Looking on a surface level, all six life histories remember the *Panchayat* regime's ruthless military operation as equivalent to police atrocity mobilized by a multi-party democratic state after 1990s. This is the reason they could feel no sense of difference in both of regimes. This way state repression taunted their life world again and again and re-produced anti-state consciousness which eventually got manifested through their participation in Maoist movement.

As the People's War gradually expanded in region by military and political mobilization. In this process, the CPN (M) established the *Jansatta* in village by establishing Thabang Special District. As is been argued above that the Maoist had deviated from original goal since 4th Plan, therefore what came into existence in Thabang was a dysfunctional Maoist government. Although, political consciousness of people was developed in this course but it was non-functional because of policy of CPN (M) was to use as a bargaining chip for peace negotiation with government. For instance, life histories of two women mentioned in Chapter-5 specifically reveal women's oppression in society of Thabang. The patriarchy ruled over this world by polygyny. The practice of jari was established practices where a man takes another wife by compensating for loss of his property. The girl child had no access to education and they did not property rights in parental property. This is the reason which made women to reach at a consciousness to assert their voice by participating with Maoist movement. This is why, narratives of Rajkumari Roka Magar and Deumaya Budha Magar sets a new political consciousness by ploughing the land and joining in guerrilla squads simultaneously. Thabang Special District had empowered Rajkumari Roka Magar by awarding her a share in parental property. But after the disbanding of the *Jansatta*, his brother as former chief of village *Jansatta* refused to give her share on a gendered basis. As she bitterly reminds us that the though she came from a middle peasant background, but she is after all woman oppressed by patriarchy. The life history of Dhan Bahadur Nepali also narrates about specific trajectories which became a reason to weaken untouchability and caste discrimination against the Dalits. The concurrent security operation by police and royal army created a circumstances in Thabang by which community feeling between peasants grow while going for safety in forests. This was later resulted in the *Jansatta*'s declaration of Thabang as untouchability liberated zone.

In this sense, formation and declarations of *Jansatta* in village and Special District was not mobilised for villager's empowerment to solve their everyday problem but rather for military mobilization. This is a basic reason as life histories of Deumaya Budha Magar narrates that illness of her father could not become a serious issue worth to get resolve which led her to desert the movement finally. The declaration of a base area in form of Thabang Special District was done without adhering to theory of Protracted People's War. Consequently, the Maoists leadership did not really thought over resolving the essential question of "semi-feudal, semi-colonial" Nepal where demand of a land distribution and livelihood questions were not worth issues to get resolved.

How come this sense of betrayal emerged among local party activists that the senior Maoist leadership was not attentive to their questions once their 'Cash Maoist' journey begun? The two life histories (3 and 6) of a Dalit activist and a village *Jansatta* deputy chief put a light on this aspect. According to them, middle and rich peasants were dominating in the local leadership where majority of population had a subsistence economic resource. Though, it was poor peasants who had actively participated in movement but they kept always in lower committees of the party and *Jansatta*. A majority of these activists came from poor background always faced livelihood question which get manifested in their demand of distribution of land. But the village and Thabang Special District government did not look at it since the CPN (M) had no policy from central level. Instead what was done on mere mechanically building of co-operatives, bank and commune and collectivization of land, which was surely had to be get failed which resulted eventually. Moreover, if they have had any policy then moneylenders would not have been emerged from local Maoist leadership.

In course of time, what came into picture was to achieve quick victory at any cost since the Maoist had left aside theory of guerrilla warfare long ago. The CPN (M) leadership caught in an ideological blunder which gets reflected in their mechanical understanding of mobilizing Maoist governance as my study of Thabang shows. It means that the CPN (M) was never serious to transforming project of building of new society. It was why as life history of Comrade Jung tells that a practice of two separate kitchen system one for senior leaders and other for lower party activists existed during the whole course of Maoist armed struggle.

Thus quick victory was its obvious outcome with tendencies of warlord. The two life histories (5 and 6) of a PLA commander Binay Pun and Comrade Jung recollects this fact very clearly that in most of battles between PLA and government security forces after royal army mobilization in 2001, the CPN (M) faced a series of defeats and heavy loss of its activists. It was why; there was no emphasis on political work within the Maoist organizations.

So politicization of activists including political organization and Maoist combatants did not take place at all. It was precisely this reason when CPN (M)'s 'Cash Maoist' journey started from the end of 1998 which later expressed in a theoretical form of "*Prachanda Path*". This gave birth to a political strategy other than fighting a protracted People's War which resulted in heavy loss of Maoist combatants. This made a mass desertion from party, PLA and also from the movement too.

This is the idea which I theorised as 'Cash Maoism' according to which the political movement led by the Maoists were not intended to transform Nepali society and state but rather focussed on using its military mobilizations as a bargaining chip to enter in parliamentary bourgeois politics. This process had already begun once they went on with formal and informal peace negotiation starting with King Birendra and during reign of King Gyanendra. Their journey was finally settled by May, 2006 Peace Treaty.

Through a thesis of Nepal's 'Cash Maoism', I have demonstrated that the People's War in Nepal emerged as an effective form of political mobilization until first stage of strategic defence whereby it drew to its fold the most oppressed and marginalised classes and communities. The people responded overwhelmingly to the call of the People's War because it fulfilled some of their long-standing political, social, economic and cultural aspirations. As long as the CPN (M) adhered to its basic principles, it could initiate a process of democratising the society in Nepal by challenging the Nepali state. Even though as a concept and a form of political mobilization the *Jansatta* attracted mass support in Nepal. It is why the villagers opposed re-entry and establishment of police post in Thabang, because they know difference between Maoist army and government security forces. Thus in conclusion of this chapter, it can be said that political consciousness of people was thus taken as for granted by the CPN (M). The fundamental social transformation which was the necessity of people – including revolutionary demand of land redistribution – remained unfulfilled due to abandonment of the protracted path of People's War and adhering to quick victory. Therefore, the embryonic forms of Maoist government could not fulfil its responsibility of emerging as an alternative to the political power of the "old state".

From Thabang's experience, it can be concluded that the political movement of People's War gave birth to 'Cash Maoism' in Nepal because in absence of correct mass line. This is why those peasants of Thabang reiterate that they have not fought for the Democratic Federal Republic of Nepal. They are ready to follow only those who will carry forward flag of liberation but not the leaders who have betrayed them by abandoning goal of the Socialist Nepal in midway.

Glossary

Abhiyan	Campaign.
Akhil Nepal Kisan Sangh	All Nepal Peasant Association.
Akhil Nepal Mahila Sangathan	All Nepal Women Organisation.
Asal Hindusthan	Pure land of Hindus.
Bahudal	Multi-party democracy/multi-party system.
Bahudaliya Janbad	Multi Party Popular Democracy.
Bhailo	A musical performance and celebration held during Dasain/Tihar festival in Nepal.
Bharuwa bandook	A homemade local gun which fire only one time.
Birta	Land granted to individual on a tax free basis.
Bist Kamaune	A tradition practice among Dalit in Thabang as similar to the *Jajmani* system in India.
Chaar Tyarri	Four preparation organised by the CPN (M) prior to the People's War.
Dalit Mukti Morcha	Dalit Liberation Front.
Chaklabandi	Collectivization of land.
Chapamar Dal	Guerrilla squad.
Dai	Elder brother.

Dal-Bhat	A standard Nepali diet of lentil *(dal)* and rice *(bhat)* which often served with fried vegetable on the side.
Desain	A Hindu festival of Nepal that celebrated for ten days. The festival also marks the beginning of harvesting.
Dhami-Jhankri	A *Shaman* priest who work as local doctor.
Dhido	Usually cooked from flour of maize by making a semi-liquid material and taking as main meal along with lentil with vegetable.
Ga-Ja-Sa	A village level Maoist government. Also refer as *Jansatta/Gaon Jansarkar/Gaon Jansatta.*
Gaon	Village.
Gramin Varg Sangarsh	Rural class struggle, a political and socio-cultural mobilization prior to the People's War.
Goth	Shepherd's hut, a hut nearby irrigated field.
Guthi	Land endowments for religious and charitable trust.
JABAS	*Jan Vargiya Sangathan*, various mass organizations based on class and oppressed nationality.
Jagir	Land assigned to government officials in lieu of cash salaries they were entitled to receive.
Jand	A home-made bear.
Janjati	Ethnic community. After 1990s, this was designated and referred to non-Hindu groups and tribal ethnic groups found in Nepal.
Sanyunkta Janmorcha	Political organization of underground CPN (Unity Centre).
Jansatta	People's Power.

Jari	A practice in the hills regions in which a man takes away another's wife by paying him compensation for the loss of his property.
Janyudha	People's War.
Jilla Jansarkar	District People's Government.
Kalo Pahar	A popular destination located in Kangada district of Indian state of Himanchal Pradesh.
Khola	Small River in hill.
Khukri	A type of *Nepali* knife.
Ladaku Dal	Fighting group/squad.
Magar Mukti Morcha	Magar Liberation Front.
Mashal Juloos	Torch light procession.
Moto Mashal	A Communist faction called CPN (*Mashal*) led by Mohan Baidya alias Kiran.
Mukhiya	Village Mayor/ headman, and revenue collector for un-irrigated land.
Muluki Ain	Civil code.
Panchayat	System of government (1960-1990) in which political parties were banned.
Phataha	Mischief/ liar.
Pradhan Panch	An elected village mayor during *Panchayat* regime.
Raikar	Land under the proprietorship of the state.
Raksi	Home-made liquor distilled from millet.
Ranga	Buffalo.
Sahid	Martyr.
Shamanta	Feudal landlord.

Sukuti	A dish made of dry meat of pig, buffalo, cow, and goat.
Sija Abhiyan	The campaign prior to People's War in Nepal. The term derives from two Mountains, the *Sisne* Mountain of Rukum district and the *Jaljala* Mountain of Rolpa district.
Singh Durbar	Office of the Prime Minister of Nepal.
Panch	Refer to the *Panchayat* politician from bottom of village to top level of centre level.
Patlo Masal	A Communist faction led by Mohan Bikram Singh.
Tamsuk	Bond paper/ loan paper of peasants issued by agricultural banks or refer to moneylenders.
Thabangi	Person living in Thabang VDC.
Thar	Clan.
Thula Gaon	Official Headquarter of the VDC.
Tihar	A festival of Hindu population in Nepal as same as Diwali in north India.
Bishes Jilla	Special district.

Photographs at Thabang

Poster issued in June, 1996 during initiation of the Janyudha in Nepal

First leaflet of People's War, issued by CPN (M) on 13 February, 1996

Barman Budha Magar, founder of Nepal Communist Party in Thabang

Communist veteran Tejman Gharti Magar alias 'Dirgh' was the first chief of Thabang Special Distrct People's Government

A Martyr's family; (from clockwise) son & wife of Tejman Gharti Magar alias 'Dirgh'

A picture showing Marxism-Leninism-Maoism-Prachandpath Zindabad

The Julmeni family own a seven story guest house in Libang, the district headquarter of Rolpa

Remains of regional police post of Thabang VDC, destroyed during the Janyudha

Rajdhan B.K. worked as Maoist militia; now engaged in traditional occupation

Proceedings of Janbadi Vivah in Thabang

Sarkeni B.K. was the first Dalit woman judge of the People's Court

Debris of household of Thabang village now used as Volleyball ground; the Royal Nepal Army had set ablaze more than 17 households on 28 March, 2002

Thabang High School

A wall painting done during Maoist movement

Celebration of Desain festival @ Ajamabri Commune, Rachibang village, 6 November, 2010

A Dalit Hotel in Thabang village; run by Jabbar Singh Sunar since 2008

A view of Thula Gaon (from top), Thabang VDC

Entrance to Thula Gaon, Thabang; Workers of All Countries, unite! - with background painting of the Communist ideologues Marx, Engels, Lenin, Stalin, Mao: wall painting done first time during establishment of Thabang Special District

A view of ThulaGaon (from top), Thabang VDC

A local shaman

Two generations of retired Gurkha pensioner; from clockwise, Ram Prasad Roka Magar of British Gurkha Regiment, aged 94 years old & Rajman Nepali of Indian Gurkha Regiment aged 64 years

The Bhume Mela at main ground, Thabang VDC

A group of villager

A group of villagers

Mules are main source of transportation of goods in mountains

Martyr's Memorial Road

Appendix

1. APPENDIX

Table-I: Revolts and rebellions against state[1]

The criterion for including events in table records is a large participation of people in collective, public political struggles in forms of revolt and rebellions that resulted in suppression and execution. More than five dozen of such activities has been documented by many scholars however the number of such revolting events are high and scattered in various works of both folk literature, songs and manuscripts. The table-1 records various revolts and rebellions from 1770s until beginning of organised political movement from 1950s.

Period	Revolts against the state until 1960s	Location
1770	Ten Limbuwan rebellion and expulsion.	Pallo Kirant (far-east)
1773-81	Majh Kirant rebellion.	Dudhkoshi-Arun region
1778	Limbu revolt against language suppression and execution of Phakosek Limbu, expulsion of many others.	Pallo Kirant (far-east)
1792	Limbu revolt against encroachment of ethnic autonomy and inherent lands rights and the execution of several Limbus, mass expulsion.	Far Kirat

1 **Source:** Mahendra Lawoti, (2007), *Contentious Politics and Democratization in Nepal*, New Delhi: Sage Publications, p. 32.

1792-93	Nepal-China war: Limbus and Bhote assist China.	Arun-Tista (Limbus) and Nuwakot (Bhote)
1793	Tamang(Murmi) revolt for autonomy: for religious freedom and mass suppression.	Nuwakot
1790	Jumla rebellion led by Sobhan Shahi.	Jumla
1808	Khambu (Rai) revolt against ancestral land expropriation and usurpation of local autonomy and execution of 2 Khambus, enslavement and property confiscation of 15 families and mass exodus of Khambu peasantry.	Majh Kirat, Bhojpur
1858	Sukhdev Gurung rebellion for land rights, autonomy and religious freedom: execution of Sukhdev Gurung after 15 years in jail and property confiscation of many persons.	Lamjung
1867	Dashain (festival) boycott: Ramlihang and Ridima killed.	Dhankuta
1870	Limbu rebellion: for community land (Kipat system) and language repression.	Pallo Kirant (far-east)
1876	Magar rebellion: Lakhan Thapa Magar and his seven associates hanged and hundreds of Magar families fled from the country to avoid execution/incarceration.	Gorkha
1877	Supati Gurung rebellion: for local autonomy, religious freedom. Execution of Supati Gurung and many others and their property confiscation.	Gorkha
1908	Limbu rebellion: for Kipat land. Atal Rai, Bharatsing Rai and Kanthabir Rai were executed.	Manjh Kirant
1910	Cultural resistance of various ethnic groups and theirs incineration of almost 30000 copies of genealogies, copper plates, stone inscription, manuscripts and other documents of historical, linguistics, cultural and religious importance.	Throughout Nepal

1914	Cultural revivalist movement against suppression of Limbu language: execution of several Limbu language speakers and expulsion of several Limbus including Lalsor Sendang and his disciples.	Throughout Nepal
1925	Buddhist revivalism to resist Hindu hegemony and suppression of Buddhist, Pragyaratna Mahasthavir and other eight monks sent into exile.	Patan and Kathmandu
1927	Religious freedom movement by Newar of Kathmandu valley: Buddhist monks expelled.	Kathmandu
1941	Buddhist religion suppression: four rebel (including 3 Newars) given capital punishment.	Kathmandu
1950	Literary movement for democracy & Newar language suppression and incarceration of eminent poets/ authors Chittadhar Hridaya, Siddhicharan Shrestha, Phutte Bahadur Singh for 10 years and confiscation of their property.	Kathmandu
1950-51	Kiranti rebellion for local autonomy and Kipat land: suppression of Kirant leaders.	Majh & Pallo Kirant (east & west hill
1956	Tamang rebellion (Khaniyabash Kanda) against Hindu high caste exploitation and suppression of local Tamang people (several executed, incarcerated and run away).	Dhading, Nuwakot and Rasuwa
1961	Movement against making Nepali the only language of instruction.	Terai

Table-II: Social movements in Nepal since 1950s[2]

In addition to above documentation, a series of social movements (i.e., student, Dalit and peasant) got organised with a direct influence of Nepal Communist Party. The below table is based on these events.

2 *Ibid.*, p. 33.

Peasant Movement	**Student Movement**	**Dalit Movement**
18 November 1950: Firing at a rally organized by Kisan Sangh, several killed in districts of Gaur and Routhat	1947: Jayatu Sanskratam Movement led by different student groups in Kathmandu	1947: Anti-untouch-ability movement lead by Bhagat Sarabjit mainly centred in mid-western Nepal; suppressed and failed
3 May 1951, Anti-landlord movement: several killed in police firing in Bardiya district	1951: Student movement lead by Chiniya Kaji against Rana regume; Kaji was killed by government	1954: Dalit temple entry movement by entering in Pashupati temple in Kathmandu and Shaileshowri temple in Doti district; suppressed by state and several injured
1952: Peasant Movement organized by Kisan Sangh in several districts of Terai mainly in Rauthat, Bara, Parsa, Sarlahi and Mahottari (began from Rauthat); brutal suppression, several killed by the police	1966: student movement for organizing Free Student Unions mainly focused in Kathmandu and few urban centre	1965: Dalit temple entry movement at Sidhkali in Bhojpur district of eastern Nepal; failed
January 1952: revolt lead by Dr. KI Singh in Kathmandu; brutally suppressed, several killed	1976: four months long student movement for democracy, inconclusive result, focused in Kathmandu only	

1953: Peasant-landlord conflict erupted in hill region mainly in Pyuthan district; brutally suppressed by state	April 1979: Bhutto death protest that turned into a student movement ; forced king's controlled Panchayat government to organize national referendum	
August 1953: Peasant movement led by Bhim Datt Pant in Dhangarhi district of far-western Nepal; Indian Army intervened and suppressed this movement by killing him and several of his associates		
1964: Peasant revolt against abolish of Kipat (community land) in eastern hills		
1965-69: Peasant movement in western and mid eastern Nepal		
1979: peasant protest, Chintag killing in Dhankuta by landlords		

2. APPENDIX

40 Points Demand

4 February, 1996
Right Honourable Prime Minister
Prime Minister's Office
Singha Darbar, Kathmandu

Sub: Memorandum

Sir,

It has been six years since the autocratic monarchical partyless Panchayat system was ended by the 1990s People's Movement and a constitutional monarchical multiparty parliamentary system established. During this period state control has been exercised by a tripartite interim government, a single-party government of the Nepali Congress, a minority government of UML and a present Nepali Congress-RPP-Sadbhavana coalition. That, instead of making progress, the situation of the country and the people is going downhill is evident from the fact that Nepal has slid to being the second poorest country in the world; people living below the absolute poverty line has gone up to 71 per cent; the number of unemployed has reached more than 10 per cent while the number of people who are semi-employed or in disguised employment has crossed 60 per cent; the country is on the verge of bankruptcy due to rising foreign loans and deficit trade; economic and cultural encroachment within the country by foreign, and especially Indian, expansionists is increasing by the day; the gap between the rich and the poor and between towns and villages is growing wider. On the other hand, parliamentary parties that have formed the government by various means have shown that they are more interested in remaining in power with the blessings of foreign imperialist and expansionist masters than in the welfare of the country and the people. This is clear from their blindly adopting so-called privatization and liberalization to fulfil the interests of all imperialists and from the recent 'national consensus' reached in handing over the rights over Nepal's water resources to Indian expansionists. Since 6 April, 1992, the United People's Front has been involved in various struggles to fulfil relevant demands related to nationalism, democracy and livelihood, either by itself or with others. But rather than fulfil those demands, the governments formed at different times have violently suppressed the agitators and taken the lives of hundreds; the most recent example of this is the armed police operation in Rolpa a few months back. In this context, we would like to once again present to the current coalition government demands related to nationalism, democracy and livelihood, which have been raised in the past and many of which have become relevant in the present context.

Our demands

Concerning nationality

1. All discriminatory treaties, including the 1950 Nepal-India Treaty, should be abrogated.
2. The so-called Integrated Mahakali Treaty concluded on 29 January, 1996 should be repealed immediately, as it is designated to conceal the disastrous Tanakpur Treaty and allows Indian imperialist monopoly over Nepal's water resources.
3. The open border between Nepal and India should be regulated, controlled and systematised. All vehicles with Indian licence plates should be banned from Nepal.
4. The Gurkha/Gorkha Recruitment Centres should be closed. Nepali citizens should be provided dignified employment in the country.
5. Nepali workers should be given priority in different sectors.

A 'work permit' system should be strictly implemented if foreign workers are required in the country.

6. The domination of foreign capital in Nepali industries, business and finance should be stopped.
7. An appropriate customs policy should be devised and implemented so that economic development helps the nation become self-reliant.
8. The invasion of imperialist and colonial culture should be banned. Vulgar Hindi films, videos and magazines should be immediately outlawed.
9. The invasion of colonial and imperial elements in the name of NGOs and INGOs should be stopped.

Concerning people's democracy

10. A new constitution should be drafted by representatives elected for the establishment of a people's democratic system.
11. All special privileges of the king and the royal family should be abolished.
12. The army, the police and the bureaucracy should be completely under people's control.
13. All repressive acts, including the Security Act, should be repealed.
14. Everyone arrested extra-judicially for political reasons or revenge in Rukum, Rolpa, Jajarkot, Gorkha, Kabhre, Sindhupalchowk, Sindhuli, Dhanusa, Ramechhap, and so on should be immediately released. All false cases should be immediately withdrawn.
15. The operation of armed police, repression and state-sponsored terror should be immediately stopped.

16. The whereabouts of citizens who disappeared in police custody at different times, namely Dilip Chaudhary, Bhuwan Thapa Magar, Prabhakar Subedi and others, should be investigated and those responsible brought to justice. The families of victims should be duly compensated.
17. All those killed during the People's Movement should be declared martyrs. The families of the martyrs and those injured and deformed should be duly compensated, and the murderers brought to justice.
18. Nepal should be declared a secular state.
19 Patriarchal exploitation and discrimination against women should be stopped. Daughters should be allowed access to paternal property.
20. All racial exploitation and suppression should be stopped. Where ethnic communities are in the majority, they should be allowed to form their own autonomous governments.
21. Discrimination against downtrodden and backward people should be stopped. The system of untouchability should be eliminated.
22. All languages and dialects should be given equal opportunities to prosper. The right to education in the mother tongue up to higher levels should be guaranteed.
23. The right to expression and freedom of press and publication should be guaranteed. The government mass media should be completely autonomous.
24. Academic and professional freedom of scholars, writers, artists and cultural workers should be guaranteed.
25. Regional discrimination between the hills and the tarai should be eliminated. Backward areas should be given

regional autonomy. Rural and urban areas should be treated at par.

26. Local bodies should be empowered and appropriately equipped.

Concerning livelihood

27. Land should be belong to 'tenants'. Land under control of the feudal system should be confiscated and distributed to the landless and the homeless.
28. The property of middlemen and comprador capitalists should be confiscated and nationalised. Capital lying unproductive should be invested to promote industrialisation.
29. Employment should be guaranteed for all. Until such time as employment can be arranged, an employment allowances should be provided.
30. A minimum wage for workers in industries, agriculture and so on should be fixed and strictly implemented.
31. The homeless should be rehabilitated. No one should be relocated until alternative infrastructure is guaranteed.
32. Poor farmers should be exempt from loan repayments. Loans taken by small farmers from the Agricultural Development Bank should be written off. Appropriate provisions should be made to provide loans for small farmers.
33. Fertiliser and seeds should be easily available and at a cheap rate. Farmers should be provided with appropriate prices and markets for their produce.
34. People in the flood- and drought-affected areas should be provided with appropriate relief materials.

35. Free and scientific health services and education should be available to all. The commercialisation of education should be stopped.
36. Inflation should be checked. Wages should be increased proportionate to inflation. Essential goods should be cheaply and easily available to everyone.
37. Drinking water, roads, and electricity should be provided to all villagers.
38. Domestic and cottage industries should be protected and promoted.
39. Corruption, smuggling, black marketing, bribery, and the practices of middlemen and so on should be eliminated.
40. Orphans, the disabled, the elderly and children should be duly honoured and protected.

We would like to request the present coalition government to immediately initiate steps to fulfil these demands which are inextricably linked with the Nepali nation and the life of the people. If there are no positive indications towards this from the government by 17 February, 1996, we would like to inform you that we will be forced to adopt the path of armed struggle against the existing state power.

Thank you.

Dr. Baburam Bhattarai

Chairman

Central Committee, United People's Front, Nepal

3. APPENDIX: CHRONOLOGY OF TEN YEARS OF PEOPLE'S WAR[3]

1996

- 13 February: Initiation of the People's War in Nepal by the CPN (M) following 1st Plan of "March along the path of People's War to smash the reactionary state and establish a New Democratic State!"
- First propaganda raid by the Maoist's guerrillas on the state-owned Bank in Chyangli, Gorkha district. The guerrillas burnt down hundreds of bond & debt papers of the peasants. Another 3 simultaneous attacks on police post were carried out in three different districts namely Rolpa (Holeri), Rukum (Athbiskot) and Sindhuli (Sindhuligari).
- 19 February: Press statement by Prachanda, General Secretary of the CPN (M) taking responsibility of nationwide armed strikes.
- June: 2nd Plan starts. Slogan: "Let us develop guerrilla war in a planned way!"

1997

- 3 January: First successful attack by the guerrillas in Bethan police post of Ramechap district. At least 4 policemen and 3 guerrillas got killed.
- June: 3rd Plan of People's War with the slogan: "Let us take the guerrilla war to a new height of development."
- September: The guerrillas' raided police patrol troop in Kalikatar, Tanahun district and seized weapons.

3 This chronology has been drawn from various sources.

1998

- 14 June: Guerrilla attack on Riot police base camp at Laha in Jajarkot district.
- May: Girija Prasad Koirala government starts counter-insurgency Operation Kilo-Sierra-2 by deploying thousands of specially trained security forces in 20 districts.
- August-September: The CPN (M) call for 4th Plan to "Advance in the great direction of creating base area".
- 27 October: Various police posts in three districts of Kavre, Parsa and Dhanusha were successfully raided.

1999

- 3 January: Successful guerrilla attack on Bhattedanda police post in Lalitpur district.
- 23 January: Two police posts were attacked by the guerrillas in Kalikot district.
- 23 April: Gualichour police post in Baglung district attacked and looted.
- May: The Maoist boycotted general election; Nepali Congress leaders KP Bhattarai was elected Prime Minister
- 2 May: Police base camp in Janbang, Rolpa was attacked.
- 10 May- 28 May: Three police posts in districts of Kalikot, Gorkha and Jumla.
- 4 June: Guerrilla action on a local branch of Nepal Bank Ltd. in Khimti, Ramechhap and burning of loan papers of the peasants.
- 11 June: The Guerrilla attack on policepost in Odanakhu Padam, Jumla.

- 14 June: A commando police post in Laha, Jajarkot captured by guerrillas.
- 30 June: A police post in Machhae VDC of Kavre district was attacked by Maoist squad and looted arms.
- August: The 5th Plan begun by calling to "Go forward a bit more in great direction of building base area".
- 21 September: The guerrillas raided Mahat police base camp in Rukum district. More than half a dozen of policemen killed and a DSP with dozens of policemen detained and kept in Thabang.
- 2 November: The Maoist combatants attacked 2 police posts successfully one each in districts of Kalikot and Dolpa.

2000

- January: Two police posts were raided successfully in Jumla district and Nuwakot. 3 policemen killed including a guerrilla commander.
- 20 February: Successful raid by the guerrilla squads on riot area police camp in GhartigaunVDC of Rolpa.
- March: Guerrilla attacks on police posts in Bhengri in Pyuthaan, and Dhurkot in Gulmi district.
- 2 April-5 April: Tworiot area police base camp raided in Taksera and Takma in Rukum.
- 13 April: Harmi Bhanjyang police post in Gorkha district was successfully raided.
- June: The Maoist call for 6th Plan with a aim to consolidate base area in their influence area.
- 3 July: Riot police base camp in Jajarkot was attacked.
- 23 August: Dhawadi police post was successfully raided in Nawalparasi

- 30 August-31 August: an area police office and forest guards post was raided successfully in districts of eastern Terai of Jhapa and Morang.
- 24 September: First attack on a district headquarters in Dunai of Dolpa district. 14 police force killed, leaving 40 of them injured.
- 25 September: Maoist leader Prachanda appeal for Peace Talks with government of Nepal.
- 26 September: Guerrilla raid on the Bhorletar area police office in Lamjung, killing 8 policemen. A national bank was also raided and burning of bonds papers of peasants.
- 20 December: Declaration of first District People's Government in Rukum.

2001

- February: The CPN (Maoist) adopted party's ideological and political line, Marxism-Leninism-Maoism and "*Prachanda Path*" through Second National Conference held in India. Now onwards designation of Party's General Sectary is replaced by Chairman.
- 30 March: Successful jailbreak by 7 women guerrillas in Gorkha district.
- 1 April: The guerrillas successfully attacked on three police base camp in Rukumkot, Naumule and Mainapokhari.
- June: A Coordination Committee of the Maoist Parties and organizations of South Asia (CCOMPOSA) formed.
- 1 June: Massacre at Royal Palace.
- 6 July: Raid on area police post in Bichaur in Lamjung district.
- 12 July: The guerrilla squad attacked on Holeripolice post

in Rolpa. 71 policemen taken into custody.

- 30 August: First Peace Talk with the Nepal government began.
- September: a national convention held in Kureli VDC of Rolpa call for formation of United Revolutionary People's Council (URPC) and People's Liberation Army (PLA).
- 21 November: Chairman Prachanda announced an end to Peace Talks.
- 23 November: First large scale military attack by the PLA in Ghorahi, district headquarters of Dang. 14 RNA men with 11 policemen killed including a Major. 7 PLA were also killed. The PLA also seized many sophisticated weapons i.e. rocket launchers and mortars etc.
- 23 November: Another military attack by PLA on district headquarters of Syangja district. 14 policemen were killed and over a dozen injured. A hundred rifles and a large quantity of ammunitions were seized.
- 25 November: District Headquarter of Solukhumbu district raided by PLA. 33 policemen including 4 RNA men and 2 government officers died. 15 PLA were also killed.
- 7 December: Unsuccessful PLA attack communication towers in Rolpa and Salyan districts.

2002

- February: A series of successful PLA attacks on police posts in different district of Kavre, Sarlahi, Salyan and Aacham. It also included a notable attack by destructing of Mangalsen Palace in Aacham district leaving 132 security personnel (including RNA too) dead. The Maoist also lost its 24 PLA combatants.

- 11 April: PLA attack on armed police force in Satbaria, and police post in Lamahi of Dang district. 34 armed security personnel killed with many injured.
- 2 May: First incident positional battle between the PLA and the RNA in Tewang VDC of Rolpa district.
- 7 May: A RNA military base camp in Gam VDC of Rolpa district was destroyed by the PLA. 31 RNA personnel with a dozens of PLA were killed.
- 27 May: The first unsuccessful Khara battle in Rukum district where hundred of PLA combatants dead.
- 8 September: A successful military strike by the PLA on armed police post in Bhiman of Sindhuli district. 49 police personnel dead and more than three dozens injured.
- 10 September: A big PLA attack on Sandhikharka, the district headquarters of Arghakhanchi. 81 security personnel were killed. Many loss on PLA side too.
- 4 October: King Gyanendra sacked Prime Minister Sher Bahadur Deuba, suspend parliament and assumed executive power.
- 27 October: A failed PLA strike on RNA soldiers in Okhaldhunga district where many of Maoist combatants left dead.
- 14 November: PLA attack in Khalanga, the district headquarters of Jumla. Many as more than a dozen PLA activists got killed including 33 security personnel including a CDO. Millions of cash money and large quantities of arms and ammunitions seized.
- 4 December: Two area police posts and local branch of Nepal Bank Ltd. in Siraha and Dang district respectively is attacked by the PLA. Around a dozen policemen killed.

2003

- January: In first week two PLA ambushes on government forces in Kusum, Banke district leaving 6 policemen dead and 14 injured. And on RNA patrol in Banke district. 2 RNA personnel and 3 policemen killed.
- 25 January: Krishna Mohan Shrestha, IGP of Armed Police Force, killed by special task force of PLA in day light in Kathmandu.
- 28 January: The Second Peace Talk between the CPN (M) and Nepal government begun in Kathmandu.
- 27 April- 16 July: Three rounds of Peace Talks held until Doramba massacre took place on 16 July.
- 27 August: Break down of seven month long ceasefire and Peace Talks.
- September: A series of PLA attacks on the RNA camps in different parts of country where hundreds of losses for both sides. 41 RNA were killed in Kailali; 9 RNA killed in Goganpani, Doti; PLA battle with RNA in Kerabari and in Saptari district.
- 10 October: Unsuccessful attack on armed police base camp in Kusum which resulted in heavy losses for PLA.
- 12 October: The armed police training camp in Bhaluwang was attacked by killing 25 RNA personnel. Significant quantity of arms seized by PLA but also lost more than a dozen combatants.
- 15 October: A RNA company force in Gaira of Ghanteshower is attacked in national highway leaving 21 RNA dead.
- 15 November: A RNA Brigadier General and 3 other army officers were blown up in a mining ambush in Makwanpur district; 12 RNA personnel killed and 15 were seriously injured in a PLA attack in Bajhang district.

- 18 November: 11 police personnel got killed in a road ambush in Morang district.
- 1 December: 15 RNA men killed and 35 injured in a PLA attack in Kailali district. A high ranking PLA commander reported dead.
- 3 December: 4 RNA personnel died in road ambush in Morang district.
- 13 December: A fierce encounter between the RNA and the PLA at Pachhawang of Rolpa in which 10 RNA soldiers dead. Four Maoist combatants including a senior commander died.

2004

- January: 79 RNA personnel killed in various PLA ambushes in different location of national highways. This includes Hetauda-Narayangarh national highway, Narayangarh-Mughling highway in Chitwan district and eastern and far-western Nepal districts of Khotang, Morang and Dadeldhura. More than a dozen PLA combatants also left dead.
- 21 February: A 14 hours long battle between the PLA and the RNA at Khotang district. One dozen RNA personnel and 6 PLA combatants get killed.
- 2 March: The district headquarters of Bhojpur district was attacked leaving more than 30 government security personnel dead and many injured.
- 20 March: One of the biggest and successful military actions by the PLA on Beni. 150 RNA and police personnel dead.
- April: a series of PLA attacks in first week of April in Dhanusha and Ilam district. 13 Policemen were killed and 20 injured.

- May: 25 RNA personnel and 1 policeman killed in a PLA attack in two different incidents of Kabhre VDC in Dolkha and Doti district.
- 19 June: 14 police personnel were killed in a PLA ambush in Dang district.
- July: 24 security personnel (including RNA too) were killed in two different attacks in Parsa and Salyan district. Heavy loss for the PLA too.
- 5 September: Two high ranking PLA brigade commanders got killed in a battle with the RNA in forests of Siraha district.
- 16 November: 7 RNA personnel killed and 5 injured in an encounter at Prithvi national highway in Dhading district. Many losses for the PLA too including a senior battalion commander.
- 17 November: PLA attacked by a road ambush on RNA made 8 security personnel dead.
- 20 November: many hours long battle between the RNA and the PLA at Pandaun forest in Kailali district. 19 RNA soldiers dead whereas 10 PLA activists also died.
- 15 December: Positional battle with RNA in Arghakanchi district made 34 RNA men dead on the spot and many injured. Heavy losses for the PLA side too.
- 18 December: 4 police personnel died in a daylight PLA attack on police camp at Sankhu, a nearby town of national capital Kathmandu.
- 19 December: The PLA gunned down 9 RNA personnel in an encounter in Dolkha district. 3 Maoist combatants also died and many more injured.
- 22 December: 15 RNA soldiers died in a PLA attack in Bardia.

2005

- January: 47 RNA soldiers died in different PLA attacks in districts of Dhankuta, Ilam and Parbat.
- 1 February: Military coup by King Gyanendra.
- 9 February: Dhangadhi jailbreak in Kailali by the PLA and set free 130 Maoist activists.
- 7 April: The Second Khara attack by PLA. Heaviest and largely unreported losses for the PLA in the history of People's War.
- 9 May: A failed military strike by the PLA on the RNA base camp at Bandipur in Siraha. Many losses for the PLA side.
- 11 May: 22 RNA personnel killed in a PLA attack in Kavre district.
- 25 June: Encounter between the PLA and RNA leaves 19 royal soldiers dead in Arghakanchi district.
- 7 August: PLA military raid on the RNA base camp at Pili in Kalikot district made 70 government security personnel dead.
- 22 November: Twelve Points Agreement signed in New Delhi between the CPN (M) and Seven Parliamentary Parties to jointly launch Anti-Monarchy People's Movement.

2006

- 14 January: A PLA strike in two police check posts at Thankot and Dadhikot simultaneously at the periphery of national capital of Kathmandu valley.
- 21 January: A 19 hours long battle held between the PLA and the RNA in Makawanpur district. 64 army soldiers killed whereas 26 Maoist combatants dead.

- 1 February: A PLA attack on Tansen, district headquarters of Palpa, leaving 47 RNA soldiers dead.129 prisoners, mostly Maoist activists were set free from the district jail.
- 6 February: PLA attacks two districts simultaneously in Uadypur and Kavre. 23 RNA soldiers get killed.
- 9 February: 25 RNA personnel died in a PLA ambush in Rambhapur of Nawalparasi district.
- 6 April: 19 days April People's Movement began from Kathmandu.
- 24 April: King Gyanendra recedes from power and announced that Parliament would be reinstated.
- 25 April: Girija Prasad Koirala appointed as interim Prime Minister of Nepal.
- 26 May: Peace Talks between the Nepal government and the CPN (M) began.

4. APPENDIX

Table-iii: Organizational structure of the People's War in Nepal

Party	People's Liberation Army (PLA)	United front (Jansatta)
General Headquarter (Chairman)	Central Military Commission (including Party Chairman)	United Revolutionary People's Council (Central level People's Government)
Standing committee (5 member)	General Staff (including division commanders)	Autonomous Regional People's Government
Politburo (17 members)	Division (7)	District People's Government (including Special District)

Central Committee (35 members)	Brigade (29)	Village People's Government
Command (west, east, special)	Battalion	Ward level People's council
Regional Bureau	Company	
District Committee	Platoon	
Area Committee	Section/ Squad	
Village Committee	Militia	
Cell Committee		

Numerical figure of Maoist guerrillas in PLA structure:

1 Division = several thousand combatants.

1 Brigade = 1,350 of minimum 3 battalions;

1 Battalion = 450 of minimum 3 companies;

1 Company = 150 of minimum 3 platoons;

1 Platoon = 30-45 of minimum 3 squads;

1 Squad/ section = 9-15 guerrillas;

Name of seven divisional headquarters of PLA duly located in UNMIN's supervision:

First Division: Chulachuli, Ilam

Second Division: Dudhauli, Sindhuli

Third Division: Shaktikhor, Chitwan

Fourth Division: Jhyaltungdanda, Nawalparasi

Fifth Division: Dahban, Rolpa

Sixth Division: Dasrathpur, Surkhet

Seventh Division: Talband, Kailali

5. APPENDIX: MAJOR EVENTS IN THABANG

- **June, 1955:** Barman Budha Magar & associates arrested on false charges of allegedly being 'communist' because of their clash and fight with *Mukhiya* of Thabang village.
- **1956:** Arrival of Communist leader Mohan Bikram Singh in Thabang. Thabang village branch of All Nepal Peasant Association was founded on 3 July, 1956.
- **1958:** Barman Budha Magar appointed as *Mukhiya* of Thabang village.
- **1959:** In Nepal's first general election, Thabang village unanimously voted for CPN candidate Khagulal Gurung from Pyuthan constituency.
- **1959:** Opening of Primary School in Thabang village which later get extended into Thabang High School.
- **1973:** Barman Budha Magar, then village mayor and Kaman Jhankri Magar get arrested for allegedly promoting seditious activities against the *Panchayat* government.
- **1974:** An anti-brewery women's movement gets organised in Thabang.
- **1976:** Producing crops of Hashish/Marijuana was banned by the *Panchayat* regime.
- **1979:** Student Movement in Thabang was a result of nationwide student protest demonstration against hanging of Julfikar Ali Bhutto by government of Pakistan.
- **1980:** National Referendum held in Nepal; Thabang village unanimously vote for the *Bahudal* system instead of the *Panchayat* system.
- **1980:** Village mayor Barman Budha gets arrested for allegedly opposing the *Panchayat* system and put in prison for two years.

- **1981:** Thabang village unanimously boycott the countrywide general elections organised by the *Panchayat* government.
- **October, 1981:** Military crackdown of Thabang village by Royal Nepal Army. An area police station was established in village.
- **1990:** People's Movement held and the party less *Panchayat* government was replaced by multi-party democracy in country.
- **June, 1991:** General election held in country; Thabang's Barman Budha Magar gets elected as Member of Parliament.
- **1992-1993:** Commencement of rural class struggle in Rolpa & Rukum amid police crackdown by Operation Romeo.
- **1995:** *Sija* campaign in Thabang and adjoining region; Four Preparations began to resist against state repression.
- **15 February, 1996:** First guerrilla action in Thabang by destructing Julmeni apple nursery after People's War broke on 13 February.
- **17 January, 1997:** A women activist Lali Roka Magar with Dilman Roka Magar was killed by police in a gruesome incident after gang rape in police custody in Thabang.
- **8 March, 1997:** A village fighting squad kill two police informer in retaliation of Lali Roka's massacre.
- **13 March-28 March, 1997:** A 15 day's jungle search operation by police in Thabang.
- **June, 1997:** Thabang village including dozens of VDCs of Rapti region boycotted mid-term general election.

- **May-November, 1998:** A counter-insurgency operation Kilo Sierra-2 held against the Maoist guerrillas in region.
- **21 September, 1999:** The guerrillas raided Mahat police camp an adjoining to Thabang village. Many policemen killed and a DSP with a dozens of policemen detained and kept in Thabang.
- **October, 1999:** A village level committee of *Jansatta* was founded in Thabang.
- **November, 1999:** The Maoist guerrillas attack and destroy Thabang Area police post completely.
- **April, 2001:** Two successful Maoist attacks on Nepal police at Namule and Rukumkot force government to relocated police stations to District Headquarter.
- **March, 2002:** The CPN (M) passes a resolution to form Thabang Special District in Thabang VDC.
- **30 March, 2002:** RNA's weeks long counter insurgency operation in Thabang village; army burned down more than two dozen houses of suspected Maoist activists.
- **September, 2002:** Village *Jansatta* gets established in Thabang. The Jaljala Co-operative bank (i.e., Janbadi bank) also founded.
- **25 February, 2003:** Thabang Special District People's Government founded in Thabang village.
- **June, 2003:** Ajambari Commune gets established in Rachibang hamlet of Thabang VDC.
- **9 January, 2004:** Magarat Autonomous Region People's Government is declared in a huge rally in Thabang.
- **October, 2004:** Radio People's Republic established at Jaljala Mountains.

- **11 October, 2004:** Tejman Gharti Magar alias Comrade Dirgh dies in Nepal's Tarai district of Kapilvastu during an encounter of government security forces. He was first chief of Thabang Special District Maoist Government and a member of advisory board to CPN (M).
- **20 November, 2004:** Inaugural ceremony of the Martyr's Road connecting Nuwagaun-Thabang-Chunbang was held by convening a rally at Thabang.
- **12 February, 2005:** A Martyrs Memorial School was founded in village.
- **April, 2006:** A 19 days April People's Movement begun from Kathmandu.
- **21 November, 2006:** Official declaration to end People's War in Nepal. A Comprehensive Peace Agreement was signed between the government and the Maoist. Village *Jansatta* gets disbanded.
- **August, 2007:** The Peasants of Thabang held a protest demonstration at Libang district headquarter to oppose government's effort to re-establish area police station in village; however police post get re-established at end of the year in view of holding constituent assembly elections.

6. APPENDIX: PEOPLE KILLED DURING PEOPLE'S WAR (1996-2006)

Year	By the Nepali State	By the CPN (M)	Total
1996	59	22	81
1997	16	32	48
1998	334	75	409
1999	328	141	469
2000	180	219	399
2001	243	390	633
2002	3296	1351	4647
2003	1217	646	1863
2004	1606	1113	2719
2005	1031	600	1631
Total	**8310**	**4589**	**12899**

Source: *CPN (M) (2006), The Worker: Organ of the Communist Party of Nepal (Maoist), No. 10, p. 140, (May Issue).*

Bibliography

PRIMARY SOURCES:

Unpublished Documents (Nepali)

Purn Bahadur Roka Magar (2008), Documentation of Purn Bahadur Roka Magar, Thabang.

CPN (M) (1999 [2055 B.S.]), '*Prativaden, Samkuta Gaon Jan Samiti*,' Thabang: Rolpa.

Published Documents (Nepali & English)

GON, (2008 [2065 B.S.]), *Antim Prativaden (Final Report)*, Babarmahal, Kathmandu: Ministry of Physical Planning & Building.

CBS, Nepal (1985), *Statistics on Rolpa, Rapti Zone*, HMG: National Planning Commission Secretariat.

CPN (M) (1997), *The Worker, Organ of the Communist Party of Nepal (Maoist)*, No. 3, (February issue).

CPN (M) (2001 [2057 B.S.]), '*Niti Tatha Krayakram, Gaon Jan Samiti*', 2057 (Policy and Program, United Village People's Committee, 2001).

CPN (M) (2002a), *Maoist Information Bulletin-1,* Occasional Information Bulletin of Communist Party of Nepal (Maoist), (January Issue).

CPN (M) (2002b), *Maoist Information Bulletin*-3, Occasional Information Bulletin of Communist Party of Nepal (Maoist), (April Issue).

CPN (M), (2003), *Maoist Information Bulletin-4,* Occasional Information Bulletin of Communist Party of Nepal (Maoist) (September Issue).

CPN (M) (2004a), *Problem and Prospects of Revolution in Nepal: A Collection of Articles by Com. Prachanda and Other Leaders of the CPN (Maoist)*, Nepal: Jandisha Prakashan.

CPN (M) (2004b), *Some Important Documents of Communist Party of Nepal (Maoist),* Nepal: Jandisha Publications.

CPN (M) (2004c), *Naya Chetna: Jansasharta Pustak*, Kshtriya Janshiksha Bibhag: Kendriya Aadhar Ilaka.

CPN (M) (2004d), '*Prativaden, Ajambari Jan Commune Thabang*', Thabang,

CPN (M) (2005a)), '*Niti Ra Karyakram*', *Magarant Syayattya Gantantra Jan Pratinidhi Sabha.*

CPN (M) (2005b), '*Pathyakram, Naya Janbadi Shiksha- Kaksha 1 Dekhi Kaksha 5 Samm*', Kshtriya Janshiksha Bibhag, Kendriya Aadhar Ilaka.

CPN (M), (2006), *The Worker: Organ of the CPN (Maoist)*, No. 10, (May Issue).

Onesto, Li (2001), 'Interview with Comrade Prachanda', *A World to Win*, No. 27.

Pun, Nirmal (1995 [2051]) 'Gramin Varg Sangharsh: Kehi Anubhibhuti Ra Shiksha', *Sisne: Akhil Jilla Sanagathan Samiti*, Rolpa, No. 3, (December issue), pp. 11-18.

Secondary Sources:

Acharya, Baburam and Yogi Narharinath (2010 [2061 BS]) (ed.), *Rashtrapita Badamaharajadhiraj Shri 5 Prithvinarayan Shahko Dibya Upadesh*, Antarrashtriya Manch Chhapakhana.

Adams, Vincanne (1998), *Doctors for Democracy: Health Professionals in the Nepali Revolution*, Cambridge: Cambridge University Press.

Adhikari, Aditya (2010), 'The Ideological Evolution of the Nepali Maoists', *Studies in Nepali History and Society*, Vol. 15, No. 2, pp. 217-251.

Adhikari, Kamal (1996), 'Naming Ceremonies as Rituals of Development', *Studies in Nepali History and Society,* Vol. 1, No. 2, pp. 345-364.

Kessel, Patrick (2008 [1974]), A Basic Understanding of the Communist Party, Rahul Foundation: Lucknow.

Alavi, Hamza (1979 [1965]), 'Peasants and Revolution', in A. R. Desai (ed.), *Peasant Struggles in India*, Bombay: Oxford University Press, p. 671-718.

Beteille, Andre (1974), *Studies in Agrarian Structures*, Delhi: Oxford University Press.

Bhandari, Khil Bahadur (2006 [2063 B.S.]), (ed.) *Krantiko Killa Thabang,* (in Nepali, Thabang: Fort of Revolution), Kathmandu: Vision Media.

Bhattarai, Baburam (2005 [2001]), 'Lets' Not Legitimize New Kot Massacre', in *Monarchy vs. Democracy: The Epic Fight in Nepal,* Noida: Samkaleen Teesari Duniya, pp. 17-25.

Bhattarai, Baburam (2003a), 'Political Economy of the People's War', in Arjun Karki and David Seddon (eds.), *The People's War in Nepal: Left Perspectives*, Delhi: Adroit Publishers, 117-164.

Bhattarai, Baburam (2003b), *The Nature of Underdevelopment and Regional Structure of Nepal: A Marxist Analysis,* Delhi: Adroit Publishers.

Bista, Dor Bahadur (2008 [1991]), *Fatalism and Development: Nepal's Struggle for Modernization*, Kolkata: Orient Longman.

Blaikie, Piers, John Cameron and David Seddon (2005 [1980]), *Nepal in Crisis: Growth and Stagnation at Periphery*, New Delhi: Adroit Publishers.

Brown, T. Louise (1996), *The Challenge to Democracy: A Political History*, London: Routledge.

Byres, T. J. (1986), 'Foreword: The Agrarian Question and Differentiation of the Peasantry', in Atiur Rahman (1986), *Peasants and Classes: A Study in Differentiation in Bangladesh*, London: Zed Books Ltd, pp. ix-xxxvii.

Cameron, Mary M. (1997), 'The Riti-Bhagya System in Western Nepal: Farmers And Artisans, Caste and Gender', in Mahanta K.C. (ed.), *People of the Himalayas: Ecology, Culture, Development and Change*, J. Hum. Ecol. Special Issue No. 6, pp. 189-194.

Caplan, Lionel (2007 [1970]), *Land and Social Change in East Nepal: A Study of Hindu-Tribal Relations*, Lalitpur: Himal Books.

Cowen, Sam (2010), 'Inside the People's Liberation Army', *European Bulletin of Himalayan Research*, Vol. 37, pp. 82-116.

Deutsch, Karl (1961), 'Social Mobilization and Political Development', *American Political Science Review*, Vol. 55, No. 3, pp. pp. 493-514.

'Dipak', Udaybahadur Chalune (2009 [2066 B.S.]), *Janyudha Ra Janmukti Sena: Saidhantik Aadhar Ra Karyaniti,(People's War and People's Liberation Army: Theoretical Basis and Tactics)*, People's Liberation Army, Nepal: Sixth Division.

Draper, Hal (1978), *Karl Marx's Theory of Revolution, Vol. 2*, Monthly Review Press: New York & London.

Engels, F. (1977), *The Origin of the Family, Private Property and the State: In the Light of the Researches of Lewis H. Morgan*, Moscow: Progress Publishers.

Etzioni, Amitai (1969), *The Active Society*, New York: Free Press.

Fanon, Franz (1971 [1961]), *The Wretched of the Earth*, Penguin Books: Middlesex.

Frank, Andre Gunder and Marta Fuetens (2002 [1987]), 'Nine Theses on Social Movements', in Ghanshyam Shah (ed.), *Social Movements and the State: Readings in Indian Government and Politics*, New Delhi: Sage Publications, pp. 32-55.

Fujikura, Tatsuro (1996), 'Technologies of Improvement, Locations of Culture: American Discourses of Democracy and 'Community Development' in Nepal', *Studies in Nepali History and Society*, Vol. 1, No. 2, pp. 271-311.

Gaige, Frederick H. (1975), *Regionalism and Nationalism in Nepal*, New Delhi: Vikas Publishing House.

Gautam, Shoba, Amrita Banskota and Rita Manchanda (2003), 'Where There Are No Men: Women in the Maoist Insurgency', in Deepak Thapa (ed.), *Understanding the Maoist Movement of Nepal*, Kathmandu: Martin Chautari, pp. 93-124.

Gellner, David N. (2007), 'Caste, Ethnicity and Inequality in Nepal', *Economic and Political Weekly*, Vol. XLII, No. 20, pp. 1823-1827.

Gurung, Harka (2008 [1997]), 'State and Society in Nepal', in David N. Gellner, Joanna Pfaff-Czarnecka with John Whelpton (eds.), *Nationalism and Ethnicity in Nepal*, Kathmandu: Vajra Publications, pp. 495-532.

Gurr, Ted Robert (1970), *Why Men Rebel?*, Princeton: Princeton University Press.

Heberle, Rudolf (1951), *Social Movements: An Introduction to Political Sociology*, New York: Appleton-Century-Crofts.

Hitchcock, John T. (1966), *The Magars of Banyan Hills*, New York: Holt, Rinehart & Winston.

Hobsbawm, Erich J. (1965 [1959]), *Primitive Rebels: Studies in Archaic Forms of Social Movement in the Nineteenth and Twentieth Centuries*, New York: W. W. Norton and Company.

Hofer, Andras (2004 [1979]), *The Caste Hierarchy and the State in Nepal: A study of the Muluki Ain of 1854*, Lalitpur: Himal Publication.

Hoftun Martin, William Reaper and John Whelpton (1999), *People, Politics and Ideology*, Kathmandu: Mandala Books.

Hutt, Michael (ed.) (2005), *Himalayan 'People's War': Nepal's Maoist Rebellion*, London: Hurst & Company.

International Crisis Group (2012), Nepal: From Two Armies To One, available at http://www.crisisgroup.org/~/media/Files/asia/south-asia/nepal/211----%20Nepal%20-%20From%20Two%20Armies%20to%20One.pdf

Joshi, Bhuwan Lal and Leo E. Rose (1966), *Democratic Innovations in Nepal: A Case Study of Political Acculturation*, Berkeley: University of California Press.

Karki, Arjun and David Seddon (2003) (eds.), *The People's War in Nepal: Left Perspectives*, Delhi: Adroit Publishers.

K. C., Surendra (2001), *Nepalma Communist Andolanko Itihas (History of Communist Movement in Nepal)*, Kathmandu: Bidyarthi Pustak Bhandar.

Kumar, S. (1967), *Rana Polity in Nepal: Origin and Growth*, Bombay: Asia Publishing House.

Laquerur, Walter (1977), *Guerrilla: A Historical and Critical Study*, London: Weidenfeld and Nicolsen.

Lawoti, Mahendra (2007) *Contentious Politics and Democratization in Nepal*, New Delhi: Sage Publications.

Lenin, Vladimir I. (1964), 'Development of Capitalism in Russia', in *Collected Works of Lenin, Vol-3*, Moscow: Progress Publishers.

Lenin, V.I. (1968a), 'Imperialism, The Highest Stage of Capitalism', in *Selected Works* of Lenin, Moscow: Progress Publishers, pp. 169-262.

Lenin, V.I. (1968b), 'The State And Revolution' in Selected Works of Lenin', in *Selected Works of Lenin*, Moscow: Progress Publishers, pp. 263-348.

Lenin, V.I. (1968c), 'Two Tactics of Social-Democracy in the Democratic Revolution', in *Selected Works of Lenin*, Moscow: Progress Publishers, pp. 50-147.

Magar, Purn Bahadur Roka (2011 [2068 B.S.]), *Krantikari Itihas Bokeko Thabang (Thabang that Carries a Revolutionary History)*, Nayabazar: Ganga Jamuna Press.

Map of Nepal (n.d.), available at www.ncthakur.itgo.com.

Marx, Karl (1955), *The Poverty of Philosophy*, Moscow: Progress Publishers.

Friedrich Engels (1974), *The German Ideology*, London: Lawrence and Wishart.

Marx, K. (1976), 'Theses On Feuerbach', in K. Marx, F. Engels, V. Lenin, *On Historical Materialism: A Collection*, Moscow: Progress Publishers.

Marx, Karl and Frederick Engels, (1977), *Manifesto of the Communist Party*, Peking: Foreign Language Press.

Marx, Karl (1977), *The Eighteenth Brumaire of Louis Bonaparte*, Moscow: Progress Publishers.

McLellan, David (1986), *Ideology*, Open University Press: Milton Keynes.

Mishra, Chaitanya (2004), 'Locating the 'Causes' of the Maoist Struggle', *Studies in Nepali History and Society*, Vol. 9, No. 1, (June issue), pp. 3-56.

Mishra, Chaitanya (2006), *Essays on the Sociology of Nepal*, Kathmandu: Fine Prints.

Mohanty, Manoranjan (2012 [1978]), *The Political Philosophy of Mao Zedong*, Delhi: Aakar Books.

Molnar, Augusta (1981), *The Kham Magar Women of Thabang*, Kathmandu: CEDA.

Myrdal, Jan (1965), *Report from a Chinese Village*, London: Heinemann.

Mikesell, Lawrence Stephen (1999), *Class, State, and Struggle in Nepal: Writings 1989-1995*, New Delhi: Manohar Publications.

Mikesell, Stephen (2007), 'Prajatantra' in Mary Des Chene, and Pratyoush Onta (eds.), *Nepalko Sandarbhma Samajsastriya Chintan*, Lalitpur: Social Science Baha, pp. 1-41.

Ogura, Kiyoko (2004), 'Realities and Images of Nepal's Maoists after the Attack on Beni', *European Bulletin of Himalayan Research*, Vol. 27, pp. 67-125.

Ogura, Kiyoko (2007), 'Maoist, People, and the State as Seen from Rolpa and Rukum', in H. Ishi, D. Gellner and K. Nawa (ed.), *Political and Social Transformation in North India and Nepal*, Delhi: Manohar Publications, pp. 435-475.

Ogura, Kiyoko (2008a), 'Maoist People's Governments, 2001-05: The Power in Wartime', in D.N. Gellner and K. Hachhethu (ed.), *Local Democracy in South Asia: Micro Process of Democratization in Nepal and its Neighbours*, New Delhi: Sage Publications, 175-231.

Ogura, Kiyoko (2008b), *Seeking State Power: The Communist Party of Nepal (Maoist),* available at http://edoc.vifapol.de/opus/volltexte/2011/2550/pdf/transitions_cpnm.pdf.

Onesto, Li (2005), *Dispatches from People's War in Nepal,* London: Pluto Press.

Onta, Pratyoush (1996a), 'Creating a Brave Nepali Nation in British India: The Rhetoric of Jati Improvement, Rediscovery of Bhanunhakta and the Writing of Bir History', *Studies in Nepali History and Society*, Vol.1, No. 1, (June isse), pp. 37-76.

Onta, Pratyoush (1996b), 'Ambivalence Denied: The Making of *Rastriya Itihas* in Panchayat Era Textbooks', *Contributions to Nepalese Studies*, Vol. 23, No. 1, pp. 213-254.

Oommen, T. K. (1990), *Protest and Change: Studies in Social Movements*, New Delhi: Sage Publications.

Pasang (2008), *Red Strides of the History: Significant Military Raids of the People's War*, Kathmandu: Agnipariksha Janprakashan Graha.

Patel, Pawan (2015), 'Nepal: 'Naya' Jange Sambidhan, 'Brahmanwadi Marxwad' Aur 'Cash Maowad' Ka Cocktail', Filhaal, Vol. 21-22, pp. 15-19.

Pathak, Bishnu (2005), *Politics of People's War and Human Rights in Nepal*, Kathmandu: Bimipa Publications.

Petras, James and Henry Veltmeyer (2005), *Social Movement and State Power: Argentina, Brazil, Bolivia, Ecuador*, London: Pluto Press.

Plummer, Ken (2001), 'The Call of Life Stories in Ethnographic Research', in Paul Atkinson et al (eds.), *Handbook of Ethnography*, London: Sage Publications, pp. 395-406.

Pradhan, Kumar (1991), *The Gorkha Conquests: The Process And Consequences Of The Unification Of Nepal, With Particular Reference To Eastern Nepal*, Calcutta: Oxford University Press.

Pradhan, Rajendra (2002), 'Ethnicity, Caste and a Plural Society', in Kanak Mani Dixit and Shastri Ramachandaran (eds.), *State of Nepal*, Kathmandu: Himal Books.

Pratt, Jeff (2003), *Class, Nation and Identity: The Anthropology of Political Movements*, London: Pluto Press.

Rawat, P. C. (1974), *Indo-Nepal Economic Relations*, New Delhi: National Publishing House.

Redfield, Robert (1956), *Peasant Society and Culture: An Anthropological Approach to Civilization*, Chicago & London: The University of Chicago Press.

Regmi, Mahesh Chandra (1971), *A Study in Nepali Economic History 1768-1846*, New Delhi: Manjusri Publishing House.

Regmi, Mahesh C. (1978), *Thatched Huts and Stucco Palaces: Peasants and Landlords in the 19th Century Nepal*, New Delhi: Vikas Publishing House.

Seddon, David, P. Blaikie and J. Cameron (1979), *Peasants and Workers in Nepal*, New Delhi: Vikas Publishing House.

Seddon, David (1995), 'Aids in Nepal: Issues for Consideration', *Himalayan Research Bulletin*, Vol. 15, No.2, pp. 2-11.

Seddon, David with Jagannath Adhikari and Ganesh Gurung (2001), *The New Lahures: Foreign Employment and Remittance Economy of Nepal*, Kathmandu: Nepal Institute of Development Studies (NIDS).

Sales, Anne De (2003a), 'Remarks on Revolutionary Songs and Iconography', *European Bulletin of Himalayan Research*, Vol. 24, pp. 5-24

Sales, Anne De (2003b), The Kham Magar Country, Nepal Between Ethnic Claims and Maoism', in Deepak Thapa, (ed.), *Understanding the Maoist Movement of Nepal*, Kathmandu: Martin Chautari, pp. 59-88.

Schneiderman, Sara and Mark Turin (2004), '"The Path to *Jansarkaar*", in Dolakha District: Towards an Ethnography of the Maoist Movement', in Michael Hutt (ed.), *Himalayan 'People's War': Nepal's Maoist Rebellion*, London: Hurst & Company, pp. 79-111.

Semmel, Bernand (1981) (ed.), *Marxism and the Science of War*, London: Oxford University Press.

Shah, Ghanshyam (2002) (ed.), *Social Movements and State: Readings in Indian Government and Politics*, New Delhi: Sage Publications.

Shah, Saubhagya (2008), 'Revolution and Reaction in the Himalayas: Cultural Resistance and the Maoist "New Regime" in Western Nepal', *American Ethnologist*, Vol. 35, No. 3, pp. 481–499.

Shanin, Teodor (1971) (ed.), 'Peasantry as a Political Factor', in *Peasants and Peasant Societies: Selected Readings*, New York: Penguin Books, pp. 238-263.

Sharma, Pitambar (2008), *Unravelling The Mosaic: Spatial Aspects of Ethnicity in Nepal*, Kathmandu: Social Science Baha.

Singh, Randhir (2011), *The World After Collapse of Soviet Union*, Delhi: Aakar Books.

Shrestha, Nandra Raj (1982), *The Process of Rural-To-Urban Migration in the Agrarian Economy of Nepal*, Unpublished Ph.D Dissertation submitted to Department of Geography, Indiana University.

Shrestha, Nanda R. (1999), *In the Name of Bikas: A Reflection from Nepal*, Kathmandu: Ekta Books.

Shrestha, Nanda R. (2001), *The Political Economy of Land, Landlessness and Migration in Nepal*, New Delhi: Nirala Publications.

Shrestha, Nanda (2008), 'Misery is My Company Now': Nepal's Peasantry in the Face of Failed Development, *The Journal of Peasant Studies*, Vol.35, No.3, (July issue), pp. 452-475.

Silverman, Sydel (1979), 'The Peasant Concept in Anthropology', *The Journal of Peasant Studies*, Vol. 7, No. 1, (October issue), pp. 49-69.

Stiller S.J., L. F. (1989 [1968]), *Prithvinarayan Shah in the Light of Dibya Updesh*, Kathmandu: Himalaya Book Centre.

Stiller, L.F. (1976), *The Silent Cry: The People of Nepal 1816-39*, Kathmandu: Sahyogi Prakashan.

Tamang, S.R. (2000), *Nepal in Feudal Order*, Kathmandu: Sangam Publication.

Thapa, Deepak (2007) (ed.), *Understanding the Maoist Movement of Nepal*, Kathmandu: Martin Chautari.

Thapa, Deepak and Bandita Sijapati (2004), *A Kingdom Under siege: Nepal's Maoist Insurgency, 1996 to 2003*, Kathmandu: The Print House.

Tilly, Charles (1977), *From Mobilization To Revolution*, Michigan: University of Michigan.

Tse-Tung, Mao (1965), 'Problems of Strategy in Guerrilla War Against Japan', in *Selected Works of Mao Tse-Tung*, Vol. II, Peking: Foreign Language Press, pp. 79-112.

Tse-Tung, Mao (1966), 'The Present Situation and Our Tasks (excerpts)', in *Selected Military Writings of Mao Tse-Tung*, Peking: Foreign Language Press, pp. 345-352.

Tse-Tung, Mao (1967), *Selected Works of Mao Tse-Tung,* Peking: Foreign Language Press.

Tse-Tung, Mao (1971a), 'On Practice', in *Selected Works of Mao Tse-Tung,* Peking: Foreign Language Press, pp. 65-84.

Tse-Tung, Mao (1971b),'Report of an Investigation of the Peasant Movement in Hunan', in *Selected Works of Mao Tse-Tung,* Peking: Foreign Language Press, pp. 23-39.

Tse-Tung, Mao (1971c), "Some Questions Concerning Methods of Leadership' in *Selected Works of Mao Tse-Tung,* Peking: Foreign Language Press, pp. 287-294.

Verma, Anand Swaroop (2001), *Rolpa se Dolpa Tak*, Noida: Samkaleen Teesari Duniya.

Wallerstein, Immanuel (1990), 'Antisystemic Movements: History And Dilemmas', in Samir Amin, Giovanni Arrighi, Andre Gunder Frank and Immanuel Wallerstein (eds.), T*ransforming the Revolution: Social Movements And The World-System*, New York: Monthly Review Press, pp. 13-53.

Whelpton, John (2005), *A History of Nepal*, Cambridge, UK: Cambridge University Press.

Wilkinson, Paul (1971), *Social movements*, London: Pall Mall.

Williams, Raymond (2016 [1977]), *Marxism and Literature*, New Delhi: Oxford University Press.

Wolf, Eric R. (1966), *Peasants*, Englewood Cliffs, N.J.: Prentice-Hall.

Xaxa, Virginus (1989), 'Some Problems in Defining Peasants', in M. N. Karna (ed.), Peasant and Peasant Protests in India, New Delhi: Intellectual Publishing House, pp. 21-32.

Index

D

E

F

G

H

T

U

V

W